D1330020

VICTORIAN POETS AND ROMANTIC POEMS

Intertextuality and Ideology

by

Antony H. Harrison

UNIVERSITY PRESS OF VIRGINIA

Charlottesville

This is a title in the
Victorian Literature and Culture Series

THE UNIVERSITY PRESS OF VIRGINIA
Copyright © 1990 by the Rector and Visitors
of the University of Virginia

First published 1990
First paperback edition 1992

Library of Congress Cataloging-in-Publication Data

Harrison, Antony H.
Victorian poets and romantic poems : intertextuality and ideology /
Antony H. Harrison.
p. cm.
Includes bibliographical references.
ISBN 0–8139–1253–9 (cloth); 0–8139–1364–0 (paper)

1. English poetry—19th century—History and criticism.
2. Romanticism—England—History—19th century. 3. Influence
(Literary, artistic, etc.) 4. Intertextuality. 5. Historicism. I. Title.
PR595.R6H37 1990
821'.809—dc20   89-22443
CIP

Printed in the United States of America

For Francesca Juliet Harrison Vaala—
"There is no friend like a sister"

Contents

Acknowledgments

Jerome J. McGann and Elizabeth Helsinger have read earlier
versions of this manuscript, and I am grateful for their careful
criticisms. Other friends and colleagues have provided incisive
comments on individual chapters. For their generous assistance
I would like to thank Deborah Wyrick, Mary Ellis Gibson,
Judith Ferster, John Wall, David Riede, Florence Boos, and Jim
Kincaid. At the University Press of Virginia, John McGuigan
and Cynthia Foote have been model editors, dependably
helpful and efficient. This book could not have been completed
without the help of a semester's leave from my normal teaching
duties at North Carolina State University, for which I am
grateful to my department. Finally, for the most important
kinds of help and support during the last stages of editing and
production, I thank Louise Dolan Harris.

Portions of several chapters have been previously
published and appear here much revised. I am grateful for
permission to republish material from the following articles:
"Introduction" to *The Metaphysical Poets in the Nineteenth
Century,* a special issue of *The John Donne Journal* (vol. 4, no. 2
[1985]: 163–80); "Cleon's Joy-Hunger and the Empedoclean
Context," *Studies in Browning and His Circle* 9 (1981): 57–68;
and "Irony in Tennyson's Little *Hamlet,*" *Journal of General
Education* 32 (1981): 271–86. Chapter four was published in
Studies in English Literature 29 (1989): 745–61.

VICTORIAN POETS AND ROMANTIC POEMS
Intertextuality and Ideology

Introduction:
Intertextuality, Ideology,
and the New Historicism

*The living utterance, having taken meaning and
shape at a particular historical moment in a socially specific environment, cannot fail to brush up
against thousands of living dialogic threads,
woven by socio-ideological consciousness around
the given object of an utterance; it cannot fail to
become an active participant in social dialogue.*
Mikhail Bakhtin, The Dialogic Imagination

THIS STUDY investigates a complex of issues that emerge when
authors refer, either explicitly or in less immediately visible ways,
to the work of earlier writers. Texts produced by such precursors
thus often become palimpsests as they are appropriated by successive generations of authors. The fabric of literary relationships
determined in this way has come to be discussed under the rubric of
"intertextuality" by such theorists as Roland Barthes, Julia Kristeva, Gerard Genette, and Michael Riffaterre. Writers of richly
intertextual works may allude to precursors for varied reasons: to
demonstrate admiration, to make use of the earlier writer (or even a
contemporary) as an authenticating authority, to enter into a debate, or to subvert or transvalue a specific system of beliefs he or
she might have held. In this study I scrutinize the ways in which
self-consciously intertextual uses of precursors by Victorian poets
serve to reveal ideology, that is, to expose a system of sociopolitical—as well as moral and aesthetic—values embedded in the work
of each writer and deployed to influence readers in specific ways.
These may include designs to supplant, subvert, or correct the

ideology of an authoritative pre-text. Sometimes, as well, a work's intertextual operations accomplish what Harold Bloom has described as a "metalepsis," the appropriation of a text in a corrective fashion so as to reestablish the values or tradition (or ideology) of a work or writer common as a precursor to both the present author and the one whose work he appropriates.

Investigating Victorian poems along these lines reveals how fully Victorian poets attempted either to escape or to embrace the ideological constraints of their culture in order to redirect or reinforce existing social, religious, economic, political, or aesthetic values. Often these poets self-consciously reinscribed specific texts that had assumed clearly defined significance for their culture in order to subvert accepted interpretations of those texts, restore to them some earlier and "purer" significance, or set the accepted understanding of such a precursory literary work in new and unexpected contexts so as to present a critique of values held by Victorian readers. Such is the case, for instance, in Tennyson's *Maud,* where allusions to *Hamlet* proliferate. The protagonist of this poem, which Tennyson designated his "little *Hamlet,*" serially adopts ostensibly conflicting ideological stances. At the poem's beginning he condemns Britain for its materialism and Darwinian class struggles. At the end, he joins the army to fight in the Crimea for the country he has earlier disparaged. But by means of deft and often ironic manipulations of allusions to *Hamlet,* a very popular play on the mid-Victorian stage, Tennyson presents in *Maud* a simultaneously specific and highly generalized cultural critique. Because of the speaker's fluctuating values and perspectives, the reader is forced to ask difficult questions about economic, social, political, and amatory, as well as literary, matters. In one view, the poem itself presents only inconsistent answers to them. *Maud* thus finally interrogates both the process of accepting an imposed ideology and that of formulating and adhering to one's own.

By contrast, Matthew Arnold attempts in *Empedocles on Etna* to debunk the influence of Keats in contemporary philosophical poetry, especially the immensely popular work of the "Spasmodic" school. He does so by creating a failed "hero" as his protagonist, who is Keatsian in many of his concerns and in many aspects of his character. But as Arnold's preface to the second edition of his *Poems* intimates, *Empedocles* itself fails in its attempt to subvert the Keatsian literary ideology (with its important social and political ramifications) because his protagonist achieves an originally unintended titanic stature. Partially because Arnold realized the great strength of the "Keatsian school" in his era as well as the real power of Keats over his own poetry, in 1853 he effectively renounced poetry and turned to the writing of criticism in hopes of rehabilitating the literary values of his culture.

These two examples suggest the range of intertextual operations in Victorian poetry that this study explores. Its chapters are designed to be heuristic. That is, no organically structured unitary argument evolves over the course of the book. Rather, the essays here cohere methodologically. In them I attempt consistently to apply a new historicist approach to familiar, often canonical, poems of the Victorian period in order to demonstrate how this methodology can revise traditional interpretations of these texts and their sociopolitical operations.

The first three chapters largely focus on single Victorian poems in their relations with Romantic pre-texts or works that are ideologically derivative from the work of the Romantics. These chapters identify Spasmodicism as a crucial force in mid-Victorian cultural politics, one that threatened Arnold, Browning, and Tennyson. Each poet responded differently to that threat, but did so in a work that, additionally, demonstrates a deeply conflicted relationship with a famous precursor. The remaining four chapters range more widely over the poetry of the writers they take as their focus. The chapters on Dante and Christina Rossetti explain how brother and sister alike wrote poems that deployed identifiable strategies, albeit very different ones, in order to escape particular ideological constraints of their culture and to offer critiques of what they perceived as hegemonic aesthetic, political, and social (specifically amatory and domestic) ideologies. In his attempt, Dante Rossetti reinscribed texts of Romantic writers from Keats and Shelley to Ruskin and Browning. Christina Rossetti succeeded rather better than her brother in a parallel endeavor to elude the dominant ideologies of her day, and for reasons that have, according to the standard criticism of her works, made her appear imprisoned rather than liberated by her devout Anglo-Catholic religious beliefs. Positioning the work of Christina Rossetti in its intertextual relations with that of Elizabeth Barrett Browning (whom she clearly perceived as her most important female precursor) generates a full and coherent perspective on Rossetti's countercultural project as a writer.

The final two chapters, on Morris and Swinburne, return to discussions of intertextuality as a mode of specifically political engagement for writers. For Morris in 1872 that engagement took the form of a challenge to the amatory ideologies of poets in his immediate circle, Rossetti and Swinburne. In *Love Is Enough* Morris attempted, as a political gesture, to escape his entrapment by late Keatsian amatory ideologies dominant in the work of his two friends. By the time he composed *The Pilgrims of Hope* thirteen years later, however, Morris had realized that such a purely aesthetic gesture was helpless in the face of political realities. The last chapter moves to a discussion of Swinburne, who was, unlike Morris, an avowedly political poet from the earliest days of his public career. I argue that although Swinburne appears scandalously anti-Victorian in his sexual, religious, and political dispositions, he was nonetheless stunted and finally subverted as a radical poet by the power of Wordsworth's influence over him.

In effect, these chapters are ordered chronologically according to the publication dates of the major poems they discuss. My intent is, in part, to recreate the public dialogues in which some of the most visible writers of the era engaged through their poetry. Thus, the first three chapters focus on works published from 1852 to 1855—*Empedocles on Etna,* "Cleon," and *Maud.* Investigating the relations of these poems to specific pre-texts and to the particular historical contexts of their production, I attempt to enhance, if not to entirely revise, the image of mid-Victorian literary politics that has come down to us. Chapter four concentrates largely on poems that appeared in Dante Rossetti's 1870 *Poems.* In chapter five, coming to historicist terms with the work of Christina Rossetti requires some commentary on poems published by Elizabeth Barrett Browning between 1838 and 1856, but the texts by Rossetti that I present as responses to some of these were all published after 1862. At the heart of my discussion is her sonnet of sonnets, the *Monna Innominata,* which did not appear until 1881. The two poems by Morris that occupy chapter six, *Love Is Enough* and *The Pilgrims of Hope,* were published in 1872 and 1885, respectively. Finally, the works crucial to my argument about Swinburne in chapter seven appeared over the course of two decades, from "The Triumph of Time" and other works from his 1866 volume *Poems and Ballads, First Series* to "Neap-Tide" from *Poems and Ballads, Third Series* (1889).

These chapters participate in the much larger project of "new historicist" literary archaeology that was begun, especially for Anglo-American critics and theorists, in the early 1980s with the work of Marilyn Butler, Jerome McGann, and David Simpson (among others) in the field of nineteenth-century studies and the work of Louis Montrose, Stephen Greenblatt, Jean Howard, and Leah Marcus in Renaissance studies. Among theorized critical methodologies that have vied for adherents during the last two decades, the new historicism has, according to some reports, come to dominate the American critical scene. In a review of recent studies in the nineteenth century (1988), for instance, David Riede casually acknowledges the "triumph of the New Historicism."[1] Nonetheless, given the number of practitioners affiliated with the methodology these days, it is doubtless more accurate to refer to new historicisms. Much about this critical methodology remains to be clarified, and the phenomenon of its swift rise to a position of dominance sanctioned by all the academic apparatuses of our culture (journals, presses, professional organizations, and even the awarding of endowed chairs) remains to be scrutinized. Indeed, the new historicism has been under attack for some time and continues to draw fire, particularly because new historicist studies have not been consistently implemented with the rigor the methodology implicitly (and perhaps impossibly) demands.[2] Such attacks should continue. They will keep us honest. As David Simpson has recently argued, a "stringent skepticism about the nature of historical claims can perfectly well coexist with an absolute commitment to historical methods,"[3] and such skepticism is essential if the new historicism is to succeed in making a genuine contribution not only to the historical understanding of cultures and subcultures but also to a historicized awareness of the ideological predispositions that mold critical approaches to literary production and the particular contexts in which it takes place. If we admit the possibility of objectivity in historical knowledge and strive to attain it, then, as Simpson observes, "it is an essential condition of the analysis that users of the historical method are honest about what they *do not know,* and about the forms of information that would modify the terms of knowing."[4]

Agreeing with these stipulations, I must acknowledge from the outset that the conclusions reached in the following chapters are speculative and tentative to the degree that the historical inquiries from which they emerge are incomplete. Given the "triumph of the New Historicism" and the number of helpful new historicist studies in Romantic poetry and the Victorian novel, it is surprising that rigorous interrogations of the historical contexts, particularly the sociopolitical contexts, surrounding the production and reception of Victorian poems have been very few indeed. To my knowledge, this study is the first extended new historicist project to take Victorian poetry as its subject, and it is deliberately limited to analysis of the historical relations among the ideologies particular poems and their authors respond to and propagate. A vast amount of work in the field remains to be done.

This book raises a number of theoretical and historical questions, while making certain assumptions about the reader's familiarity with recent developments in critical theory. It may be helpful briefly to rehearse some of those developments, particularly the ones upon which my critical premises and methodology depend. A word about my use of the vexed and often vexing terms *intertextuality* and *ideology* is in order, as is a more extensive review of the recent history of the new historicism as a critical "school" emerging over the last two decades.

Ideology is a term that is vexed because of its remarkably varied constructions since being coined by Antoine Destutt de Tracy in his *Elements d'Ideologie* (written between 1801 and 1815). De Tracy's optimistic rationalism inaugurated one tradition of interpreting the term: the study of ideas and their interactions, based on a belief in reason and observation and the possibility of general social agreement about the constitution of "truth." The tradition of analysis established by de Tracy has largely come to dominate the Anglo-American discipline of sociology today. An alternate tradition derives from the work of Hegel, Marx, Mannheim, and Habermas. For thinkers in this tradition, ideologies are multiple and heterogeneous, in conflict with one another and dynamic rather than consensual and static. Generally speaking, my use of the term emerges from this latter tradition, in which *ideology* becomes very broadly defined by Louis Althusser as the "reproduction of the conditions of production."[5] More specifically, I use *ideology* (and contextually refine its definition) as Karl Mannheim attempted to do in establishing a sociology of knowledge that investigated the relationship between emerging or evolving structures of thought in society, on the one hand, and historically changing political and social circumstances, on the other. As should become clear, I believe that social and political events in Victorian England were in part determined by the interaction of multiple and heterogeneous belief and value systems, some of which were dominant and widely accepted, indeed virtually monolithic and inescapable. Others were largely subcultural or countercultural. Moreover, I would contend that separately identifiable (but usually complementary) value systems dominated separate areas of an individual's activity in the world. Thus, in the pages that follow I speak variously of internally consistent "aesthetic," "domestic," "religious," and even "amatory" ideologies. In no case do I adopt the term (in the fashion of early Marxists) to mean "false consciousness." Beyond these remarks, in order to avoid repeating recent and helpful summary discussions explaining the history of the term *ideology* and the controversies surrounding it, I would refer readers to David McLellan's *Ideology* and Lennard Davis's *Ideology and Fiction*.[6]

The chapters in this book are concerned with the ways in which works of literature perpetually reconstitute themselves, both *as* they are experienced over history by readers with changing horizons of expectations and *in* the works of subsequent writers, where the originary text serves as "palimpsest." Claus Uhlig has usefully positioned this by-now familiar term in connection with Michel Foucault's program of cultural archaeology and Julia Kristeva's semiological formulation of *intertextualité*. In brief, Uhlig understands the evolving relations between literary texts and their precursors as a process of "palingenesis," or the founding of new texts upon stratified layers of (formally, stylistically, or thematically) related antecedent ones. Palimpsests are texts that have been repeatedly reinscribed in discrete texts by new authors and are thus "saturated with history."[7] From the point of view of the new historical critic concerned with the operations of reception, all texts which outlive the immediate historical moment of production (that is, all texts which remain available for "recovery" and reconstitution) might function as palimpsests, but only those that have been repeatedly appropriated are true palimpsests and largely comprise the canon. The works that appropriate them become intertexts.

Like *ideology*, *intertextuality* is a term variously construed by recent literary critics. Also as with *ideology*, a number of recent theorists have discussed the evolution of the concept of intertextuality, beginning with the work of structuralists such as Juri Lotman in the early 1970s and moving to the recent writings of Genette and Riffaterre.[8] To these commentaries, I would only add that employing intertextuality for the primary purpose of sociohistorical literary analysis, as I do in this study, is an uncommon critical practice. Indeed, the design of semioticians and structuralists who first applied the concept was precisely to escape the perceived dangers of earlier psychological and historical criticism, as Thaïs Morgan has explained:

> *"Intertextuality" has been touted since the late 1960s as the panacea for many of the critical pitfalls involved in historically oriented approaches to literature and in the New Criticism. As a structural analysis of texts in relation to the larger system of signifying practices . . . in culture, intertextuality seems by definition to deliver [critics] from old controversies over the psychology of individual authors and readers, the tracing of literary origins, and the relative value of imitation or originality. By*

> *shifting . . . attention from the triangle of author/work/tradition
> to that of text/discourse/culture, intertextuality replaces the evo-
> lutionary model of literary history with a structural or synchronic
> model of literature as sign system. The most salient effect of this
> strategic change is to free the literary text from psychological,
> sociological, and historical determinisms, opening it up to an
> apparently infinite play of relationships with other texts, or semi-
> osis.*

But, as Morgan acknowledges, intertextuality is, in fact, "no more
a value-free, innocent critical practice than historicism or New
Criticism."[9] I would extend this admission to insist that intertextuality as the study of interrelated signs and sign systems, whether
synchronic or diachronic, can only artificially and arbitrarily extricate itself from the historically particular situations of the systems
that are its objects of analysis.[10] Indeed, it is precisely the situated-
ness of such systems that gives them intelligible "meaning."

The arguments of this book operate on the assumption that all
literary works are, as Robert Weimann described them in 1976,
"structures" that "function in terms of a . . . profound dialectic of
objectivity and subjectivity." That dialectic implicitly involves a
writer as both creator and respondent whose work often reinscribes, under particular material circumstances, elements of past
texts. In doing so he generates, so to speak, a new stratum of texts,
artifacts that have an objectively definable existence in contexts that
can be described at a high level of particularity. The historical critic
can thus relate "the activities of writing and those of reading to
some comprehensive social context." By extension, he or she must
"view literature as both the (objective) product and the (subjective)
'producer' of a culture." "Structure" thus

> *reflects the mode of representation of a given reality; as such it is
> related to both the expressive and mimetic dimensions of literature,
> which, necessarily, reflect the premises, needs, and perspectives of
> the age in which it is created. At the same time, structure is related
> to the complex process of mediation (between author and reader,
> but also between past writing and new writing), and it reflects the*

> *historicity of this process itself. In other words, the creation and the*
> *interpretation of structure are affected by the changing dialectic of*
> *tradition and originality that is characteristic of the writing as well*
> *as of the reading of literature.*[11]

The important issues Weimann addresses here were first raised in 1969 by Hans Robert Jauss, who concluded his essay "Literary History as a Challenge to Literary Theory" with a provocative question: "toward what end and with what right can one today still—or again—study literary history?"[12] Delivered originally as a lecture at the University of Constance entitled "Literary History as Provocation," Jauss's "challenge" almost immediately evoked heated responses in Europe, initiating a debate, the texts of which over the last twenty years largely comprise the literature of reception theory and to a lesser extent, reader-response criticism.[13]

Jauss opens his essay with a discussion of the bankruptcy of traditional literary historical studies, whose practitioners, he claims, have been trammeled by their acceptance of an already sanctioned canon.[14] For the sake of convenience they have attempted to present their discussions within closed historical "periods," setting the lives and works of writers one after another chronologically or presenting literature by genres and registering changes from work to work as each follows or departs from the unique laws of form governing the genre to which it belongs. Such historical studies tend to frame "the unclarified character of the literary development with a general observation . . . concerning the *Zeitgeist* and the political tendencies of the age." In an attempt to attain an ideal of "objective" historiography, authors of these studies avoid judging the quality of past literary works, thus eluding the "difficult" task of asserting criteria of "influence, reception, and posthumous fame." In place of this tradition of literary historiography, Jauss elaborates seven theses that set out "what . . . a historical study of literature [should] be today."[15]

Borrowing from the work of Karl Kosik, Jauss emphasizes in his theory the "ongoing influence of the work of art as a process formative of history," nonliterary as well as literary. Jauss cites Kosik's insistence that, "the work [of art] lives to the extent that it has influence."[16] Kosik's thesis thus has two consequences for any new literary history:

> *If the life of the work results 'not from its autonomous existence but rather from the reciprocal interaction of work and mankind,' th[e] perpetual labor of understanding and of the active reproduction of the past cannot remain limited to the single work. On the contrary, the relationship of work to work must now be brought into this interaction between work and mankind, and the historical coherence of works among themselves must be seen in the interrelations of production and reception.*[17]

The world of human social relations is never quite the same once a given work has been "consumed." That work enters into history and reconstitutes the "facts" of history as well as its processes. One aspect of this phenomenon is intertextual, involving the assimilation of a (literary) text by subsequent authors who, in various ways and to varying degrees, might reinscribe its elements. This ongoing process is what Uhlig has termed "textual palingenesis," and it is a process, as Weimann makes clear, subject to every sort of cultural and ideological pressure.

Because Jauss's theory is still unfamiliar in many English and American critical circles, a summary recapitulation of his seven theses may be helpful:

1.   To revise the bases of literary history, "the prejudices of historical objectivism" must be abandoned and the traditional aesthetics of production and representation must be grounded in an aesthetics of reception and influence."[18] Any useful literary history must concern itself with the experience of literary texts by readers and by authors in the continuing process of production.

2.   Analysis of such experience begins by describing an "objectifiable system of expectations that arises for each work in the historical moment of its appearance, from a pre-understanding of the genre, from the form and themes of already familiar works, and from the opposition between poetic and practical language." A reader's response to a given work is thus not at all merely a series of subjective impressions, but rather the result of carrying out "specific instructions in a process of directed perception, which can be

comprehended according to its constitutive motivations and triggering signals."

3. Entering society and the individual reader's world at a
particular historical moment, therefore, a work sustains an "aesthetic distance": the "disparity between the given horizon of expectations" and the constitution of the new work itself. Its reception
can "result in a 'change of horizons.' "[19]

4. Reconstructing horizons of expectations not only exposes
as valueless traditional attempts to produce generalized statements
about the spirit of an age, but it enables literary historians to enter
specific sociohistorical moments in a highly particularized way,
formulating "questions that the text gave an answer to" at the time
of its production and thereby discovering "how the contemporary
reader could have viewed and understood the work." Of equal
importance, such a procedure "brings to view the hermeneutic
differences" between the understanding of a work at every historical moment of its existence up to the present. It calls into question
the "platonizing dogma" that a literary work has a single "objective
meaning" accessible at all times to the interpreter.

5. Ascertaining the horizon of expectations for a work also
enables the literary historian to place it in its proper "literary series," that is, "to recognize its historical position and significance in
the context of the experience of literature," in which authors respond to works of their predecessors. Such an approach to literary
history, however, must be scrupulously nonteleological and es-
chew concepts of literary "evolution": "The standpoint of the literary historian becomes the vanishing point—but not the goal—of
the process."[20]

6. Unlike traditional literary history whose perspective is
largely diachronic, reception historians must integrate synchronic
and diachronic perspectives on literary works in order "to discover
an overarching system of relationships in the literature of a historical moment." A new literary history can be developed if "cross
sections" of reception history "diachronically before and after" the
appearance of a work "were so arranged as to articulate historically
the change in literary structures in epoch-making moments."

7. The historian's final representation of literary production

and reception must appear not only as a self-contained "succession of systems" but also as a " 'special history' in its own unique relationship to 'general history.' "[21]

In recent years the new historicism has emerged as a prospectively strong ally of Jauss's reception theory. Not surprisingly, both have deep roots in Marxist critical thought.[22] In response to Jauss, for instance, Marilyn Butler has extrapolated five principles for a "genuinely historical" method in criticism. She insists: 1. that literary works be examined "as far as [is] possible from within their own discourse or code or cultural system"; 2. that "the definition of literature . . . should not be exclusive," because "canons" are determined by readers and institutions with ideological biases—all texts are possible objects of the critic's scrutiny, including letters, sermons, and advertisements, as well as what are traditionally considered to be great or major works; 3. that the full complexity of intertextual relations, that is, a work's or author's relationship to precursors—whether dependent, revisionist, or competitive—must be carefully examined; 4. that the modern historicist critic must "acknowledge his own position . . . as bound in time and place," aware that his task is not the impossible one of reconstructing the past but rather of understanding "how writing functions in its world, in order to understand writing, the world, and ourselves"; and 5. that "a genuinely historical perspective discourages dogmatism, by obliging us to foreground the difference between our circumstances, aims, and language, and those of the past."[23] These general principles are fundamental to the endeavors of new historicist criticism and guide my own inquiries in the chapters of this book.[24]

Like Butler, Jerome McGann has argued for a thoroughgoing renovation of the original (nineteenth-century) program for historical literary criticism, properly insisting that such criticism can "no longer . . . treat any of its details in an untheorized way." It can not be satisfied to paint a static "picture of great detail," because the significance of literary works has always "remained in process of realization."[25] McGann, after the fashion of Jauss, sees a literary work as always self-evolving while existing in a dialectical relationship with each cultural moment through which it evolves. Because art serves, alongside other cultural activities, to construct "human nature" in the course of mankind's social history, what it "imitates" or "has reference to" finally is the

> *totality of human changes in all its diverse and particular man-*
> *ifestations. Since the totality neither is nor ever can be concep-*
> *tually completed, however, art works must always intersect with*
> *it at a differential. That is to say, art must establish its referential*
> *systems—including its reference to the totality—in the forms of*
> *dynamic particulars which at once gesture toward the place of these*
> *particulars in the ceaseless process of totalization, and also assert*
> *their freedom within the process. Such freedom is relational, and it*
> *illustrates a key element in the maintenance of the process of*
> *dynamic totalization: that the particulars which are to count in art,*
> *the particular acts, events, circumstances, details, and so forth,*
> *along with the textualizations through which they are constituted,*
> *are those which in fact* make (and/or have made) *a differ-*
> *ence—particulars which will be seen to have been (and to be still)*
> *positively engaged in processes of change.*[26]

As distinct from traditional historicist and philological critics, the new historicist thus displays an awareness of the dynamic and dialectical relations between a work and the historical particulars that partially constituted its "meaning" upon composition or first publication. He or she must also demonstrate such an awareness in attending to subsequent moments in the history of the work's existence, including the critic's own historical moment, for a text's meanings and interpretations clearly change according to the expectations, values, and social milieu of the reader. Moreover, any attempt critically to explore a work's meanings over history will be influenced by these same considerations as they relate to the critic. His project, therefore, must be undertaken at a high level of self-consciousness.[27]

The chapters that follow bring together the critical strategies of the new historicism and intertextual analysis in order to interrogate the ideological operations of Victorian poems and the ideological dispositions of their authors, particularly in relation to Romantic precursors and pre-texts. In doing so, they will, I hope, inaugurate a larger new historicist movement in the criticism of Victorian poetry, setting it fully in the contexts of ideologies competing for dominance during an era in which conflicts within the social and institutional structures of society, as well as its structures of thought, became more numerous, more visible, and yet more subtle and complex than ever before.

I

Arnold, Keats, and the Ideologies of *Empedocles on Etna*

MATTHEW ARNOLD is the most pervasively intertextual of Victorian poets. Not only does he allude repeatedly to precursors through verbal, thematic, and formal echoes in his poems, but, unlike most canonical poets of the nineteenth century, he also names such influential figures openly. He does so in such commendatory and elegiac pieces as "Shakespeare," "Heine's Grave," "Stanzas in Memory of the Author of Obermann" (and its sequel), "Memorial Verses," and "Stanzas from the Grand Chartreuse." Most often with unmixed admiration, he calls upon the ghosts of Goethe, Senancour, Sophocles, and Wordsworth, while he directly criticizes the deficiencies of Byron and Shelley. Arnold also pays tribute in his poetry to Homer, Milton, and Epictetus. Not once in his poems, however, does he refer by name to John Keats (although he frequently discusses Keats in his prose works). But Keats, it may be argued, was second only to Wordsworth in the power and persistence of his influence upon Arnold. Appropriations of Keats's sensuous image patterns, his stanzaic forms, his stylistic mannerisms, and even such frequent themes as the crisis of poetic vocation are common in Arnold's poetry, but any direct reference to Keats is elided.

Keats's ubiquitous present absence in Arnold's poetry has been much discussed, as have Arnold's various employments of other major precursors, especially Wordsworth.[1] The first critic to explore at length the depth of Keats's influence on Arnold, George Ford, observed that, "of Keats's importance [to other writers] he must have been aware, but whole-hearted recognition he was not prepared to offer." This statement holds true not only for Arnold's estimate of Keats's significance to the work of other poets, but also to Arnold's own poetry. Speaking "qualitatively rather than quantitatively," Ford insists that in Arnold's finest poems, "the stamp of Keats is most marked, whereas in the great bulk of his minor work it is conspicuous by its absence. What is more, the influence of Keats was, in Arnold's case, almost entirely beneficial."[2] Yet until 1863, especially in his letters and in the Preface to *Poems, a New Edition* (1853), Arnold consistently disparaged Keats's work and influence or at least seriously qualified his admiration for Keats. Although by 1863 Arnold's attitude toward Keats is far more positive than previously, such qualifications surface even in his two essays of that year which discuss Keats in largely laudatory terms, "Heinrich Heine" and "Maurice de Guérin." Arnold's 1880 essay "John Keats," by contrast, offers Arnold's most strongly positive and complete estimate of Keats's work.

Arnold's complex position on Keats finally emerges, nonetheless, not in his criticism, but in his poetry, as Ford acknowledges: "however much he might badger and quarrel with the Keatsian current in Victorian poetry, he himself failed to remain outside it. His words on the influence of Tennyson apply even more to Tennyson's influential predecessor, John Keats. 'One has him so in one's head, one cannot help imitating him sometimes.' "[3] Critics since Ford have clearly agreed, and they have made eloquent and illuminating cases for the influence of Keats on numerous major poems, with the baffling exception of *Empedocles*. None of these commentators has, however, perceived the ideological ramifications of Keats's influence or the perplexing and profound ways in which the ideological strife between the two poets significantly influenced the shape of Arnold's career.

In the essay written to preface his selections from Keats's poetry (1880), Arnold quotes from what proves to be—in the vexed history of Arnold's relationship with Keats—a letter by Keats that powerfully illuminates Arnold's various appropriations of him. The letter is to J. H. Reynolds (April 9, 1818) and was first printed in R. M. Milnes's *Life, Letters, and Literary Remains of John Keats* (1848), which Arnold had read when it first appeared:

I have not the slightest feel of humility towards the Public—or to anything in existence—but the eternal Being, the Principle of Beauty,—and the Memory of great Men. . . . I would be subdued before my friends, and thank them for subduing me—but among Multitudes of men—I have no feel of stooping, I hate the ideal of humility to them—

I never wrote one single Line of Poetry with the least Shadow of public thought.

Forgive me for vexing you. . . . but it eases me to tell you— I could not live without the love of my friends—I would jump down Ætna for any great Public good—but I hate a Mawkish Popularity.—I cannot be subdued before them—My glory would be to daunt and dazzle the thousand jabberers about Pictures and Books.[4]

This letter has, of course, important political overtones. In it Keats presents himself as a rebel against the middle-class "jabberers" who review books and establish public taste, including those for *Blackwood's* and the *Quarterly* who had recently attacked *Endymion*. The distinction between petulance and confident self-sufficiency blurs here, as the lower-class Cockney—whose work Byron labeled in 1820 as "Johnny Keats's '*p-ss a bed*' poetry"[5]—defies the middle-class philistinism of the culture-determining institutions of his time. But unlike Arnold, who emerges from the same class as these reviewers and devotes the major part of his career to reforming middle-class tastes, Keats shows no inclination to rehabilitate the misguided values of his poetry's prospective audience.

The volume in which this letter first appeared greatly disturbed Arnold. Soon after Milnes's book came out, Arnold wrote to Arthur Hugh Clough:

What a brute you were to tell me to read Keats' Letters. However it is over now: and reflexion resumes her power over agitation. What harm he has done in English Poetry. As Browning is a man with a moderate gift passionately desiring movement and fulness, and obtaining but a confused multitudinousness, so Keats with a very high gift, is yet also consumed by this desire: and cannot produce the truly living and moving, as his conscience keeps telling him.

*They will not . . . understand that they must begin with an Idea
of the world in order not to be prevailed over by the world's multitudinousness: or if they cannot get that, at least with isolated ideas:
and all other things shall (perhaps) be added unto them. . . . I
have had that desire of fulness without respect of the means, which
may become almost maniacal: but nature had placed a bar thereto
not only in the conscience (as with all men) but in a great numbness
in that direction. But what perplexity Keats Tennyson et id genus
omne must occasion to young writers of the [Greek] sort: yes and
those d----d Elizabethan poets generally. Those who cannot read
G[ree]k sh[ou]ld read nothing but Milton and parts of Wordsworth: the state should see to it.*[6]

This letter suggests the profound ideological tensions that plague
Arnold's attempts to grapple with the inescapable influence upon
him of Keats's "very high gift," one important aspect of which was
what Arnold described in his essay on Maurice de Guérin as the
ability of Keats to write a poetry of "natural magic."

That poetry is a product of what Geoffrey Hartman has
loosely termed Keats's "sensory ideology," the pervasiveness of
images of sensory apprehension, of "sensible ecstasy," in the work
of Keats.[7] The sensuousness of Keats's language and imagery frequently occupies Arnold in his essays after 1852 and is a major
concern when he attempts to explain the aesthetic "confusion of the
present times" in his famous 1853 Preface.[8]

In mid-Victorian England, according to Arnold, "the multitude of voices counselling different things [is] bewildering, the
number of existing works capable of attracting a young writer's
attention and of becoming his models, immense. What he wants is
a hand to guide him through the confusion" (*Prose*, 1:8). Arnold
proceeds to disparage Keats as one of those recent "imitators of
Shakespeare" who might serve as a dangerous model for contemporary poets (*Prose*, 1:10). In all of his Preface, in fact, Arnold
discusses at length just one monitory example from the "multitude" available, and it is Keats's *Isabella*. Arnold concedes that, "the
poem . . . is a perfect treasure-house of graceful and felicitous
words and images: almost in every stanza there occurs one of those

vivid and picturesque turns of expression, by which the object is made to flash upon the eye of the mind, and which thrill the reader with a sudden delight. This one short poem contains, perhaps, a greater number of happy single expressions which one could quote than all the extant tragedies of Sophocles." But the problem with this poem, as with all Keats's poems for Arnold, is one of "action" or "story," by which he means architectonic conception, the inseparability of structure and *idea:* "the action itself is an excellent one; but so feebly is it conceived by the poet, so loosely constructed, that the effect produced by it . . . is absolutely null" (*Prose,* 1:10). Arnold's equivocal commentaries on Keats until "Maurice de Guérin" (including these remarks from the 1853 Preface) dependably reflect his discomfort at the fact that Keats possessed "a very high gift" but no perceptible "Idea of the world," no ideology, in fact, that would unify and give shape to his "multitudinous" perceptions. Keats's responses to the world seemed fragmentary to Arnold, his unfiltered sensory receptivity to phenomena potentially dangerous because disorderly—a sign even of moral turpitude.

Arnold's use of Keats as his central negative example betrays the extent of Keats's power over him. And it seems no mere coincidence that this extraordinary display of intertextual self-consciousness on Arnold's part should appear in that very important preface in which he attempts to eject from his own corpus the poem that later generations have come to revere as Arnold's most important work. In *Empedocles on Etna* the "sensory ideology" of Callicles serves as a counterpoint to the frustrated Wordsworthian ideology of transcendence that Empedocles on first glance seems to embody. In fact, the whole conception of the work may well have originated from Arnold's reading in 1848 or 1849 of Keats's letter to Reynolds. Responding to the corrupt popular values of "the times," Empedocles does indeed "jump down Ætna." The "public good" his poetic example serves, Arnold may originally have thought, would be to present reciprocally a critique of an era and of a prospective hero driven to desperation by his society and its false values. But Empedocles is a failed hero who betrays his own best potential to redeem that society and perhaps to redirect cultural history.

Shortly I will present a substantial analysis of the Keatsian subtexts of *Empedocles on Etna*. In his most important poem Arnold's mix of open as well as subtle and covert appropriations of Keats's poetic values and practices exposes Arnold's own "perplexities" through the counterpointed and often self-subverting ideological stances the work presents. In order better to understand this poem's difficult intertextual operations, however, it is essential to explore several particular contexts of Arnold's relationship to Keats's poetry and of Arnold's perceptions of his important precursor during the late 1840s and early 1850s. In those years Arnold was working strenuously to develop a historically grounded system of social, moral, and literary values.

Any discussion of this vexed relationship might well begin with Arnold's Preface and his own suicide as a poet.[9] As we have seen, in the Preface Arnold for the first time attacked Keats publicly, while announcing to his audience the impossibility of writing poetry "in these bad times." If Empedocles's leap down Etna thus has come to represent the death of Arnold the poet, the work in which it appears may be seen to constitute a symbolic act of patricide, especially (as we shall see more fully later on) since aspects of Keats are bound up in both Empedocles and Callicles. While Empedocles kills himself, Arnold kills off the surviving Callicles by repudiating his poem entirely. Neither the poetry of introspection nor the poetry of natural magic, which Callicles comes to represent, is adequate to Arnold's age, it would seem. But as Arnold himself acknowledges, the entire treatment of his subject in this poem is "vaguely conceived and loosely drawn." It is "indeterminate, and faint, instead of being particular, precise, and firm" (*Prose*, 1:2). These characteristics of *Empedocles* result in part from Arnold's typical ambivalence in absorbing and transvaluing the work of the two major Romantic precursors appropriated in the poem, Wordsworth and Keats. Arnold's perplexity about what to make of Keats afflicted him at least to some extent for the rest of his career, but to an extreme and painful degree up to 1863, as his prose writings openly reveal and as the major commentators on the relationship between Keats and Arnold have readily noted.

In his prose writings Arnold therefore moves between denigration and praise of Keats. If Arnold's early remarks dependably berate his precursor, by the time of his last commentary on Keats (1880) he is able—with the help of newly published materials, including the *Letters to Fanny Brawne*—finally to detect a genuine ideology informing Keats's work, and it is something more than what Hartman has termed the "sensory ideology." It might be better designated as the "aesthetic ideology," what the Pre-Raphaelite poets in fact perceived it to be.

Arnold begins his 1880 essay on Keats by repeating what he has said elsewhere, that "Keats as a poet is abundantly and enchantingly sensuous" (*Prose*, 9:205). After disturbed remarks on Keats's "underbred" and "ignoble" "relaxed self-abandonment" displayed in the letters to Fanny Brawne (to which I shall later return), Arnold recovers his strongly positive attitude toward Keats the poet, who possesses "something more, something better" than the "sensuous strain" (*Prose*, 9:207). "By his promise . . . , if not fully by his performance," Keats is "one of the very greatest of English poets, and . . . a merely sensuous man cannot either by promise or by performance be a very great poet, because poetry interprets life" for us. By 1880 Arnold has discovered in Keats "elements of high character . . . and the effort to develop them; the effort is frustrated and cut short by misfortune, and disease, and time, but for the due understanding of Keats's worth the recognition of this effort, and of the elements on which it worked, is necessary" (*Prose*, 9:207). Keats's awareness of his own deficiencies, moreover, prompts Arnold to assert that he "had flint and iron in him . . . character." But also, "nothing is more remarkable in Keats than his clear-sightedness, his lucidity" (*Prose*, 9:211). Arnold can conclude that, although "Keats was not ripe" during his lifetime for "the faculty of moral interpretation," nor for "the architectonics of poetry" (*Prose*, 9:215),

(*Prose*, 9:213)

> the truth is that "the yearning for the Beautiful," which was with Keats, as he himself truly says, the master-passion, is not a passion of the sensuous or sentimental man, is not a passion of the sensuous or sentimental poet. It is an intellectual and spiritual passion. It is "connected and made one," as Keats declares that in his case it was, "with the ambition of the intellect." It is, as he again says, "the

mighty abstract idea *of Beauty in all things." And in his last days
Keats wrote: "If I should die, I have left no immortal work behind
me—nothing to make my friends proud of my memory;* but I
have loved the principle of beauty in all things, *and if I had
had time I would have made myself remembered." He* has *made
himself remembered. . . . For to see things in their beauty is to see
things in their truth, and Keats knew it.*

In the end it is Keats's ability to assimilate, reformulate, and transmit beauty *intellectually*—to generate a virtual ideology of transvalued sensory perception—that yields Arnold's admiration for
him.

Arnold anticipates the position expressed here in 1880 in his
essay "Maurice de Guérin," first published in 1863. In it he designates a category of poets who possess the faculty of "natural
magic." Such poets, including Guérin and Keats, as he describes
them, have the unique "power of so dealing with things as to
awaken in us a wonderfully full, new, and intimate sense of them,
and of our relations with them. When this sense is awakened in us,
as to objects without us, we feel ourselves to be in contact with the
essential nature of those objects, to be no longer bewildered and
oppressed by them, but to have their secret, and to be in harmony
with them; and this feeling calms and satisfies us as no other can"
(*Prose*, 3:13). For Arnold, "manifestations of this magical power of
poetry are very rare and very precious" (*Prose*, 3:14). But the
temperament which enables such magical power, does not, significantly, give rise to "active virtues"; rather, it "indisposes for the
discharge of them." It is characterized by "something morbid and
excessive"; ultimately, the temperament "is *devouring*; it uses vital
power too hard and too fast, paying the penalty in long hours of
unutterable exhaustion and in premature death" (*Prose*, 3:32). Still,
it gives a "unique brilliancy and flavour" (*Prose*, 3:33) to the work
of such writers as Keats and Guérin. When they "speak of the world
they speak like Adam naming by divine inspiration the creatures;
their expression corresponds with the thing's essential reality." But
Keats distinguishes himself from Guérin in Arnold's mind by his
superior "sense of what is pleasurable and open in the life of Nature; for him she is the *Alma Parens;* his expression has, therefore,

more than Guérin's something genial, outward, and sensuous"
(*Prose*, 3:34). Such comments, so specific in designating the particular virtues of Keats's poetry and so powerful in their praise of
Keats, compel us to ask the reasons for Arnold's remarkable change
in attitude toward the value of Keats's work between 1853 and
1863.

How and why during this period was Arnold able to un-
perplex his praise from his earlier criticism of Keats's "d----d"
Elizabethan sensuousness, his lack of "an Idea of the world," his
chaotic "multitudinousness" so dangerous that "the state should
see to it" that he and his type remain unread? The answer to this
question, I will argue, lies in a crucial change in Arnold's political
values that occurred in 1859 and crystallized fully in the early
1860s. The relevance of such a change to Arnold's estimate of
Keats's work is to be found in a portion of his 1880 essay on Keats,
his only significant prose commentary on Keats after 1863. The
early paragraphs of that essay display the residual effects of Arnold's earlier, more conservative ideology—his partially unself-
conscious fabric of political, social, moral, and aesthetic values.

As Arnold begins "John Keats" with a discussion of the recently
published *Letters to Fanny Brawne* (1878), he is clearly as "agitated"
by them as he was by Milnes's *Life* when he read it some thirty
years earlier. He finds the letters' publication "inexcusable," in part
because they threaten to undermine the generally positive view of
Keats and his work Arnold had with some difficulty arrived at by
1863. Arnold quotes Keats's famous letter to Fanny of October 13,
1819: "You have absorb'd me. I have a sensation . . . as though I
was dissolving—I should be exquisitely miserable without hope of
soon seeing you. . . . I have no limit now to my love. . . . I could
die for you. . . . You have ravished me away by a power I cannot
resist." For Arnold the "real point of remark" in this letter is

(*Prose*,
9:206–7)

*the complete enervation of the writer. We have the tone, or rather
the entire want of tone, the abandonment of all reticence and all
dignity, of the merely sensuous man, of the man who "is passion's
slave." Nay, we have them in such wise that one is tempted to*

speak even as Blackwood *or the* Quarterly *were in the old days wont to speak; one is tempted to say that Keats's love-letter is the love-letter of a surgeon's apprentice. It has in its relaxed self-abandonment something underbred and ignoble, as of a youth ill brought up, without the training which teaches us that we must put some constraint upon our feelings and upon the expression of them. It is the sort of love-letter of a surgeon's apprentice which one might hear read out in a breach of promise case, or in the Divorce Court. The sensuous man speaks in it, and the sensuous man of a badly bred and badly trained sort.*

As we have seen, Arnold quickly overcomes the temptation to speak of Keats as the reviewers had done in 1817, insisting on "something more, something better" in Keats's "poetic powers." But Arnold *was* intimately familiar with the reviews he mentions, having described them as "merciless" in his biographical sketch of Keats for *Ward's English Poets* (*Prose,* 11:547–48). Indeed, Arnold was personally acquainted with the *Quarterly* reviewer, John Wilson Croker.[10]

Knowing the reviews of *Endymion* so thoroughly, Arnold would have understood—perhaps better than most Keatsians have until recently—the full extent of the reactionary political motivations behind them and the full political implications of the reviews themselves.[11] Indeed, until the early 1860s he would have shared the ideology upon which they were founded. Even Arnold's diction in the passage quoted above betrays such a sympathy. His description of Keats's "complete enervation" in the letter to Fanny Brawne echoes J. G. Lockhart's attack (in *Blackwood's*) upon Keats's "loose, nerveless versification" along with the "Cockney rhymes" (*Endymion*'s couplets) Lockhart associates with the liberal Leigh Hunt, "The poet of Rimini," whose protégé he assumed Keats to be.[12] Croker, too, had attacked Keats's "Cockney" couplets. As William Keach has recently observed, they constituted "an affront to the orthodoxy of the closed Augustan couplet and to the social and moral traditions it symbolizes." For both Lockhart and Croker, it would seem, the attempt "to reform the heroic couplet is an exact image of [Hunt's and Keats's] reformist politics."[13] Such an association is hardly surprising, given that Lockhart stops to quote at length from the opening lines of book 3 of *Endymion,* which demonstrate "how [Hunt's] bantling has already learned to lisp sedition."[14] In these lines from *Endymion* Keats was insisting upon a concept of genius that eschews worldly honors and, by implication, would abolish arbitrary hierarchies of wealth and station upon which Arnold's early career actively depended.[15]

> There are those who lord it o'er their fellow-men
> With most prevailing tinsel: who unpen
> Their baaing vanities, to browse away
> The comfortable green and juicy hay
> From human pastures; or, O torturing fact!
> Who, through an idiot blink, will see unpack'd
> Fire-branded foxes to sear up and singe
> Our gold and ripe-ear'd hopes. With not one tinge
> Of sanctuary splendour, not a sight
> Able to face an owl's, they still are dight
> By the blear-eyed nations in empurpled vests,
> And crowns, and turbans. With unladen breasts,
> Save of blown self-applause, they proudly mount
> To their spirit's perch, their being's high account,
> Their tiptop nothings, their dull skies, their thrones—
> Amid the fierce intoxicating tones
> Of trumpets, shoutings, and belabour'd drums,
> And sudden cannon. . . .
> Are then regalities all gilded masks?[16]

Keats's political standing "on the liberal side of the question" is asserted more directly in his letters. To Dilke (on September 22, 1819), for instance, Keats wrote, "I hope sincerely I shall be able to put a Mite of help to the Liberal side of the Question before I die."[17] As Arnold would have realized, Keats's liberalism was far more radical than the essentially middle-class political values of the Whigs who surrounded Lord Lansdowne when Matthew Arnold served as his secretary from April 1847 to June 1851—the years of and just preceding Arnold's period of greatest poetic productivity. Lansdowne himself, whom Arnold came to admire enormously, was an early Victorian embodiment of the perfect gentlemen. A connoisseur of the arts, he frequently played host to distinguished literary and scientific men as well as politicians. Indeed, Lansdowne held considerable political power. In theory a defender of liberty and toleration, he by no means believed in equality, however.[18] Keats presents a complete contrast with such a figure: "when Keats used the word 'liberal' he did not mean what the enlightened Whig meant. He had in view a liberal-mindedness like Robin Hood's, the pursuit of which implied a thorough reformation of sexual mores and economic arrangements."[19] With these considerations in mind, we are less shocked to recall G. B. Shaw's remarks when praising Keats's *Isabella:* "Keats achieved the very curious feat of writing one poem of which it may be said that if Karl Marx can be imagined as writing a poem instead of a treatise on Capital, he would have written *Isabella.*"[20] *Isabella* is, of course, the poem singled out for condemnation not only by Lockhart in his review of Keats but also by Arnold in his 1853 Preface.

It is at precisely that point in his career—with the repudiation of *Empedocles* and, virtually, of the poetic vocation—that Arnold began to establish himself as what John Storey has termed, after Antonio Gramsci, an "organic intellectual," one of the elite "men of culture, who have the function of providing leadership of a cultural and general ideological nature."[21] Gramsci's concept of this functionary derives from Marx, who in *The German Ideology* argues that "each new class . . . is compelled . . . to represent its interest as the common interest of all the members of society, put in an ideal form; it will give its ideas the form of universality, and represent them as the only rational, universally valid ones."[22] For Arnold, of course, the class in question is the middle class. As he explains in *Culture and Anarchy,* "almost all my attention has naturally been concentrated on my own class, the middle class, with which I am in closest sympathy, and which has been, besides, the great power of our day." As an "organizer" of the middle class, Arnold saw it as his duty to reprove and rehabilitate it, especially by guiding it away from its false values and transforming it into a "cultured, liberalised, ennobled" class to which the working classes might happily aspire. His goal then becomes the hegemony of a reformed middle class, of which Arnold speaks admiringly and hopefully in *A French Eton:*

(Prose,
2:322)

> *In that great class strong by its numbers, its energy, its industry, strong by its freedom from frivolity, not by any law of nature prone to immobility of mind . . . in that class, liberalised by an ampler culture, admitted to a wider sphere of thought, living by larger ideas, with its provincialism dissipated, its intolerance cured, its pettiness purged away—what a power there will be, what an element of new life for England! Then let the middle class rule, then let it affirm its own spirit, when it has thus perfected itself.*

Up to the 1860s Arnold's affiliation with the middle class carried with it a generally Whig political ideology. But his mission in 1859 to assist in reporting on the state of popular education in France had a powerful effect upon his political values. The experience was as close to an epiphany as Arnold came during his career, and it inspired him to write three important works: *England and the Italian Question, The Popular Education of France,* and *A French Eton.* In them, as Park Honan acknowledges, he is "less dogmatic and more open to plural values and observable facts" than ever before.[23] It seems clear, despite Arnold's ranting against the lower classes as late as 1867 in *Culture and Anarchy,* that Arnold's illumination during the French tour led him gradually toward a more liberal political ideology, as is reflected with special clarity in his essays "Democracy" (1861) and "Equality" (1878).[24] R. H. Super describes "Equality" as "a remarkable corrective for those who fancy that *Culture and Anarchy* savors too much of the elite" (*Prose,* 8:451). Before 1859, however, Arnold's Whig politics were clearly elitist in ways most often determined, it seems, by the company he kept and by immediate political events that made him, like so many members of Victorian England's middle class, fearful of "the lower orders" with whom Arnold still associates Keats, the "ignoble" and "underbred" surgeon's apprentice, in 1880.

When he served as secretary to Lansdowne, Arnold's surroundings and acquaintances had been distinctly aristocratic. But these were hardly uncongenial to him at twenty-five. After all, Balliol, his college at Oxford, had traditionally been a Tory stronghold. At Lansdowne's house in Berkeley Square he was also in an upper-class preserve. Arnold's elitist predispositions were only strengthened in these surroundings, although he was fully aware of the "bounded and ineffective" state of the aristocracy. It was the spectacle of power, charm, and elegance in Whig society that first captured his attention: from "the nearer view provided by his secretarial post" he was confronted by a "society fallen from its highest peak of grandeur but still impressive, cultivated, and brilliant; a ruling caste faltering, weak, and unenlightened but still responsible, tenacious, instinct with authority . . . above all, a government capable of maintaining order and of lending itself to gradual reform."[25] Moreover, despite Arnold's conscientious efforts to remain objective, even aloof, in his new position, the extraordinary events of 1848 necessarily reinforced his conservative political tendencies, especially since the latest news from France passed immediately to Lansdowne House, and the threats from abroad were strengthened by the presence of Chartist mobs gathering nearby in Trafalgar Square, where they engaged in sporadic conflicts with police. These were tumultuous times, of course, when many feared the revolutionary fervor of the lower classes. As happened again (but briefly) during events surrounding the Governor Eyre controversy in 1866, Arnold "was too emotional to see politics in the near view steadily."[26] Although predicting the fall of the landed and privileged in March of 1848, he was, nonetheless, convinced that England must turn for leadership to the aristocracy. "He could express only consternation at George Sand's adulation of '*a people*.'"[27]

By contrast, as a result of his experiences during the French tour of 1859, Arnold subsequently believed that the era of "the people" and of "ideas" had come to replace the era of aristocracy and "character." Such ideas arose turbulently from the dissatisfied lower classes, but this group could be organized, trained, and controlled—in short, civilized—by the modern state, which itself must be molded by the power of a rehabilitated middle class. Very significant for Arnold's changing attitude toward Keats, too, is his new admiration—discussed in *The Popular Education of France*—for a "crude primitive vigor" as the underlying power of a nation. As

Arnold had now come to see the matter, the strength of England derives, not from learning, but from the people's *"constitutional preference for the animal over the intellectual life"* (*Prose*, 2:158–62). As Honan observes, because Arnold "is assured of the primitive sensuous quality in the English . . . he can recommend to them later Swift's 'sweetness and light.' "[28] It is, of course, precisely Keats's sensuousness that he acclaims as the poet's greatest virtue one year later in "Maurice de Guérin."

Arnold can view Keats's work and character in a new light by 1863 not only because of his altered political and social values, however. Apart from Keats's Cockney origins, another factor had powerfully influenced Arnold's condemnations of him between 1848 and 1853, and that was the remarkable success of the Spasmodic poets—who were most often perceived as "Keatsian"—just as Arnold was attempting to launch his own poetic career. By 1855 they were out of vogue.

Exactly ten years before Arnold published *The Strayed Reveller and Other Poems* in 1849, Philip James Bailey's *Festus* had been enthusiastically received by reviewers and the public. For the next fifteen years Spasmodic poetry exerted a powerful influence on British literary taste. Writers including Bailey, J. Westland Marston, Ebenezer Jones, John Stanyon Bigg, Sidney Dobell, and Alexander Smith largely dominated the scene.[29] It was with the highly emotive and introspective, vigorous and extravagant, work of such writers, along with Tennyson and the Brownings, that Arnold entered into competition with his first two volumes of poetry.[30] Indeed, his early work was often compared unfavorably with the "enthusiastic" Spasmodic poets, especially Alexander Smith—a lower-class muslin designer from Glasgow—whose *A Life-Drama* appeared early in 1853, on the heels of *Empedocles* (October 1852). During the spring of 1853, according to William Michael Rossetti, "nothing [was] talked of . . . but Alexander Smith."[31] The crucial Preface to the new edition of Arnold's *Poems* was completed in October of 1853.

Arnold's Preface was, to a significant extent, a response to the popular success of the Spasmodics.[32] The reactionary literary values Arnold advocates in it—especially his preference for classical rather than modern "actions"—not only demonstrate his desire to be controversial (defying the general cry in his day for poetry that is optimistic and speaks to the age), but they also parallel his conservative political ideology. As we have seen, the Preface disparages all romantic excesses in poetry as well, including those of Alexander Smith and his predecessors.[33]

The first in the perceived lineage of such predecessors was Keats. In 1853 Arthur Hugh Clough, for instance, reviewed Smith's *A Life-Drama* together with Arnold's *Empedocles on Etna and Other Poems*. Responding with considerably more enthusiasm to Smith's poem than to Arnold's work, he designated Smith as "the latest disciple of the school of Keats, who was . . . the fountainhead of a true poetic stream."[34] Similarly, George Gilfillan, the untiring proponent of Spasmodicism, claimed that he had discovered in Smith, "another Keats."[35] Arnold himself could not forebear making the same comparison in telling Clough that Smith's "kind does not go far: it dies like Keats."[36] Arnold even obliquely carries the comparison into his Preface. G. H. Lewes had hailed Alexander Smith's "luxuriant imagery and exquisite felicity of expression" as a promise of "the great poet he will be when age and ripe experience lend their graver accent to his verse."[37] Describing *Isabella* in the Preface as "a perfect treasure house of graceful and felicitous words and images," Arnold appears to be ironically echoing Lewes's description.[38]

By contrast with their commentaries on the valuable Keatsian qualities of Smith's *A Life-Drama,* reviewers of Arnold's first two volumes saw his poems as "unintelligible," "strange," stale, derivative, and imitative of Tennyson. Even Clough accused him of "obscurity" and "pseudo-Greek inflation."[39] Understandably, Arnold rankled under such criticism, but rather than succumbing to it and attempting to write as the public apparently demanded, Arnold was determined to make his conservative stand even more firmly in favor of "the ancients." Specifically he admires their emphasis on "actions" that (echoing Wordsworth) "appeal to the great primary human affections," regardless of the historical era in which they are set; on architectonics; and on stylistic austerity. In

affirming these poetic principles, Arnold felt compelled to eject
from his collection the poem which seemed to him to have most in
common with the popular poetry of his day—the Keatsian strain of
Spasmodicism—whose most important characteristic, according
to one reviewer (quoted by Arnold in his Preface), is that it presents
a "true allegory of the state of one's own mind" as a "representative
history" (*Prose,* 1:4, 8). By 1853, because of Spasmodic transvaluations of Keats and Spasmodic corruptions of Keatsian stylistic mannerisms, Arnold saw Keats as in many respects the arch-villain
among Romantic poets. That "the dialogue of the mind with itself
has commenced" (*Prose,* 1:1) is, by association, the fault of Keats,
whose Cockney literary values do appear, in Arnold's view, to have
accomplished a lamentable revolution in popular taste.

Keats and Empedocles on Etna

Over the years the philosophical and literary sources of *Empedocles*
have been carefully studied. The poem is, in fact, a kind of intertextual medley, a potpourri of interacting literary influences. According to Miriam Allott, those "most deeply affecting the central
thought and feeling in the poem . . . [include] Lucretius, Marcus
Aurelius and Epictetus among the ancients, Spinoza among later
writers, and Carlyle among his contemporaries, together with
strong injections of Romantic melancholy from nineteenth-century
writers ranging from Byron to George Sand and from Foscolo to
the Senancour of *Obermann.*"[40] One could safely add other precursors as well, especially Pindar among the ancients, as Paul Zietlow
has recently shown.[41] Among the Romantics, however, Keats's
relevance to the complexities and perplexities of Arnold's greatest
poem has been barely touched upon. That Arnold had Keats (as
well as Tennyson) "so much in [his] head, [he couldn't] help imitating him sometimes" is as true in connection with *Empedocles on Etna*
as with the works whose various debts to Keats are most frequently
discussed, "The Scholar-Gipsy," *Tristram and Iseult,* and "Thyrsis."
As William Ulmer has asserted when discussing "The Scholar-
Gipsy," all of these works interrogate Keatsian poetic values. So
does *Empedocles,* and it initiates the ongoing dialogue with Keats
that occupies all Arnold's longer poems up to *Merope.*

As we have seen, this dialogue in one of its aspects involves matters of reception and reputation: in the 1853 Preface Arnold strenuously attempted to repudiate the Keatsian strain in modern poetry that spawned works flaunting "the dialogue of the mind with itself." Indeed, Arnold goes to extraordinary lengths to distinguish his own literary ideology from the "poetic credo" that "Keats had helped to establish" and that "was the very essence of Alexander Smith and of his confreres of the Spasmodic school."[42] At the same time, of course, Arnold jettisons *Empedocles* from his volume, suggesting the extent of his own very recent contamination by the Keatsian strain that (as we have also seen) Arnold could not help but associate with Cockneyism, threatening liberal political values, and (most recently for him) a Glasgow muslin designer.

As a complex of interacting intertexts, *Empedocles* is a poetic inscription of "the confusion of the present times, . . . the multitude of voices counselling different things, . . . the number of existing works capable of attracting a young writer's attention and of becoming his models" (1853 Preface, *Prose,* 1:8). Arnold therefore deprecates his own work as "vaguely conceived and loosely drawn," as "general, indeterminate, and faint, instead of being particular, precise, and firm" (*Prose,* 1:2). The world of the poem is, as Zietlow has recognized, "one of irreconcilable disparities, paradoxical inconsistencies, and ironic reversals."[43] It appears this way, one might argue, because Arnold has—apparently despite himself—been too avid a student of Keats's poetics of negative capability. Empedocles is hardly a traditional hero (or, it has been insisted, any hero at all), and his suicide results from his persistent "irritable reaching after fact and reason" and his incapacity to remain "content with half knowledge,"[44] as his Keatsian creator is ostensibly able to do. Like Keats himself, whom Arnold decried in his 1849 letter to Clough, this highly dialogical poem seems overwhelmed by the "multitudinousness" of literature and philosophy. It presents no single, coherent "Idea of the world." It is self-subverting and inconclusive in its attempt to address a number of the issues that dominate Keats's major poetry and his letters—how best to pursue the "*mighty abstract* idea of beauty," how to value one's exclusively sensuous responses to the world, how to deal with the difficulties and dangers of the poetic vocation, how to understand the mytho-historical and political problem of revolutions in power, the supplanting of one generation and/or ideology by another.

In treating these issues *Empedocles* presents not only "a dialogue of the mind with itself" but a host of other dialogues as well. The two-act structure of the play has frequently been described as dialectical, but it is in fact dialogical: the play's acts hardly build to any synthesis of the philosophical views or the differing social, moral, aesthetic, and political values expressed by its three characters. Instead, the issues in each act reciprocally interrogate one another, as do its characters (directly or by the juxtaposition of their speeches), leaving all ideological conflicts unresolved. At the same time, the substantive and stylistic borrowings in the poem— from Pindar, Epictetus, Lucretius, Spinoza, Byron, Wordsworth, Keats, etc.—establish a highly complex and inconclusive dialogue among Arnold's precursors.[45] By contrasting the splendid days of his youth with "the swelling evil of this time" (1.1.113),[46] Empedocles himself presents a dialogue between past and present, youth and maturity, one that is also embodied in the counterpointed speeches of Empedocles and songs of Callicles in act 2. Empedocles further implies a dialogue between himself and the "new swarm of sophists" that "has got empire in our schools" (1.1.121–22). Even within his long homily in act 1, Empedocles sets up a dialogue among a number of general philosophies of life. Though this dialogue appears conclusive, it ends with advice for attaining human happiness that in act 2 Empedocles emphatically cannot follow: "trust the joys there are."

> . . . Fear Not! Life still
> Leaves human effort scope.
> But, since life teems with ill,
> Nurse no extravagant hope;
> Because thou must not dream, thou need'st not then
>   despair!

(1.2.421–26)

Empedocles himself personifies the dialogical thematic structure of the play. Because of his self-contradictions, his misanthropy, his despair, his failure to find any "vent in action" except suicide, Empedocles is more like a failed Wordsworth or a Byronic antihero (without the gusto of a Manfred) than a classical hero. But, as we shall see, his Keatsian qualities finally outnumber and redefine the other, "multitudinous," fragments of precursive literary personalities that together constitute his character. Similarly, as we shall also see, it is predominantly Arnold's response to what he perceived as limitations in Keats's poetic and political values that determines his depiction of Callicles.

Callicles reflects both Arnold's strong attraction to Keats's "very high gift" and his distress at Keats's "confused multitudinousness" when composing *Empedocles* between 1849 and 1852. As Zietlow argues, throughout the play Callicles "remains in the ethos of 'the old religion of Delphi' and speaks with 'the calm, cheerfulness, the disinterested objectivity' of 'early Greek genius.' "[47] In that respect only, Callicles embodies the most conservative elements of the play. But like Keats, Callicles sings songs (in the form of Pindaric odes) concerned with such issues as the poetic vocation and revolutions in the power structures of the world. Callicles' songs about Marsyas and Apollo and Typho and Zeus are, in these respects, not merely responses to issues that preoccupy Empedocles, but works parallel to Keats's "Greek" *Hyperion*. Moreover, like Keats, the poet of "natural magic," Callicles is wholly attentive to the beauty of the world around him. In sensuous descriptions he dependably replicates that beauty:

> Here in the valley, is the shade; the sward
> Is dark, and on the stream the mist still hangs;
> One sees one's footprints crush'd in the wet grass,
> One's breath curls in the air; and on these pines
> That climb from the stream's edge, the long grey tufts,
> Which the goats love, are jewell'd thick with dew.

(1.1.12–17)

Callicles' blank verse, his diction ("crush'd," "jewell'd"), and his rhymes here generally echo Keats's style as surely as the first line of this passage specifically echoes the first line of *Hyperion*: "Deep in the shady sadness of a vale." Callicles is Arnold's Strayed Reveller—who grappled with the difficulties of choosing the poetic vocation—now fully reconstituted as a poet. Both figures have a conspicuously Keatsian lineage.

Even Callicles' name, which is Greek for "beauty," confirms the fact. While rereading Keats in the mid-1840s and looking into Milnes's *Life* of Keats just as he was beginning to write *Empedocles* in 1848–49,[48] Arnold was fairly obsessed with the proper pursuit of poetic beauty. In Milnes's volume he confronted the letter he quotes prominently in his essay on Keats in which Keats mentions the "mighty *abstract idea* of Beauty in all things" that dominates him. Keats confesses his "yearning passion for the Beautiful, connected and made one with the ambition of my intellect."[49] Similarly, in a letter to Clough in February 1848, Arnold himself insists that only "the *beautiful*" is "*poetical*." And at the beginning of 1849, while discussing Clough's poems, he advises his friend primarily to "consider whether you attain the *beautiful*."[50]

Throughout *Empedocles* Callicles consistently assimilates the beauty of the external world and generates it anew in the self-sufficient mythical structures of his verse. Callicles is a perfect "camelion Poet," as Keats describes that figure: "he has no Identity—he is continually . . . filling some other Body."[51] Uncommitted to particular positions and values, he is wholly disinterested. Moreover, his songs operate precisely as "natural magic," "so dealing with things as to awaken in us a wonderfully full, new, and intimate sense of them, and of our relations with them." Such poetry not only "calms" the reader (as Callicles' detached songs clearly aim to calm Empedocles), but it also possesses a "grand . . . interpretive power." It "interprets by expressing with magical felicity the physiognomy and movement of the outward world" (*Prose*, 3:33). But poetry at its best, for Arnold in the essay on Maurice de Guérin, also possesses "*moral profundity*." It also "interprets by expressing, with inspired conviction, the ideas and laws of the inward world of man's moral and spiritual nature" (ibid.). In its imperturbable resignation to such laws, Callicles' poetry is that of both natural magic and moral profundity. He is fully the ideal poet whose work "illuminates man . . . gives him a satisfying sense of reality . . . [and] reconciles him with himself and the universe" (ibid.), whereas Empedocles only half fulfills Arnold's criteria for such a figure.

When we encounter him, Empedocles is no longer the poet of natural magic he apparently once was:

> yet what days were those, Parmenides!
> When we were young, when we could number friends
> In all the Italian cities like ourselves,
> When with elated hearts we join'd your train,
> Ye Sun-born Virgins! on the road of truth.
> Then we could still enjoy, then neither thought
> Nor outward things were closed and dead to us;
(2.235–49)
> But we received the shock of mighty thoughts
> On simple minds with a pure natural joy;
> And if the sacred load oppress'd our brain,
> We had the power to feel the pressure eased,
> The brow unbound, the thoughts flow free again,
> In the delightful commerce of the world.
> We had not lost our balance then, nor grown
> Thought's slaves, and dead to every natural joy.

Like Wordsworth as Keats viewed him, however, Empedocles now appears merely to be a poet attempting moral profundity. But he is flawed even in that role by a growing uncertainty about the true structure of "man's moral and spiritual nature." Like Wordsworth in the first four stanzas of the Intimations Ode, he is a poet with a diminished "faculty of joy."[52] He has lost his "power of feeling" and his sense of the "fulness of life." But unlike Wordsworth, he cannot recover what he has lost. Rather, like Keats's Hyperion about to fall from power, he turns his eyes to the stars and appeals to them as symbols of the vitality he has lost and the immortality he feels is inaccessible to him:

> No, no, ye stars! there is no death with you,
(2.301–3)
> No languor, no decay! languor and death,
> They are with me, not you! ye are alive—[53]

Nonetheless, in act 1 at least, Empedocles has been willing to exercise his talents to moralize on the subject of others' misguided values and false philosophies. Like Wordsworth as Keats caricatures him in *Sleep and Poetry,* his "themes / Are ugly clubs, the Poet's Polyphemes / Disturbing" the tranquil harmony of his natural surroundings (ll. 232–34). Moreover, the philosophy of "moderate bliss" he hypocritically rehearses in concluding his otherwise skeptical homily to Pausanias is untenable for him, a matter only of paying a "debt."

Despite his ostensibly Wordsworthian characteristics and despite his present deficiency of natural magic, Empedocles is a figure far more derivative of Keats than of Wordsworth. In the very first paragraph of his essay on Keats, Arnold disparagingly quotes Keats's ejaculation, "O for a life of sensations rather than of thoughts!" (*Prose,* 9:205). As he briefly introduces his negative comments on the letters to Fanny Brawne here, Arnold is concerned that "character and self-control"—indispensable "for every kind of greatness, and for the great artist, too"—give way in Keats to sheer sensuousness. But Arnold's citation of Keats is ironically inappropriate in this context. In the letter from which Arnold quotes (to Benjamin Bailey, November 22, 1817),[54] Keats is in a wholly speculative state of mind. Discussing how "all our Passions . . are in their sublime, creative of essential Beauty" and trying urgently to come to grips with the operations of the imagination, Keats is, at the point of Arnold's quotation, extremely frustrated that "even the greatest Philosopher" must put aside "numerous objections" to arrive "at his goal." In this as in so many of his speculative and philosophical letters, Keats represents himself as one of "Thought's slaves," a "devouring flame of thought," a "naked, eternally restless mind!" (*Empedocles,* 2.249, 329–30). Having read many of these letters in 1848–49, Arnold was obviously aware that, at least in this creative medium, Keats was a kind of immature and unpolished—indeed, at times undignified—version of the figure that developed as his own Empedocles. The more closely we inspect the character of Empedocles, the more strongly we are compelled to realize the similarities between his own temperament and that of Keats. Empedocles is a poet of natural magic vanquished by age.

In his essay on Maurice de Guérin, we recall, Arnold describes the temperament that Guérin shares with Keats as "*devouring; it uses vital power too hard and too fast, paying the penalty in long hours of unutterable exhaustion and in premature death*" (*Prose,*

3:32). He goes on to discuss at length Guérin's intense and chronic
state of depression, quoting Guérin's remarks on his "sense profound, near, immense, of my misery" (ibid.). Like Keats (and
Empedocles) in temperament, Guérin explains that "Mental work
brings on, not drowsiness, but an irritable and nervous disgust
which drives me out, I know not where, into the streets and public
places" (*Prose,* 3:32–33). Similarly, Empedocles flies "back to men"
to "help him to unbend his too tense thought" (9.220, 222), but
with as little permanent effect as Guérin achieves. The magic of
nature has also failed Guérin: "The Spring, whose delights used to
come every year stealthily and mysteriously to charm me in my
retreat, crushes me this year under a weight" (*Prose,* 3:33). Arnold
concludes, "certainly it was not for Guérin's happiness, or for
Keats's . . . to be as they were" (ibid.). The logical end to such
overpowering depression, if "premature death" did not come naturally, would be suicide. That Arnold can in 1863 retrospectively
draw such clear connections between the depressed, "devouring"
temperaments of Keats and Guérin, each afflicted with a mind
"preying upon itself" and "Some secret and unfollow'd vein of
woe"(1.1.152)—as Callicles describes Empedocles's ailment—suggests that Arnold's original model for Empedocles was Keats.

Indeed, Empedocles fulfills Keats's own prophecy for himself
as a depressed and recalcitrant poet, who feels trodden down by
"hungry generations" (Pausanias's "swarms of sophists") and who
resists the corrupt values of his time. He refuses a "mawkish popularity" in favor of "jump[ing] down Ætna." In this view, then,
Empedocles appears as a classical incarnation of the Keatsian temperament—a Keats rescued from his Cockney contexts and made
respectable, indeed ennobled. But his youthful powers of natural
magic have deserted him, and his intellectual confusion reveals that
he has never had the power to be a poet of "moral profundity." He
lacks not only a "self-sufficing font of joy" but also a clear "Idea of
the world" that would yield a sense of its orderliness and of personal calm. Such a unified conception of "the ideas and laws of the
inward world of man's moral and spiritual nature," in connection
with an "intimate sense" of the "essential nature" of the external
world, would also give him, as it gives Arnold's Scholar-Gipsy,

"*one* aim, *one* business, *one* desire." It would yield the sense of purpose and direction Callicles possesses, healing his "mental strife"
and providing an antidote to the "strange disease of modern life."
("The Scholar-Gipsy," ll .152, 222, 203).

If these speculations approach a true description of the originary contexts for *Empedocles,* then it may have been far less difficult
than one first imagines for Arnold in 1853 to repudiate the most
ambitious work he had written up to 1852. Indeed, the fate of the
poem, like that of its hero, appears to have been predetermined by
its very constitution.[55] Having set out to present a critique of the
Keatsian (and Spasmodic) poetic values he condemns so vocifer-
ously in his 1849 letter to Clough, Arnold succumbed too fully to
the effects of Keats's "very high gift." From his poem's conception
Arnold was working with a (Keatsian and Spasmodic) "hero"
whose deficiencies as an exhausted poet of "natural magic" were his
intended subject. But Arnold had become more captivated than he
wished to be by the Keatsian (and Empedoclean) temperament. In
his final poetic product Empedocles attains an unanticipated titanic
stature, which the figure of Callicles—the ideal poet—is inadequate to overshadow. As a result the play ends up presenting an
equivocal dialogue rather than an "Idea of the world," and its
"failure," in Arnold's view, tells us more than he could admit to in
his Preface—or perhaps more than he truly understood—about the
ideological conflicts out of which the poem emerged.

Those conflicts become especially apparent if we begin to
think of *Empedocles* as young Arnold's attempt to rewrite and
supersede Keats's *Hyperion,* which he knew well.[56] In his essay on
Keats Arnold insists that "*Hyperion,* fine things as it contains, is not
a success" (*Prose,* 9:215). Yet, in his attempt to reinscribe the essential structural and thematic patterns of *Hyperion* in *Empedocles,* Arnold repeatedly echoes Keats's poem. Both works concern themselves at a fundamental level with "the sure revolutions of the
world" that Empedocles alludes to at the end of act 1 (l. 472).

I have already observed, for instance, that Empedocles, like
Hyperion, turns his gaze upon the stars—in both poems symbols
of permanence—in his climactic moment of crisis. Both heroes,
too, are "unused to bend" and in different ways succumb to "the

sorrow of the time" (*Hyperion,* book 1, ll. 300–301). Moreover, *Empedocles'* "charr'd, blacken'd, melancholy waste," where vapors "boil up" and the "sea of fire" "leap[s] and roar[s]" is a parodic topographical reflex of Saturn's lost "thunder, conscious of the new command," which "rumbles reluctant o'er our fallen house" and his "sharp lightning in unpracticed hands," which "scorches and burns our once serene domain" (book 1, ll. 60–63). Empedocles, like Saturn, has lost his efficacy in the world: he is banished, while Saturn laments the loss of his "godlike exercise / Of influence" (book 1, ll. 107–8). Both, too, are self-alienated. Empedocles cannot "live with men nor with [him]self" (2.23), and Saturn claims to be

	gone
(Hyperion, book 1, ll. 112–15)	Away from my own bosom; I have left My strong identity, my real self, Somewhere.

Empedocles can be seen to derive alternately from Saturn and Hyperion, because both were once powers and both are victims of the world's "sure revolutions."

Such parallels begin to suggest that the intertextual relations between *Hyperion* and *Empedocles* function at the level of political ideology as well as characterization. Like Keats, the historical Empedocles was "on the liberal side of the question," as Paul Zietlow has reminded us. Arnold might well have expected his educated audience to know that Empedocles's attempt to encourage a form of democracy in Acragas after Theron's death in 472 B.C. precipitated his banishment. Therefore, when Callicles, in his crucial song about Zeus and Typho, appears to "extol the actions of tyrants whom Empedocles, according to tradition, found inimical . . . , Empedocles' romantic identification with Typho as Titan greatness subdued by 'littleness united' resonates with complex irony."[57]

In the contexts I have attempted to establish here, the irony is complex indeed. If we read Keats's *Hyperion* as something of a political allegory (and how could Arnold *not* think of doing so when contemplating Keats during the politically tumultuous last years of the 1840s?), then clearly some of its lines, including those of Oceanus, "speak for Keats against the order that excluded him from political enfranchisement as well as poetic recognition; and one may feel that he admires the new gods at least to the extent that they help to overthrow it forever."[58] In Arnold's representation, however, the otherwise Keatsian Empedocles cannot welcome the overthrow of the established order that has recently occurred in Catana because he has been a dominant member of that order, just as—in Arnold's view—the strain of Keats has for too many years dominated the Victorian literary scene. Empedocles' misinterpretation of Callicles' song about Typho is ironic in his present circumstances—a type of mindless, automatic, and antagonistic "liberal" response in principle to the control by newly dominant forces of those they have superseded and who have now become rebellious. Empedocles's response thus reflects an inability, like that of Hyperion and of Saturn, to accept the ongoing cyclical patterns of "sure revolutions" in human history. Another irony here, then, is that Empedocles has more in common with intransigent titans—Typho and Keats's Saturn and Hyperion—than he does with the historical Empedocles, or with Zeus, Apollo, and Arnold's own Callicles, the true "revolutionaries" in the particular histories these two works take up.

Within one of the three passages from *Hyperion* that Arnold chose to include in Ward's *English Poets,* Oceanus counsels Saturn to accept the inevitability of revolution: "thou was not the first of powers, / So art thou not the last" (*Hyperion,* book 2, ll. 188–89). He further insists that Saturn "Mark well!" that "to bear all naked truths, / And to envisage circumstance, all calm, / That is the top of sovereignty" (*Hyperion,* book 2, ll. 203–5). Callicles, who has perfectly attained such detachment, resignation, and calm, is in fact ordained to supplant Empedocles as the sovereign poet, just as Apollo—whom Callicles invokes and envisions in his last song— will supplant Hyperion in Keats's poem. Callicles possesses not only natural magic and moral profundity but also the wide vision of the ideal poet Arnold describes in "Resignation" and in a letter to Clough.[59] In the last words of the play, with his vision of Apollo and the muses, Callicles demonstrates that he is the new poet laureate who can replicate the muses' hymns of

>   . . . the Father
> Of all things: and then,
> The rest of immortals,
> The action of men.
>
> The day in his hotness,
> The strife with the palm;
> The night in her silence,
> The stars in their calm.

(2.461–68)

The ideal poet who possesses the natural magic that Empedocles
has lost and the moral profundity he could never attain, Callicles
here implicitly announces his new domain. Similarly, Callicles'
creator, by means of his poem on "sure revolutions," attempts to
announce his own supersession of the exhausted and defunct lineage of Keatsian poets on the Victorian scene. But as Arnold well
knew, his project failed in part because he became what he beheld.
The "perplexity" Keats "occasion[ed]" to this "young writer of the
[Greek] sort" proved insuperable. After 1853, therefore, *Empedocles*
serves only to announce that a true Callicles is "powerless to be
born" in mid-Victorian England.

II

———•••⟨∞⟩•••———

"Cleon" and Its Contexts

As Arnold begins to demonstrate in the virtual monodrama of act 2 of *Empedocles,* the dramatic monologue is a highly self-conscious and intellectual poetic form.[1] Since the intended targets of a monologue's author may be quite other than those of its speaker, a dramatic monologue inevitably and spontaneously evokes a subtextual question in most readers' minds: What is the poet as artificer attempting to accomplish by devising this elaborate mode of self-disguise? What values and beliefs does he (really) wish to support, criticize, or propound? And to what end?[2] Because such questioning and traces of anticipatory authorial response to it inhere in the operations of the dramatic monologue, this literary form that on its surface appears determined to suppress ideology, instead complexly draws attention—through its self-conscious elisions—to the subtle ways in which both poet and reader are entrapped in webs of ideology that demand interrogation or defense. Further, because of the inherent complexities of the dramatic monologue, discussions of intertextual relations in this poetic form can frequently yield surprising insights, especially with a master monologuist like Robert Browning, for whom the monologue becomes the most cerebral of poetic forms.

Roland Barthes has suggested that for every poem, every reader must be conceived as "une pluralité d'autres textes, de codes infinis"[3] because he bears a history of reading texts, some of which he perforce associates as intertexts with whatever work happens to be before him. It is thus the reader who "establishes a relationship between a focused text and its intertext, and forges its intertextual identity."[4] But, as is clear, readers are given guidance in seeking meaningful pre-texts for a poem that is demonstrably intertextual by the echoes and allusions embedded by an author in his text. Browning's monologues, informed by a wealth of (often obscure)

allusions, repeatedly demand intertextual readings, and their ideological complications are—like metaphors drawn out to conceits—
insistently extended in this way. Preeminent among such poems by
Browning (as Harold Bloom has observed)[5] is "Cleon," a monologue whose speaker defiantly concerns himself with his own artistic and specifically poetic lineage, much as Browning does in his
famous essay on Shelley (1852).

Composed in 1854, "Cleon" is a monologue in the form of an
epistle written by a famed Greek poet and artist (invented by
Browning) in response to a letter from King Protus (also fic-
titious).[6] Protus has asked Cleon the truth about his artistic accomplishments and his ability to "fear death less" because his poems
and paintings will live immortally. In his letter Cleon describes his
artistic lineage and supremacy, yet acknowledges the futility of his
achievement in outstripping mortality and presents "the accurate
view" of what constitutes joy in life. Cleon hastily concludes by acknowledging that he is unable to redirect a letter Protus has written
to one "Paulus" and speculates that this person might be identical
with another reputed "barbarian Jew"—Christus—whose "doctrine could be held by no sane man."[7]

Joy is the most important conceptual term—both philosophical and aesthetic—in "Cleon." Repeated in variant forms eighteen
times, it is the key to the intertextual reaches of the work. As we
shall see, it is the poem's most important link to Arnoldian, Wordsworthian, Keatsian, and Spasmodic pre-texts and the term that positions Browning's monologue on the front lines in mid-Victorian
disputes about the value and function of poetry and, more specifically, about the precedence of particular "schools" of nineteenth-
century poetry.[8] Cleon first uses the word *joy* early in the poem,
when he describes himself disingenuously, as one "whose song
gives life its joy" (l. 21). This boast is afterwards explained in his
description of the eminence he has attained in all arts:

> I have not chanted verse like Homer, no—
(ll. 139–51)
> Nor swept string like Terpander, no—nor carved
> And painted men like Phidias and his friend:
> I am not great as they are, point by point.

But I have entered into sympathy
With these four, running these into one soul,
Who, separate, ignored each other's art.
Say, is it nothing that I know them all?
The wild flower was the larger; I have dashed
Rose-blood upon its petals, pricked its cup's
Honey with wine, and driven its seed to fruit,
And show a better flower if not so large:
I stand myself.

Cleon thus attempts to establish that he has a "greater mind / Than [his] forerunners, since more composite" (ll. 64–65). Only the product of such a mind can "give life its joy."

This passage from "Cleon" transposes into verse an important statement from the essay on Shelley ("Introductory Essay") that partially lays out Browning's understanding of the intertextual relations among poets. In his essay Browning speculates that the "two modes of poetic faculty"—the objective and the subjective—may possibly "issue hereafter from the same poet in successive perfect works, examples of which . . . we have hitherto possessed in distinct individuals only" (*Poems*, p. 1003). Browning proceeds to describe his concept of the historical process of evolution among poets and presents a virtually Hegelian theory of artistic cycles of poetic supersession, beginning with the demise of the "objective" poet:

There is a time when the general eye has, so to speak, absorbed its fill of the phenomena around it, whether spiritual or material, and desires rather to learn the exacter significance of what it possesses, than to receive any augmentation of what is possessed. Then is the opportunity for the poet of loftier vision, to lift his fellows, with their half-apprehensions, up to his own sphere, by intensifying the import of details and rounding the universal meaning. The influence of such an achievement will not soon die out. A tribe of successors (Homerides) working more or less in the same spirit, dwell on his discoveries and reinforce his doctrine; til . . . the world is found to be subsisting wholly on . . . the straw of last year's harvest. Then is the imperative call for the appearance of

(*Poems*,
pp. 1003–4)

another sort of poet, who shall . . . [get] at new substance by
breaking up the assumed wholes into parts . . . careless of the
unknown laws for re-combining them (it will be the business of yet
another poet to suggest those hereafter), . . . shaping for their uses
a new and different creation from the last . . . to endure until, in
the inevitable process, its very sufficiency to itself shall require, at
length, an exposition of its affinity to something higher.

This long passage is crucial in understanding the intertextual and ideological operations of "Cleon." But these become fully visible only when we situate the poem in its most important historical contexts, one of which is the publication of *Empedocles on Etna* in 1852 and Arnold's retraction of it in 1853.

Since 1927 a number of critics and readers have extended A. W. Crawford's observation that a relationship between "Cleon" and *Empedocles on Etna* clearly exists.[9] That Browning had read Arnold's poem with enthusiasm and had been disappointed by its suppression in 1853 is certain. On August 19, 1867, shortly after Arnold had republished *Empedocles* in his *Poems*, Browning wrote to his close friend Isabella Blagden: "I should like to know something about Arnold's new volume: he told me he had reprinted therein ['Empedocles] on Etna'—with a pretty note saying that it was done thro' my request. I am really flattered at *that*—I like the man as much as the poems."[10] "Cleon" may in fact have been written as much in reaction to Arnold's retraction of *Empedocles* and his explanations for doing so in the 1853 Preface as in response to Arnold's poem itself. If this speculation is correct, then Browning's poem situates itself in the debates about Spasmodicism raging in the early 1850s as fully as Arnold's Preface does. "Cleon" may be seen as a kind of attack upon Spasmodicism (and all it represented to the Arnoldian mind) different from Arnold's earnest and theoretical Preface or William Edmondstoune Aytoun's parodic *Firmilian* (published in 1854), but a polemic, nonetheless, against the decadent poetic practices culminating in the early fifties with the publication of Sydney Dobell's *Balder* and Alexander Smith's *A Life-Drama*. These practices Arnold assaults directly in his Preface, as Browning would certainly have realized.[11]

At the center of Browning's poem, Cleon acknowledges his epistle's confessional tone. He tells Protus, "Nay, thou art worthy of hearing my whole mind" (l. 181). Indeed, this work, like so many of Browning's monologues, takes shape—with its elaborate, often obscure and convoluted conceits and symbols—as an allegory of the state of Cleon's mind, and thus as a representative history of the fate of the consummate, misguided artist. My phrasing here comes from Arnold's 1853 Preface, where Arnold misquotes David Masson's recent critical review supporting specifically Spasmodic elements of contemporary poetry. Arnold responds: "The modern critic not only permits false practice; he absolutely prescribes false aims. — 'A true allegory of the state of one's own mind in a representative history,' the poet is told, 'is perhaps the highest thing that one can attempt in the way of poetry.' . . . An allegory of the state of one's own mind, the highest problem of an art which imitates actions! No assuredly, it is not, it never can be so: no great poetical work has ever been produced with such an aim." After stressing the preeminent value in poetry of architectonics—"the power of execution, which creates, forms, and constitutes" rather than the "profoundness of single thoughts, [or] the richness of imagery, [or] abundance of illustration"— Arnold proceeds to criticize the stylistic excesses of much contemporary poetry. As we have seen in the previous chapter, he locates the most recent precedent for this malaise in the work of Keats, passing over *Endymion* as a negative model in favor of *Isabella*. *Endymion*—which explores an aesthetics of hedonism from its very first line, "A thing of beauty is a joy forever"—Arnold finds "so incoherent, as not strictly to merit the name of a poem at all." He concludes his essay, as he had begun it, insisting that the present "era of progress . . . commissioned to carry out the great ideas of industrial development and social amelioration" is wholly "wanting in moral grandeur" and therefore cannot contribute as a subject matter to the grandest goal of poetry: "to afford to [people] the highest pleasure they are capable of feeling," that is to say, the "highest enjoyment."[12]

From the very beginning of the Preface Arnold introduces into his discussion of the purposes of poetry this key term from the great poem whose retraction it is the function of the Preface to explain and justify. He does so by quoting Schiller's dictum that all art "is dedicated to Joy, and there is no higher and no more serious problem, than how to make men happy. The right Art is that alone, which creates the highest enjoyment" (*Prose*, 1:2). In the two paragraphs that follow Arnold analyzes the true sources of joy in poetry and, by extension, in life (if poetry constitutes—as Arnold later insists—a "criticism of life").

That Browning was, with "Cleon," participating in the ongoing Romantic debate concerning the true grounds and constitution of joy in poetry and in life at large—a debate that Arnold energetically enters into here—seems an inevitable conclusion, given these contexts. Further evidence for it emerges from a simple comparative analysis of "Cleon" and *Empedocles,* especially each poem's employment and interrogation of the term *joy* and each poem's implicit revision of its uses in seminal poems by Wordsworth and Keats.[13] These works—including the Intimations Ode, *The Prelude, Endymion,* and the "Ode on Melancholy"—establish a philosophical dialogue surrounding the term, one that has important implications for the politics of poetic achievement and supersession in the nineteenth century.[14]

Like Empedocles, Cleon is a philosopher-poet. Like Arnold's hero, too, Cleon confessionally laments the loss of joy in his life. This loss, and that of Empedocles, results from both poets' painful obsession with mortality. Both Arnold and Browning set up as the central dialectic of their respective poems the opposition between youth and age, though Arnold embeds that dialectic both within Empedocles (who wistfully recalls the "days . . . / When we were young" and "could still enjoy,"[15] and between Empedocles and Callicles. Following Arnold's direction, Browning chooses to focus his poem, not in the modern world or on contemporary events, but—in defiance of mid-century calls for relevancy in poetry—in Greece, the cradle of Western aesthetic culture. Again like Arnold, Browning fastens upon the term *joy* as the pivotal conceptual and philosophic term in Cleon's epistle.

"Cleon" is a poem that finally despairs over the materialism of its titular hero's historical era, as does *Empedocles.* Arnold's drama instructs in the value of the "natural joy" and spiritual fulfillment

that Empedocles had temporarily attained in his youth, while
"Cleon" exposes the moral, intellectual, and spiritual deficiencies
of its speaker, whose concept of joy is entirely hedonistic. Cleon
serves the reader as a negative example. In *Empedocles,* as well as in
poems like "The Buried Life" and "Stanzas in Memory of the
Author of *Obermann,"* joy clearly refers to an ideal state of spiritual
fulfillment, self-completion, and affinity with Arnold's version of
Wordsworth's "Immortal Sea," man's transcendent spiritual matrix
(the "general life" of "Resignation"). In Browning's poem, however, *joy* and terms associated with it refer exclusively to the effects
of sensory and aesthetic experience. Cleon has no conception of the
"soul" beyond such experience. Hence, his inaccessibility to Christian truth and revelation. He is, philosophically, the most sophisticated and refined of materialists, for whom a belief in the value of
Christian renunciation would indeed seem insane.

Before we can determine the significance of Cleon's moral,
aesthetic, and spiritual failures, we must understand—as Browning did—the success of Empedocles in sustaining right moral, aesthetic, and spiritual values. This he can accomplish only through
his suicide, thus (like Byron's Prometheus) making death a vic-
tory.[16] Empedocles' obsessive aim is to preserve what remains of
his spirit's "self-sufficing fount of joy" (2.23). He wishes to die

Ere quite the being of man, ere quite the world
Be disarray'd of their divinity—
(2.31–35)   Before the soul lose all her solemn joys,
And awe be dead, and hope impossible
And the soul's deep eternal night come on.

Empedocles is wrenchingly preoccupied with his "dwindling faculty of joy" (2.273). Using grand and simple Wordsworthian abstractions, he associates "joy" with his early days, with the "shock
of mighty thoughts" that derived from elementary, commonplace
experiences. In those days, "on the road of truth,"

(2.240–43,   . . . we could still enjoy, then neither thought
248–49)   Nor outward things were closed and dead to us.

But we received the shock of mighty thoughts
On simple minds with a pure natural joy;

. . . . .

We had not lost our balance then, nor grown
Thought's slaves, and dead to every natural joy.

For Empedocles the most sublime and valuable human experiences
are these which reveal the "primary affections of the human heart,"
the spiritual affinities of men to which "the imperious lonely thinking power" (2.375), when overindulged and overly refined, becomes antagonistic. The overactive intellect impedes access to spiritual fulfillment, to "being one with the whole world" (2.372).
Sophisticated intellectuals, from Empedocles' point of view, are
blind to spiritual knowledge and impervious to communion with
the ultimate truths of human nature and experience which are
derived from the "smallest" things:

The sports of the country-people,
A flute note from the woods,
Sunset over the sea;
(1.2.251– Seed time and harvest,
58) The reapers in the corn,
The vinedresser in his vineyard,
The village-girl at her wheel.

While Empedocles disparages excessive intellectual refinement, he also rejects most major schools of philosophical thought
in the crucial concluding section of his homily in act 1. Significantly, his attack culminates with a diatribe against hedonism that
seems especially applicable to Cleon. Empedocles reminisces on
"Our youthful blood" which inevitably "Claims raptures as its
right" and has "Pleasure" in its "hot grasp" (1.2.352–53, 357), but
which becomes discontented as we age:

Yet still, in spite of truth,
In spite of hopes entomb'd,
(1.2.367– That longing of our youth
71) Burns ever unconsumed,
Still hungrier for delight as delights grow more rare.

And thus, as we age and our senses fail, we realize our mortality with increasing urgency:

> We pause; we hush our heart,
> And thus address the Gods:
> "The world hath failed to impart
> The joy our youth forebodes,
> Failed to fill up the void which in our breasts we bear."

(1.2.372–76)

This is exactly Cleon's dilemma as he confesses to Protus his unsuccessful quest for fulfillment and the reasons for his failure. He is unable to satisfy his "joy-hunger" because he conceives of joy exclusively in terms of hedonistic and aesthetic experience. Browning's Rabbi Ben Ezra provides the perfect gloss on Cleon's fate. Cleon is the rabbi's "crop-full bird" or "maw-crammed beast," albeit disguised by his sophisticated intellect and aesthetic refinement. The rabbi comments:

> Poor vaunt of life indeed,
> Were man but formed to feed
> On joy, to solely seek and find and feast:
> Such feasting ended, then
> As sure an end to men.

(*Poems*, 1:781)

Pathetically, Cleon's ultimate spiritual fantasy is merely an aesthetic and hedonistic one: to satisfy his "joy-hunger" in an afterlife that reminds us of Keats's "favorite Speculation": that "we shall enjoy ourselves here after by having what we called happiness on Earth repeated in a finer tone and so repeated."[17] Cleon craves

> Some future state . . .
> Unlimited in capability
> For joy, as this is in desire for joy,
> —To seek which, the joy-hunger forces us.

(ll. 325–28)

Ironies cluster around Cleon's use of the word *joy,* which appears always in the context of material accomplishments and physical sensations. As I have noted, it first occurs in the poem's second stanza as part of his initial self-description. Cleon believes

one of the songs he is noted for "gives life its joy," and he immediately reveals his sense of kinship with Protus by juxtaposing that
accomplishment of his own with a discussion of "the daily building
of [Protus's] tower." Both the poet and the king, according to
Cleon, recognize "the use of life," which is the enjoyment of
sensory pleasures. Cleon assumes that Protus's goal is

. . . some eventual rest a-top [his tower],
Whence, all the tumult of the building hushed,
Thou first of men mightst look out to the East:
The vulgar saw thy tower, thou sawest the sun.

(ll. 33–36)

Since Cleon mentions the "sun-god" fourteen lines later, it is prob-
able that in these earlier lines he, nonetheless, understands Protus's
quest to be more than the creation of a material monument and the
acquisition of a sublime view. Protus wishes to "see" god's face; he
is intent upon a material quest that will effect spiritual fulfillment.
Cleon promises to celebrate Protus's aspirations, but the rest of the
poem exposes his skepticism that spiritual fulfillment can be separated from material existence. One climbs the tower "just to perish
there" (l. 236). Despite his polite expressions of admiration for
Protus's perseverance, Cleon ultimately sees the king's quest as
futile, like his own. Such a conclusion is implied shortly after
Cleon describes Protus's tower and catalogues his own material
accomplishments, *his* artifacts. One of them, an implicit critique of
Protus's labors, is "The image of the sun-god on the phare," which,
ironically, "Men turn from the sun's self to see" (ll. 51–52). For
Cleon, who rejects the possibility of spiritual revelation (ll. 115–
27), art and the sensational world it celebrates, *are* the ultimate
"spiritual" reality.

"Joy" for Cleon finally cannot exist without our material existence in which consciousness inheres, any more than it can be
sustained, according to Empedocles' opposite view, as one's consciousness expands and intensifies. In the evolutionary pattern of
Cleon's thought, the greatest joy would result from the most
highly developed and sensitized consciousness. By "making [a
creature] / Grow conscious in himself" (ll. 197–98), Cleon insists,

(ll. 217–19)
> . . . the more he gets to know
> Of his own life's adaptibilities,
> The more joy-giving will his life become.

Were man immortal, his consciousness of action and sensation, of "his own life's adaptabilities" (l. 21), would bring man the joy of complete fulfillment. But because of death, "in man there's failure" (l. 225).

From Cleon's point of view, then, consciousness benefits man, not because it allows for the perception of moral or spiritual truth, but because, as "the sense of sense" (l. 224), it enables man to savor sensations in the fashion of the Paterian aesthete, for whom "experience itself is the end," being present "always at the focus where the greatest number of vital forces unite in their purest energy." Pater defines "success in life" as Cleon defines it: a "quickened, multiplied consciousness" generated by "forever . . . courting new [sensory] impressions."[18] However, unlike Pater, for whom—in the Keatsian tradition—knowledge of mortality makes sensory impressions infinitely valuable, Cleon finds the prospect of death "horrible" (l. 323). Cleon uses metaphors with decidedly materialistic associations to describe human consciousness. It is "the pleasure-house, / Watch-tower and treasure-fortress of the soul" (ll. 231–32). And the "soul" for Cleon is simply the repository of man's aggregate sensory pleasures enjoyed in life, in combination with the potential for further (ideally infinite) enjoyments of the same sort:

(ll. 239–41)
> . . . there's a world of capability
> For joy, spread round about us, meant for us,
> Inviting us; and still the soul craves all.

Soul here becomes an illimitable appetitive organ, and as such, it is ultimately the source of Cleon's despair of life. Because we die, "life's inadequate to joy, / As the soul sees joy" (ll. 249–50).

Thus in the last section of his epistle, Cleon understandably laments his mortality and the inverse relationship that exists between the development of the soul's thirst for joy and the physical capacity to quench it:

(ll. 310–13)

> . . . every day my sense of joy
> Grows more acute, my soul (intensified
> By power and insight) more enlarged, more keen;
> While every day my hairs fall more and more.

Envying one of Protus's oarsmen, a "young man, / The muscles all a-ripple on his back," Cleon laments that he himself is "grown too gray / For being beloved" (ll. 297–99), and with self-conscious irony he conceives an appropriate epitaph for himself, "The man who loved his life so over much" (l. 322). He is the antithesis of Empedocles.

   In its intertextual relations with Arnold's poem, "Cleon" thus generates a powerful irony. For Empedocles the prospect of reincarnation—a "return . . . to this meadow of calamity" (2:365)—is excruciating. But for Cleon, who believes in progressive evolution rather than fruitless, repetitive cycles, such a prospect would constitute bliss and fulfillment. Empedocles' world of "bondage" to the flesh and mind (2.375), if made eternal, would be a state "unlimited in capability / For joy" to Cleon (ll. 326–27). Through Cleon's arrogant but pathetic negative example, Browning directly condones Empedocles' early Wordsworthian quest, his "ineffable longing for the life of life" (2.375), his implacable urge to escape sensation and consciousness in order to achieve unsullied spiritual fulfillment, to "feel the ALL" (2.353). For Browning's aesthetic and philosophical values, the implications of his poem's tacit acceptance of the Wordsworthian definition of *joy*—and, indeed, of Wordsworth as a model to be remodeled—are extensive and intriguing, as we shall see, especially in light of Browning's persistent antagonism to Wordsworth during his mature years. A full understanding of what such acceptance signifies for Browning's poetic practice and his ambitions as a poet, however, requires some preliminary discussion of particular, extra-Arnoldian, literary-historical contexts of "Cleon."

If Cleon the poet is, ultimately, a misguided hedonist blind to the revelation he (falsely) believes he craves, he nonetheless embodies—as a refashioned Paracelsus—a number of Browning's

own poetic traits and aspirations. These qualities had earned
Browning little fame, mostly disappointing reviews, and frequent
comparisons with the Spasmodic poets, whose popularity Browning envied even as he began to compose most of the poems of *Men
and Women* in 1853.[19] In this year Sydney Dobell's *Balder* and
Alexander Smith's *A Life-Drama* were published to extraordinary
critical acclaim.[20] Herbert Spencer described Smith as "*the* poet of
the age" and insisted that none better had appeared since Shakespeare, while George Meredith wrote a sonnet in Smith's honor. As
Jerome Hamilton Buckley has explained, "no poem since *Childe
Harold* had won its author such widespread acclaim."[21] *A Life-
Drama* went through four editions in two years. Similarly, *Balder*
earned Dobell accolades from many quarters. *The New Monthly
Magazine* acknowledged that rarely "has such an ovation been
offered to any modern poetical aspirant."[22]

Jerome Thrale has shown that Browning certainly knew the
Spasmodics well. He had presented Elizabeth Barrett Browning
with a copy of Bailey's *Festus* in 1845. Eight years later her letters
demonstrate a serious interest in Alexander Smith's work and its
fortunes. On April 12, 1853, she writes of having borrowed a copy
of the *Athenaeum* in order to read a review of *A Life-Drama*. Smith
is, she allows, "applauded everywhere." In June, apparently after
both she and Browning had read Smith's work, she writes that "it
strikes us . . . that he has more imagery than verity, more colour
than form." In August she comments with some satisfaction on
Tennyson's judgment of Smith's work, "*in the very words* we had
given here—'fancy and not imagination.' Also, imagery in excess;
thought in deficiency. . . . It is extraordinary . . . [that Smith] has
met with so much rapid recognition." As Thrale observes, in such
comments and elsewhere Barrett Browning's use of *us* and *we*
suggests that her opinions were shared by her husband.[23]

Like the heroes of most Spasmodic epics, Cleon is an ambitious poet and, like the Spasmodics themselves, a successful and
popular one. But the connections run deeper than this. Just as
"Popularity" is Browning's satirical response to the superficiality
and the success of Spasmodic poetry in 1853, "Cleon" constitutes

his serious critique of the inadequate aesthetic, philosophical, and spiritual values of Spasmodicism.

Cleon—master of all arts—is a projection of Browning's own earliest fantasies, in good part realized by poets like Smith and Dobell. Even before his twentieth birthday, Browning had aspired to amaze the world by producing simultaneously and anonymously a play, an opera, a novel, and a poem. With each hailed as a brilliant success, he planned to "disclose his authorship to an astonished world."[24] Although in his correspondence through the forties, Browning claimed to disdain popular success, he strongly craved it,[25] especially after it became clear that, with Wordsworth's death and the laureateship vacant, Browning himself, after twenty years as a publishing poet, was not even a contender for the post. Whereas Cleon's works, like Smith's, are the center of popular attention, Browning's had on occasion become the butt of jokes. In 1840, for instance, *Sordello* had "brought notoriety, not fame" to Browning, with reviewers and acquaintances alike despising it as "obscure," "unreadable," "trash, of the worst description."[26]

Thus when preparing *Dramatic Romances and Lyrics* for publication in 1845, Browning was anxious that these poems become popular. And eight years later, with the poems of *Men and Women* underway, he explained to his friend Joseph Milsand: "I am writing—a first step towards popularity for me—lyrics with more music and painting than before, so as to get people to hear and see."[27] But the reception of *Men and Women* was generally unfavorable. With Aytoun's exposé of the excesses of Spasmodicism the year before, Browning's new monologues were disparaged particularly for their Spasmodic obscurity.[28] Responding to the reviews, Browning wrote in exasperation to Edward Chapman, his publisher: "As to my own Poems—they must be left to Providence and that fine sense of discrimination which I never cease to meditate upon and admire in the public: they cry out for new things and when you furnish them with what they cried for, 'it's *so* new,' they grunt. The half-dozen people who know and could impose their opinions on the whole sty of grunters say nothing to *them* (I don't wonder) and speak so low in my own ear that it's lost to all intents and purposes."[29] Despite his hopes for the success of *Men and Women,* Browning had, ironically, anticipated its poor reception in "Popularity," a poem that followed "Cleon" closely in the volume. (Only "The Twins" intervened.) The speaker in "Popularity" hails a true but neglected poetic genius, "a star," "God's glow-worm," whose essential artistry—which Browning figures in an elaborate conceit of Tyrian blue, the "dye of dyes"—is popularized by a group of feeble imitators, Hobbs, Nobbs, and Nokes: the "tribe of successors" described in the essay on Shelley (*Poems,* pp. 722–23). Meanwhile the "true poet" who "fished the murex up" is starved of fame. The poem's final line—"What porridge had John Keats?" (*Poems,* p. 724)—suggests that the work is a satire of popular Spasmodicism, which Browning, like so many of his contemporaries including Arnold, saw as a development from the work of Keats, who had been critically disparaged by his contemporaries but posthumously admired.[30]

Browning's relationship with Spasmodicism is complex and, it would seem, contradictory. Donald Hair has convincingly argued that *Pauline* is a proto-Spasmodic poem.[31] *Sordello* was denounced by some reviewers for its Spasmodic excesses. And by the mid-forties William Edmonstoune Aytoun, along with other critics, had positioned Browning in the "school" of Bailey.[32] The reviews of *Men and Women* demonstrate that Browning found it impossible to shake his association with the Spasmodics and evade the damage that association continued to do to his reputation even in the late 1850s. As Mark Weinstein has observed, an important reason for the adverse reception of *Men and Women* was the volume's "absorption . . . into the reaction against Spasmodic poetry."[33] In its commentary on *Men and Women,* for instance, the *Saturday Review* castigated Browning: "Can any of his devotees be found to uphold his present elaborate experiment on the patience of the public? Take any of his worshippers you please—let him be 'well up' in the transcendental poets of the day—take him fresh from Alexander Smith, or Alfred Tennyson's *Maud,* or the *Mystic* of Bailey— and we will engage to find him at least ten passages in the first ten pages of *Men and Women,* some of which, even after profound study, he will not be able to construe at all."[34] *Blackwood's* describes

Browning as a "true brother" of Alexander Smith and Sydney Dobell; Browning is the "wild boy of the household—the boisterous noisy shouting voice."[35] Though this review was printed anonymously, Browning doubtless thought it the work of Aytoun, who was still on the offensive against the Spasmodics two years after *Firmilian* and who, in the January 1857 number of *Blackwood's* lambasted Elizabeth Barrett Browning's new *Aurora Leigh*. It is small wonder, then, that Browning maligned the "wretched organ-grinding Ayton and his like" in a letter to Edward Chapman shortly after these attacks appeared.[36]

Aytoun had been at the center of what Weinstein has aptly dubbed "the Spasmodic controversy" since its beginnings. In the early fifties the debate over poetic values and the ultimate value of poetry had fairly raged in the pages of British periodicals and, as we have seen, had engaged such luminaries as Arnold, Arthur Hugh Clough, Herbert Spencer, and Charles Kingsley, along with the lesser lights, George Gilfillan, and J. M. Ludlow. Browning in fact had entered the debate with his essay on Shelley, and the extent to which the poems of his 1855 volume extend his participation in the controversy has yet to be acknowledged. As Browning had promised Milsand, fully a fifth of these monologues (occupying a quarter of the pages of the volume) treat matters of aesthetic and poetic ideology.[37]

"Cleon" itself was composed at the climactic moment of the dispute over the proper subjects, settings, and functions of poetry in the modern age. Browning's 1853 letter to Milsand and his response to the reviews of *Men and Women* indicate that the previous year had precipitated a crisis for Browning—the serious, ambitious, but largely unappreciated poet. One factor in his reinvigorated quest for popularity may well have been the reception of Smith's *A Life-Drama* in 1853. But in May of 1854 Aytoun had delivered the coup de grâce to writers of the Spasmodic school by publishing in *Blackwood's* his effusive, parodic review of what he presented as the latest Spasmodic masterpiece, *Firmilian* by Percy Jones. (Poem and poet were both his own creations.) Shortly after, in the summer of 1854, Browning wrote "Cleon." Even if Aytoun's hoax is not viewed as the immediate occasion of Browning's poem, "Cleon" must be read, if read properly, in the context of the Spasmodic controversy. The poem follows the lead of Arnold's *Empedocles* and his Preface as a corrective response to the intense introspection, the dangerous self-absorption, and the obtuse pretentiousness of much recent Spasmodic verse, poetry extending what was universally accepted as the tradition of Keats.[38] Despite their frequent abstractions, the Spasmodics had taken Keatsian hedonism and materialism to their ultimate, absurd conclusions, especially in their works' stylistic excesses. As a serious exposé of the poetic and spiritual inadequacies of Spasmodicism, "Cleon" partially allies itself with the poetry of that school, only to subvert the poetic ideology its writers and George Gilfillan, its most important exponent among the critics, had propounded.

Browning's strategy of subversion is double-edged, involving not only the self-confessed failure of Cleon's value system, but also anti-Spasmodic elements that serve as implied correctives to Spasmodic practices. These include the Greek setting of "Cleon," its hero's overt intellectualism, and its disciplined blank verse. Since Spasmodicism embraced the critically popular insistence on contemporary settings and "relevance," the Hellenic setting of "Cleon" signals an interrogation of Spasmodic redactions of the Keatsian values Cleon propounds. This is especially the case insofar as its setting allies Browning's poem with *Empedocles* (which had been much criticized for the Greek rather than modern character portrait it presents). Nonetheless, like any number of Spasmodic poems, "Cleon" presents an intensely introspective monologuist discussing the value of poetry (and art) in its relations with religious belief and human mortality. Also in the tradition of Spasmodicism, the speaker has hedonistic propensities and self-indulgently employs elaborate and obscure metaphors. In the most prominent Spasmodic poems, as well, poetry becomes the particular medium of self-analysis through which a speaker ultimately intuits God's will and attains immortality, or attempts to do so. Such is the case, for instance, in Bailey's *Festus*, Smith's *A Life-Drama*, and Dobell's *Balder*. Dorothy Donnelly has succinctly explained how all these works

have as their protagonist a poet-hero who is at once capable of
transcendence and in the process of self-realization. In each . . .
the poet-hero-prophet-savior speculates in long passages about his
"God-given powers," his "spontaneous and inspired" thoughts,
his "emotional" needs and desires, and his high "aspirations."
Throughout the poems attention is focused on the protagonist's
attempt to establish a relationship with his universe and in so
doing to formulate what he experiences as a revelation of "truth,"
of the "secrets of the universe." In a dialogue with an interlocutor,
each protagonist expresses his conception of himself and, because
he is a poet, his "high purpose."[39]

Smith's poet-hero in fact preempts the specific aspirations Cleon
delineates for himself as the evolved master-poet "with greater
mind / Than our forerunners" ("Cleon," ll. 64–65). Smith's Walter
envisions himself as

> A mighty Poet whom this age shall choose
> To be its spokesman to all coming times.
> In the ripe full-blown season of his soul,
> He shall go forward in his spirit's strength,
> And grapple with the questions of all time,
> And wring from them their meanings.[40]

But the thrust of Browning's poem is precisely to deflate such
Spasmodic pretensions. The focus of Cleon's lament is, finally, that
revelation and immortality are unavailable to him despite his genuine accomplishments. For him, as for all men, he insists, "life's
inadequate to joy, / As the soul sees joy, tempting life to take." He
craves a sign of

> Some future state revealed to us by Zeus,
> Unlimited in capability
> For joy, as this is in desire for joy,
> —To seek which, the joy-hunger forces us.

"But no!" he concludes, "Zeus has not yet revealed it; and alas, /
"He must have done so, were it possible!" (ll. 325–35). For the

composite artist with the most refined sensibilities possible, therefore, "Most progress is most failure" (l. 272).

In addition to this deliberate subversion of the dominant ideology of Spasmodic poetry, according to which the poet-hero will
save the world, Browning also presents his poem as a critique of
Spasmodic "failures" by eschewing in both the form and substance
of "Cleon" many of the pretentious literary strategies of Spasmodic
poetry. He especially repudiates the undisciplined and rambling
epic form characteristic of works by Bailey, Dobell, Smith, John
Westland Marston, and John Stanyan Bigg.[41] Browning further
purifies Cleon of the intense passions typical of Spasmodic heroes,
along with their demonic desire to exhaust experience. Cleon thus
appears as an intellectually refined and Hellenized poet who shares
many of the impulses and ambitions common to heroes of Spasmodic poetry, as those derive from Keats. He can be seen, in fact, as
a Keats (or Callicles) who has survived into old age as an immensely successful poet. Yet his example serves finally to expose
the failure of Spasmodic transcendental aspirations by acknowledging the inadequacies even of Cleon's own (putative) supreme
achievement. Cleon cannot redeem the world, or even himself; he
cannot satisfy his "joy-hunger" and attain assurances of immortality (taken for granted by heroes of Spasmodic verse).

In this he presents a contrast to the successful Romantic example provided—for both Browning and Arnold—by Wordsworth
in his Intimations Ode. Wordsworth was, in fact, the Romantic
poet (besides the unknown Blake) who was least influential on the
Spasmodics and whose voice Browning in "Cleon" (emulating
Arnold in *Empedocles*) echoes and reinvigorates. He does so by
stressing Cleon's inability to attain Wordsworthian "joy" or any
intimations of immortality when confronted with the "horrible"
fact of mutability.

As all readers of Wordsworth's Intimations Ode know, *joy* is a
crucial term in the poem, just as it is essential to Empedocles'
recollections of his youth, and just as it is the pivotal term in
"Cleon." Repeated eight times, it initiates the Ode's final movement, as the ecphonesis at the beginning of stanza nine. The poem's

three final stanzas celebrate the recovery of the "glory and the dream" whose loss is mourned in stanzas one through four. In Wordsworth's poem, joy is in fact the emotional counterpart of idealized, visionary capacities designated by these abstractions, the emotional form in which possession of "the visionary gleam"— and certainty of immortality—expresses itself.[42] Thus, in stanza three the springtime birds sing "a joyous song"; the prelapsarian shepherd boy is a "Child of Joy"; the growing boy of stanza five beholds his originary spiritual matrix, his "life's Star," in joy; and in stanza nine all experiences and phenomena that threaten to undermine our consciousness of infinitude and immortality are "at enmity with joy." To argue that all such threats can finally be overcome is the raison d'être of this work that memorializes the permanent recovery of joy:

(stanza 9, ll. 133–36)

O joy! that in our embers
Is something that doth live,
That nature yet remembers
What was so fugitive!

Through the pattern of experience it describes, the poem implies that the recovery is permanent, precisely because it is inscribed in an always accessible work of art that can, in future, preempt the agonized process of realizing loss and recovering joy that the poem delineates. The "palm" of assured knowledge of immortality is won forever by its memorialization in a poem that dependably "gives life its joy," as Cleon would have Protus believe his own song does, before he confesses the ultimate failure of his work.

That the Intimations Ode also has a political subtext (as Marjorie Levinson has recently argued)[43] is suggested by the fact that in the same year that Wordsworth was finally able to answer the questions that conclude stanza four of his Ode (1804), he also composed a well-known section of book 11 of *The Prelude* celebrating the promise of the French Revolution. Published as a separate poem in 1809, this passage—including the famous lines "Bliss was it in that dawn to be alive, / And to be young was very heaven!"— begins with an emphasis upon the Intimation Ode's key term, *joy.* "Oh! pleasant exercise of hope and joy!" introduces a paean to the

utopian ideals of the Revolution, ideals that, of course, were bru-
tally disappointed for Wordsworth in the event and whose loss still
obsessed him in 1802 when he wrote the Ode's first four stanzas.

Unquestionably Browning was familiar with both the Ode
and *The Prelude,* Wordsworth's final monument to his own immortality, first published and much discussed only four years before
Browning composed "Cleon."[44] As a young man, Browning had
greatly admired Wordsworth's poetry and had read him carefully.
But Browning's relationship to Wordsworth is as complex as his
relationship with the Spasmodics. Browning's poem "The Lost
Leader" (1845) is a vicious attack on the laureate's political backslid-
ing. Even thirty years after the publication of this poem, Browning
could acknowledge that "the change of politics in the great poet,"
his "defection . . . was to my juvenile apprehension, and even
mature consideration, an event to deplore."[45] And in a letter to
Elizabeth Barrett the year after "The Lost Leader" appeared,
Browning insisted that he would not even "cross the room" to
obtain Wordsworth's distilled essence, a statement that has become
notorious. But, as John Maynard points out, these slurs only partially reveal Browning's attitude toward this Romantic giant:

> To the president of the Wordsworth Society, which he joined in old
> age, he set the record straight: "I keep fresh as ever the admiration
> for Wordsworth which filled me on becoming acquainted with his
> poetry in my boyhood." That his statement was not a hollow
> testimony is made clear in subsequent letters where he endorses as
> old favorites early works that even a Wordsworthian may pass
> over in rereading. . . . His repeated preference for Wordsworth's
> "first sprightly runnings" exceeds even the conventional view that
> the early poetry is best and suggests that Browning retained a
> personal and lifelong fondness for what he read as a boy.[46]

Indeed, the particular influence of the Intimations Ode on works by
Browning written throughout his career has been convincingly
established. Anya Taylor has recently made clear, for instance, that
in stanza three of "Rabbi Ben Ezra" Browning goes so far as to
repeat "not only the argument but [also the] sentence structure and
meter" of the second sentence of the Ode's ninth stanza. And W. D.

Shaw has observed how the "Prologue" to *Asolando* persistently echoes Wordsworth's poem, albeit with a corrective, orthodox thrust, when God himself emphatically responds to Asolo's vanished perception of the "glory" and "alien glow" formerly projected by "Hill, vale, tree, [and] flower": "At Nature dost thou shrink amazed / God is it who transcends" (*Poems*, 2:896).[47]

It was Wordsworth's betrayal of his early political ideology that turned Browning against him. "The Lost Leader" makes clear both the extent of Browning's admiration for Wordsworth and his anguished disappointment in him:

> Just for a handful of silver he left us,
>   Just for a riband to stick in his coat—
>   . . . . .
> We that had loved him so, followed him, honoured him,
>   Lived in his mild and magnificent eye,
>   Learned his great language, caught his clear accents,
>   Made him our pattern to live and to die!
> Shakespeare was of us, Milton was for us,
>   Burns, Shelley, were with us,—they watch from their
>   graves!
> He alone breaks from the van and the freemen,
>   —He alone sinks to the rear and the slaves!

(Poems, 1:410)

These lines are, of course, reminiscent of Byron's condemnation of Wordsworth as a "shabby fellow" in the "Dedication" to *Don Juan*. By contrast with Milton, Byron makes plain, Wordsworth, along with the other Lakers, "belie[d] his soul in songs" and "turn[ed] his very talent to a crime."[48] As "The Lost Leader" and Browning's letters demonstrate, Browning had fully idolized Wordsworth before the laureate's "defection."

Significantly, however, even in repudiating Wordsworth, Browning follows exactly the pattern of idealization and disillusionment that informs much of Wordsworth's own poetry and is repeated in the Intimations Ode. Nowhere is this pattern more powerfully expressed than in book 11 of *The Prelude*. Browning's bitterness at Wordsworth's betrayal of his early political ideology, voiced in "The Lost Leader," is modeled upon Wordsworth's re-

sponse in book 11 to France's betrayal of the revolutionary principles he had idealized in 1790. That response culminates at the end of
the book with Wordsworth's description of the crowning of Napoleon as emperor:

This last opprobrium, when we see a people,
(ll. 361–64)   That once looked up in faith, as if to Heaven
For manna, take a lesson from the dog
Returning to his vomit.

When reading *Empedocles on Etna,* and later Arnold's discussion of enduring poetic values in his 1853 Preface, Browning may
well have thought of these lines and the hundred that follow to
complete book 11 of *The Prelude.* This final passage is addressed to
Coleridge, who is described as recuperating "Where Etna, over hill
and valley, casts / His shadow stretching toward Syracuse" (ll. 377–
78). In the following lines Wordsworth, in fact, claims to discover
"solace to his grief" (a grief precipitated by recalling the events of
the revolution and his painful disillusionment at its failure) in part
by "giving utterance to a name / Of note belonging to that hon-
oured isle, / Philosopher or Bard, Empedocles" (ll. 432–34).

For Browning, the Wordsworthian resonances of Arnold's
Empedocles must have brought to mind the constellation of issues—
literary, philosophical, religious, and aesthetic—surrounding the
term *joy* which, as Browning well knew (having owned one of the
first copies of *Endymion*),[49] was a most important term in Keats's
poetry as well. But, as should by now be clear, far more than a
conflict between Keats's sensual and Wordsworth's spiritual conceptions of *joy* operates in the language, structure, and argument of
"Cleon." The term becomes the intertextual locus where historical
issues of aesthetic and political ideology, as well as issues of poetic
supremacy, intersect to accomplish multiple aims.

Thus, on one reading "Cleon" constitutes an implicit attack on
the Keatsian extravagances, the pretensions to greatness, and the
conceptual limitations of Spasmodicism and, as such, the poem is
an extension of the aesthetic ideology of Arnold's *Empedocles* and his
1853 Preface. It accomplishes this attack in part by recalling the
language and transcendental values of Wordsworth's great Ode,

while suggesting, by extension, a critique of the later values of this most "composite" of Romantic poets, who was—as the "Prospectus" to the *Excursion* (1814) makes clear—ambitious to supersede his greatest "forerunners," especially Milton. The Keatsian hedonism that blinds Cleon to true spiritual joy—a joy compatible with Christian religious values and evangelical ideas of revelation—is unquestionably at war with the transcendental intimations that are the subject of Wordsworth's internal monologue in the Intimations Ode. But Browning realized that the interrogatory mind-set that precipitated the revelations of the Ode, along with the profound and intuitive spiritual values generated for Wordsworth by the failure of political and social structures permanently to redeem mankind, ended with Wordsworth's "defection," his absorption into the Tory establishment, and finally his acceptance of the laureateship in 1843. Unlike Empedocles as Arnold depicts him (and perhaps as Wordsworth had envisioned him when composing the expanded *Prelude* in 1805), the poet of the great Ode to joy had betrayed the originary spiritual values that had made him the supreme Romantic philosopher-poet. This conclusion to Wordsworth's evolution, his progress as a poet, Browning denounces in "The Lost Leader."

But he also alludes to it through the language and elaborate evolutionary metaphors of "Cleon." These suggest an inverse relationship between the desirability of Wordsworth's early spiritual values and the trajectory of his career as a poet: "Most progress is most failure." Wordsworth attained the poetic supremacy of a Cleon only after his "defection" from the political ideology upon which his early spiritual values first depended. His complacent position atop the tower of fame during the first thirteen years of the Victorian period exposed his actual failure as the missionary of an aesthetic ideology that had profound political ramifications. During his tenure as laureate any possibility that the ideals of liberty, fraternity, and equality might continue to be transposed into popular poetry had given way to the solipsistic and hedonistic "evangelism" of the Spasmodics.

Through the intertextual ironies of "Cleon" and the example of its misguided speaker, nonetheless, Browning attempts to reconstitute, in a highly generalized form, the spiritual values of Wordsworth's early years and to do so implicitly in terms of early Christian history and doctrine. Complexly, with Wordsworth as the poem's haunting absent presence, Browning plays Paulus to the young Wordsworth's Christus.[50] In assuming the role of Wordsworth's disciple, as Arnold had provisionally done in *Empedocles* and his Preface, Browning accomplishes another goal as well. Read in the contexts established here, "Cleon" can be understood to serve, on a personal level, as Browning's preemptive denial of his own unyielding quest for popularity and poetic supremacy. Not to be positioned to become a "defector" like Wordsworth, it seems, required an anticipatory acknowledgement that "Most progress is most failure."

III

Irony and Ideology in Tennyson's "Little *Hamlet*"

The dialogue of the mind with itself has com-
menced; modern problems have presented them-
selves; we hear already the doubts, we witness the
discouragement, of Hamlet and of Faust.

(Matthew Arnold, Preface to *Poems*, 1853)

ONE HALLMARK OF Tennyson's poetry is its thematic ambivalence. Except in works where the ideological thrust appears to be transparent—reactionary poems such as "Locksley Hall Sixty Years After" or even "The Charge of the Light Brigade"—the ideological indeterminacy of his poems is consonant with the frequently symbolist modes of discourse they employ. Often, as in the case of "The Charge of the Light Brigade," exposing the historical particulars surrounding a poem's composition or discovering its specific literary or nonliterary pre-texts will expand our understanding of its ideological implications. Such contexts are often deeply buried, as Jerome McGann has shown in the case of "Tears, Idle Tears."[1] Sometimes, however, they seem quite obvious. Occasionally, Tennyson himself has referred us to them. He describes *Maud*, for instance, as

> *"a little* Hamlet,*" the history of a morbid poetic soul, under the*
> *blighting influence of a recklessly speculative age. He is the heir of*
> *madness, an egoist with the makings of a cynic, raised to sanity by*
> *a pure and holy love which elevates his whole nature, passing*
> *from the height of triumph to the lowest depth of misery, driven*
> *into madness by the loss of her whom he has loved, and, when he*
> *has at length passed through the fiery furnace, and has recovered*
> *his reason, giving himself up to work for the good of mankind*
> *through the unselfishness born of his great passion.*[2]

That "unselfishness" finds its vent in a specific "war . . . in defence of right," that is, in the Crimea, "by the side of the Black and the Baltic deep."[3] Tennyson's apparent identification in these comments with the final values of his protagonist is, however, contradicted by remarks made to Henry Van Dyke that reinforce the problem of *Maud*'s ideological ambivalence: "The speaker is wrong in thinking that war will transform the cheating tradesman into a great-souled hero, or that it will sweep away the dishonesties and lessen the miseries of humanity. The history of the Crimean War proves his error. But his very delusion is natural to him."[4]

The originary contexts of *Maud,* both literary and political, are crucial to understanding the poem's complex operations, as Tennyson's comments suggest and as commentators from the earliest reviewers to recent critics have demonstrated.[5] Yet none has managed to put all of the pieces of the poem's contextual puzzle together in a fully satisfying way. The most helpful among attempts to do so is that of Chris Vanden Bossche, who argues that the poem deliberately represents the conflicting mid-Victorian cultural codes of romance and realism, associated respectively with aristocratic and middle-class ideologies. Vanden Bossche concludes that in the poem Tennyson deliberately projects a wholly romantic and chivalric system of values because "chivalry was not ultimately an alternative to commerce so much as a means of finding a point of vantage from which to criticize it. The narrator of *Maud* provides just such a perspective." Vanden Bossche concludes that Tennyson's protagonist is a social critic and idealist who firmly believes in chivalrous behavior as a means to unite his Darwinian society. He might thus "be regarded as a Victorian prophet voicing truths with the insight of madness. Like the prophet, he sees what others cannot see, imagines as possible what others consider impossible and romantic. While Tennyson stretches the topos of the mad prophet to the breaking point, he does not undercut it. . . . the divided narrator is the spokesman of the Victorian poet whose daimonic vision enables him to see his creation as both madman and crusader."[6] Although Vanden Bossche does well to take account of the conflicting social and cultural value systems embedded in *Maud,* like nearly all of the poem's commentators he largely ignores the intertextual operations of Tennyson's poem that, along with its cultural contexts, help account for the poem's ideological ambivalence. As Tennyson himself acknowledged, one text re-inscribed in *Maud* is *Hamlet.* But Shakespeare's play is recontextualized and made meaningful for Tennyson's poetic project largely by his resituation of it in the contemporary literary context in which Spasmodic poetry was wildly successful. The year before Tennyson wrote *Maud,* Alexander Smith's *A Life-Drama* and Sydney Dobell's *Balder* had appeared, and in his poem Tennyson deliberately recalls the social concerns, the style, and especially the modes of characterization typical of these recent works by the Spasmodics. Like the heroes of their works, Tennyson's speaker is, at least until the concluding section of his monodrama, a morbid and melancholy, sometimes philosophizing and sometimes hysterical, protagonist.

Not surprisingly, behind twentieth-century critical commentaries on *Maud* is the association made by *Maud's* earliest reviewers between it and works by the Spasmodic poets, especially Alexander Smith and Sydney Dobell.[7] Attempts to immunize Tennyson from the Spasmodic contagion have been based usually upon four or five approaches to the poem that at once praise and explicate it, but none makes adequate use of Tennyson's designation of *Maud* as a reinscription of *Hamlet,* a play whose hero has much in common with Spasmodic protagonists. Although many of *Maud's* critics mention Tennyson's reference to *Hamlet* in connection with his poem, none recognizes how significant his appropriation of Shakespeare's play is to the profound critique of Spasmodic egocentrism embedded in Tennyson's poem and to the ideological ramifications of that critique. As we shall see, the most important link between *Maud* and *Hamlet* is, perhaps, the development of meaning through a proliferation of ironies. The exploration of these ironies provides a perspective on Tennyson's ability to use elements of the best as well as the worst literature available to him in order to create a monodrama whose power resides precisely in its ideological indeterminacy.

Maud succeeds, not because it presents a highly sympathetic or admirable protagonist in an affecting action, but rather because of its deliberate historicity, its engagement with mid-Victorian dialogues concerning a host of interdependent social, economic, political, and aesthetic issues. Tennyson self-consciously represents *Maud*'s speaker as one confused and afflicted voice in these dialogues. In doing so he manages not only to reify the opposed, often corrupt and self-contradictory value systems of his society, but also to call attention to their debilitating effects upon his culture's literary productions, especially those of the Spasmodic poets.

Like *Hamlet* and like *Maud,* Spasmodic poems generally depict melancholic, vacillating heroes who indulge their various passions and flaunt cosmic visions derived from solipsistic speculations on reality (as we have seen in the previous chapters). Tennyson's poem is, finally, poised between an empowering debt to *Hamlet* and a parodic confrontation with Spasmodic poetry, many general elements of which were present in his own early work and derived from a common Keatsian and Byronic literary heritage. Joseph Collins has catalogued these shared traits that "were present in Tennyson's poetry long before the phenomenon of Spasmodicism became current." They include "the use of mixed meters and violence of language; the organizational device of mirroring the action in the changing moods of a single character and the modern setting; the hero who is tangled in a web of gloomy speculation and morbid self-analysis, making his own maladjustment an indictment of society." In addition to these Byronic characteristics, the poems of Philip Bailey, Dobell, and Smith present "the theme of the alienated youth's moral restoration and reconciliation with society joined to the motif of the restorative power and redemptive function of love."[8] Given *Maud*'s similarities to the work of Smith and Dobell, especially, the early reviewers' association of *Maud* with the Spasmodic school is understandable.[9]

Indeed, Tennyson himself had admired Bailey's *Festus* in 1839 but became increasingly disenchanted with Spasmodic poems as they appeared over the years. By 1853 he was agitated enough by Smith's *A Life-Drama* to criticize its author harshly, advising that he "learn a different creed to that he preaches in those lines beginning 'Fame, fame, thou art next to God.'"[10] Tennyson could not have been unaware of the perceptible similarities between his own *Maud*

and recent works of the Spasmodics, and the design of his poem
may well have been in part to expose the superficiality and inanity
of their work. If this is the case, then Tennyson's poem constitutes a
powerfully ironic event in literary history. Aware that the excesses
of the Spasmodics were rooted in Romantic tradition, from which
his own work emerged, and aware as well that these poets might be
seen as imitators of his own early poetry, Tennyson might, justifia-
bly, have felt by 1854 a degree of kinship with the hero of Dante
Rossetti's "St. Agnes of Intercession." That artist, when asked to
evaluate a critic's poems, insists that, "when a poet strikes out for
himself a new path in style, he should first be quite convinced that it
possesses sufficient advantages to counterbalance the contempt
which the swarm of his imitators" will bring upon such poetry.[11]
Given these contexts *Maud,* it would seem, sets out to subvert
Spasmodicism and to reaffirm the (post-Romantic) originality of
Tennyson's own work, and it is empowered to do so in part by its
patent similarities to *Hamlet.* The poem also demonstrates that
neither pure tragedies nor unambiguously heroic actions were possible during an era in which the alienation of the individual in a
corrupt and fragmented society was complete.

It is hardly surprising, then, that *Maud* should have incensed
and bewildered early readers who were hard pressed to gain perspective on this devastating literary specter of the ideological conflicts within and around them. In 1892 Margaret Oliphant retrospectively explained that "the passion, the madness, the frenzy,
bringing in so many jarring elements, all the vulgar wrongs and
injustices of the day, gave as strong recoil as if we had been betrayed. What had we done in our ecstasy of wonder and admiration
to be plunged all at once into this?"[12]

Maud's complex intertextual relations—with *Hamlet* and by extension with traits common to both Spasmodic poetry and *Hamlet*—
have up to now been most usefully discussed by F. E. L. Priestly
and W. D. Shaw. Priestly notes Tennyson's inversion of the dramatic technique of *Hamlet.* He discerns in *Maud* "a kind of opposite
process to that by which we try to relate the physical action of
Hamlet to what we suppose to be its hero's state of mind. In the

latter case we start with known objective action and move from it
to psychology. . . . The action in *Maud* proceeds from the state of
mind of the hero, insofar as we are sure there *is* action. . . . The
meaning of . . . all . . . actions here is dependent, not on what the
reader thinks of them as actions, but on what the hero thinks."[13] As
I shall point out, Priestly is only partly right here, because he
ignores the fact that throughout the poem Tennyson is able to
create a uniquely ambivalent—or, more precisely, multivalent—
response on the part of the reader. That response depends upon the
poem's monodramatic form, as well as on the developing relations
between the ideology the reader brings to the poem and the conflicted and unstable ideology of the poem's speaker. In this work
"action" is more properly "interaction"—among ideological dispositions (of the protagonist and reader), psychological revelation,
and putative events. The radical changes of value within *Maud*'s
narrator—his lapses from hatred of Maud and her family to love of
her and feelings of fellowship toward her brother, from hatred of
his society to a willingness to fight in its wars—are magnetic,
because they are fervent and extreme. At the poem's conclusion,
we view the speaker from two perspectives simultaneously: we understand his conception of his own imminent heroic self-sacrifice in
a worthy "cause," yet we feel intensely the irony of his service on
behalf of the materialistic, competitive society he "hates." His
ideological stances are powerfully engaging because they are con-
frontational. But in addition, *Maud*'s irresistible imagery along
with its impressive formal gymnastics, by means of their very
virtuosity, compel a considerable degree of sympathy with the
poetic event itself on the part of the reader, while generating an
ironic distance from the speaker.[14]

Perhaps the most helpful remarks on *Maud*'s likeness to *Hamlet*
are made by W. D. Shaw, who notes that this first major tragedy by
Shakespeare is also his least Aristotelian. Moreover, Shaw correctly observes that, "*Hamlet* is a lyric that achieves as much lyric
anxiety as tragic catharsis."[15] To support this perception, Shaw
cites Northrop Frye's crucial distinction between Aristotelian and
Longinian approaches to tragedy, which suggests one formal sim-
ilarity Tennyson might have had in mind when comparing *Maud*

with *Hamlet*. Frye notes that "Just as catharsis is the central conception of the Aristotelian approach to literature, so ecstasis or absorption is the central conception of the Longinian approach. . . . The Longinian conception . . . is more useful for lyrics, just as the Aristotelian one is more useful for plays. Sometimes, however, the normal categories of approach are not the right ones. . . . *Hamlet* is best approached as a tragedy of Angst or of melancholy as a state in itself, rather than purely as an Aristotelian imitation of an action."[16] *Hamlet*'s lyricism and *Hamlet*'s melancholic morbidity clearly correspond to those same elements in *Maud* and its speaker. In addition to these resemblances, however, are numerous others between the events that occur in the two works, the circumstances and philosophical propensities of their heroes, and the proliferation of ironies by which meaning is created and conveyed in both dramas.

Thomas Harrison has briefly noted some, but hardly all, of the correspondences between *Maud* and *Hamlet*: "Each hero first appears as excessively melancholy and inclined to cynical reflections. The fathers of both have met death under strange and doubtful circumstances. Both sons suspect treachery; both witness the succession of men who are ignoble exponents of a corrupt society. Finally, both Hamlet and Tennyson's unnamed hero, resisting the impulse to suicide, seek desperately to discover a way of action." But Harrison insists that all parallels between the two works cease with Part 1, section 5, when "the erotic theme in Tennyson commences."[17] For the rest of *Maud*, Harrison finds clearer analogies in the events of *Romeo and Juliet* and *King Lear;* nor does he explore in any detail the similarities to *Hamlet* which he does note. The most important of these is, of course, the dominance in each work of a single, highly melancholy and skeptical voice that helps determine the reader's view of events as well as his view of the world of each drama.

But other similarities between *Maud* and *Hamlet* leave little doubt that Tennyson manipulated the two works' intertextual relations not only in order to enrich and lend stature to his own poem but also to make *Maud* ideologically multivalent. On the one hand *Maud*'s speaker attacks middle-class materialism and the middle-class faith in an economic hierarchy, and he never clearly relinquishes that position. On the other hand, he finally accepts traditional chivalric values and the militaristic conservatism of English foreign policy in 1855. At the same time, the poem's ambiguous, ironic tone allows each represented ideological stance of the protagonist to appear critical of the other as well as self-parodic in its extremism. *Maud*'s ideological center thus shifts with the psychological swings of its speaker, just as *Hamlet*'s philosophical center does. In *Maud* these shifts continuously engage the ideological predispositions of the reader, who must, if he is to be consistent, at some points agree with the speaker, while at other points call into question the statements, values, and beliefs the speaker articulates. As a result, the poem operates to interrogate repeatedly the very processes of formulating and accepting ideology, just as *Hamlet* interrogates the process of formulating and adhering to particular philosophical stances.

Maud also appropriates events from *Hamlet* and particular situations that arise in the course of those events. The first set of correspondences surrounds the circumstances of the nation to which each hero belongs. Both Denmark and Britain are involved in or threatened by war. Although an international war does not become an issue until the end of *Maud,* the speaker insists very early in the poem that his country endures internecine warfare: "Is it peace or war? Civil war, as I think, and that of a kind / The viler, as underhand, not openly bearing the sword" (1.27–28). Early in *Hamlet* Claudius fears that the militaristic Fortinbras will march on Denmark to reclaim lands lost by his father to King Hamlet, and, although that particular threat is soon eliminated in the play, the aura of war and the presence of internecine tensions persist. Both Britain and Denmark are also depicted as thoroughly corrupt, though for different reasons. *Maud*'s speaker repeatedly castigates his nation for its single most invasive form of corruption, materialism: the "lust of gain, in the spirit of Cain" (1.23). In Denmark, Hamlet similarly observes, "one defect"—irresponsible and disrespectful revelry—"Makes us traduc'd and tax'd of other nations." He insists that, "From that particular fault" men's "virtues else, be they as pure as grace / As infinite as man may undergo, / Shall . . . take corruption" (1.4.18–36).[18]

Parallels between events in the love relationships of *Hamlet* and *Maud* are also inescapable. Early in Tennyson's poem (1.297–300 and 1.720–23) the speaker reveals that his father had expected a marriage between his son and Maud and that the children had been betrothed. Although no such betrothal between Hamlet and Ophelia had taken place, Gertrude at Ophelia's funeral laments, "I hop'd thou shouldst have been my Hamlet's wife" (5.1.244). Early in *Maud* the speaker describes Maud as "the beloved of my mother" (1.72). But the families of both women are viewed by their lovers with suspicion, and both affairs have tragic culminations. Just as "the Sultan" in *Maud* clearly disapproves of the speaker's attentions to his sister (1.740–47), so Laertes warns Ophelia against listening credulously to Hamlet's importunities. Each brother is finally killed in a duel with his sister's lover. Each pardons his killer while dying. And the sister of each dies in the course of the drama. Finally, in each work it is the death of the hero's beloved that allows him to act redemptively. Such major events in both works are the same, although their chronology differs.

Other, ostensibly random similarities between *Maud* and *Hamlet* also emerge. Each protagonist, for instance, sees a ghost that is responsible for simultaneously prompting and delaying his revenge. Each hero at some point in his drama is compelled to leave his country; Hamlet is sent by Claudius to England, and *Maud*'s speaker seeks refuge in France after his duel with "the Sultan." In each work, too, the protagonist stands aloof from a gathering represented as a political celebration, and he comments cynically on what it means. Both heroes, of course, are afflicted by a kind of madness as a result of their circumstances, and both recover. And in both works, significant grave, garden, and star imagery appears.

The most important parallels between *Maud* and *Hamlet*, however, concern the psychological similarities between the heroes of each work and the various ironies that proliferate in each drama. Both heroes are melancholy and philosophical; immensely sensitive, but alienated and solipsistic; passionate, yet obsessed with death. Irony is the idiom of each, and appropriately, each is the victim of ironic circumstances and events. Clearly Tennyson modeled the personality of *Maud*'s speaker on his understanding of the psychopathology of Hamlet. Many Victorians viewed *Hamlet* as a play designed by Shakespeare primarily as a psychological study, and insofar as Tennyson's reading of the play may be derived from the evidence of *Maud,* it appears to have approximated that of his friend John Forster.

Tennyson had met Forster in 1837 (or perhaps earlier) at John Sterling's club in London. At the same time, he met the famous Victorian actor William Charles Macready. In subsequent years Tennyson was fond of attending private theatricals organized by Forster and Dickens, in which Macready participated.[19] Macready had played Hamlet in 1835, and his performance was sympathetically reviewed by Forster in the *Examiner* (October 11, 1835). Tennyson's own remarks on his "little *Hamlet*" suggest that the interpretation of *Hamlet* presented by these two close friends of Tennyson, both important theatrical men, either shaped or corresponded to Tennyson's own. In his review of Macready's Hamlet, Forster dwells excessively on the actor's success in conveying the psychology of the prince of Denmark. His review focuses on Macready's "sustained exhibition of single, profound, and enduring passion, cast in the yielding and varying mould of imagination." Forster asserts that the performance nearly achieves the depiction of what he fancies would be "the exact Hamlet of Shakespeare," in whom "grace, wit, chivalrous and princely bearing, profound intellect, and high faculty of imagination . . . merge . . . in a struggle of sensibility, of weakness, and of melancholy . . . 'like sweet bells jangled, out of tune and harsh.' " He twice reemphasizes the "quick and passionate sensibility" which he sees as the most important aspect of Hamlet's character, "so earnest in its faith, and so passionate in its sorrow. Here is the true Hamlet. No wonder the shock [to his] outraged sense of good should drive him nearly mad." In his general comments about the production, Forster finally praises Macready's rendering of the "subtle madness of Hamlet, which is not madness, and yet not an assumption." Forster describes the psychopathology of Hamlet as "changes of metaphysical emotion," a phrase that equally applies to the spasmodic psychological developments that occur within *Maud*'s speaker.

These correspond to the "phases of passion" that Tennyson mentions at the end of his own commentary on *Maud.*

Forster's curious phrase, "metaphysical emotion," attempts to compress what he apparently sees as the two most important aspects of *Hamlet:* its philosophical ambiguities and its depiction of intense passions. The two are for him profoundly interdependent in Shakespeare's play, and what supports and unites both is the complexly ironic mode of the play. Because of *Hamlet's* pervasive irony, ambiguities of meaning proliferate, and emotion takes on metaphysical dimensions. The same may be said of *Maud,* whose verbal ironies, dramatic ironies, and ironies of situation yield powerfully ambivalent meanings and give it a complexity missing from the Spasmodic poetry it superficially resembles.[20]

Hamlet's multifarious verbal, situational, and dramatic ironies are well known to every serious reader of the play. They are so extensive that John Weiss has called the play a "sustained gesture of irony," and Harry Levin has thoroughly explored the subject,[21] while David Bevington suggests that even Hamlet's constant wordplay constitutes a kind of ironic idiom that dominates the drama. Along with other critics, Bevington notes ironies of situation and dramatic ironies in Shakespeare's first tragedy: that Hamlet becomes suspicious of Ophelia, who genuinely loves him; that in trying to avenge a murder and accomplish justice, he himself becomes Polonius's murderer; that he misses his opportunity to kill Claudius because he mistakenly believes the king to be at prayer; that "he becomes afflicted by the ruthless mores prevailing in Denmark," and "only too late can he publicly acknowledge that he loved the fair Ophelia, stressing the tragedy of misunderstanding that has obliged him to destroy what he most cherished. Similarly, he acknowledges too late his real respect for Laertes and his regret at their fatal enmity." Bevington adds that, "A chief source of the melancholic mood in *Hamlet* derives from this sense of lost opportunity."[22] Although Dorothy Mermin does not discuss *Maud's* use of irony, she does note that its "complex and serious thematic structure" results from "an attempt to recapture the irrecoverable past, a refusal to accept the fact of loss." That such an attempt "leads to isolation, madness, and further loss" suggests the extent to which *Maud* like *Hamlet* uses irony to extend and enrich its meanings.[23]

Just as Hamlet speaks most often in an ironic idiom, the self-dramatist of *Maud* often perceives his fallen world in terms of its ironies, and when he does not, the reader views the speaker ironically. The ironic mentality of the hero is revealed shortly after the poem opens, when he declaims that the condition of England is not what it appears to be:

> Why do they prate of the blessings of peace? We have
>   made them a curse,
> Pickpockets, each hand lusting for all that is not its own;
> And lust of gain, in the spirit of Cain, is it better or
>   worse
> Than the heart of the citizen hissing in war on his own
>   hearthstone?

(1.21–24)

The speaker's pervasive cynicism early in the poem results directly from his ironic perspective on the world. He explains,

> I keep but a man and a maid, ever ready to slander and
>   steal;
> I know it, and smile a hard-set smile, like a stoic, or like
> A wiser epicurean, and let the world have its way.

(1.120–22)

Throughout the first half of the poem, *Maud*'s hero, like Hamlet, is suspicious. After he first meets Maud, who "touch'd my hand with a smile so sweet," he speculates that, "She meant to weave me a snare / Of some coquettish deceit, / Cleopatra-like" (1.200–16) in order that "A wretched vote may be gained" (1.245) to promote her brother's political career. However, with the idealistic hero of *Maud,* as with Hamlet, irony alternates with and gives way to sincerity as the drama progresses. The speaker frankly worries about the embittered condition of his soul and wishes to be other than he is:

> Ah, what shall I be at fifty
> Should Nature keep me alive,
> If I find the world so bitter
> When I am but twenty-five?

(1.220–28)

Yet, if she were not a cheat,
If Maud were all that she seem'd
And her smile were all that I dream'd,
Then the world were not so bitter
But a smile could make it sweet.

He fears desperately for himself because

(1.264–67)
. . . a morbid-hate and horror have grown
Of a world in which I have hardly mixt,
And a morbid eating lichen fixt
On a heart half-turn'd to stone.

Despite the speaker's often histrionical sincerity, verbal ironies do appear frequently in part 1 of *Maud,* as when he describes the "splendour" (1.332) of the new-made lord with whom he is competing for Maud's affections; and when irony collapses into sarcasm in his description, just before the garden soliloquy, of the "grand political dinner" at which

(1.813–16)
. . . Maud will wear her jewels,
And the bird of prey will hover,
And the titmouse hope to win her
With his chirrup at her ear.

As a result of the speaker's divided consciousness, however, verbal irony often alternates with sincerity in the very same passage. In this way Tennyson trains us to read his monodrama properly: allowing some sympathy with the speaker—despite hyperbole and histrionics—but at the same time compelling the reader to retain an ironic distance from him and his fate both because he cannot be trusted to retain that distance himself and because of his ideological, as well as emotional, instability. For instance, just before his first visit to Maud's garden, the speaker is slighted by her brother. His initially ironic response quickly modulates into a sincerity which reflects both admiration and detestation:

(1.444–56)
Scorn'd, to be scorn'd by one that I scorn.
Is that a matter to make me fret?
That a calamity hard to be borne?

> Well, he may live to hate me yet.
> Fool that I am to be vext with his pride!
> I past him, I was crossing his lands;
> He stood on the path a little aside;
> His face, as I grant, in spite of spite,
> Has a broad-blown comeliness, red and white,
> And six feet two, as I think, he stands;
> But his essences turn'd the live air sick,
> and barbarous opulence jewel-thick
> Sunn'd itself on his breast and his hands.

And then the speaker reveals his pathetic vulnerability:

> Who shall call me ungentle, unfair?
> I long'd so heartily then and there
> To give him the grasp of fellowship;
> But while I past he was humming an air,
> (1.457–65)   Stopt, and then with a riding-whip
> Leisurely tapping a glossy boot,
> And curving a contumelious lip,
> Gorgonized me from head to foot
> With a stony British stare.

Although the speaker does not employ verbal ironies as consistently as Hamlet does, he is as consistently passionate and sensitive, and we cannot help being reminded by the verbal echoes here of Hamlet's famous "mad" effusions on the "calamity of so long life," bearing "Th' oppressor's wrong, the proud man's contumely," and "the pangs of dispiz'd love" (3.1.68–71). By allusion, Hamlet's sincerity of understatement in this soliloquy on suicide to some extent redeems the histrionics of *Maud*'s speaker, while the contents of that soliloquy foreshadow the self-sacrificial fate both heroes share.

That fate and the events leading up to it are, in fact, foreshadowed throughout the first half of the monodrama in a manner that becomes ironic as soon as the speaker begins to succumb to Maud's attractiveness (1.162ff.). Dramatic irony in the poem results mainly from the conflict between the speaker's hopes for redemption through love and the predominantly deterministic

character of the early passages in *Maud* that mold the reader's
response to the speaker's hopes and his ideology. On both the
personal and the social levels, these are based upon erotic love and
brotherly love. Their achievement would result in peace of mind
on the one hand and peace in the world on the other. That these
things are impossible to accomplish in the course of the drama is
clear, however, very early on, when the speaker acknowledges
that, "My dreams are bad. She may bring me a curse" (1.73). Even
earlier *Maud*'s hero has anticipated the poem's ironic conclusion:

> Sooner or later I too may passively take the print
> Of the golden age—why not? I have neither hope nor
> trust;
> May make my heart as a millstone, set my face as a flint,
> Cheat and be cheated, and die: who knows?

(1.29–32)

The poem's deterministic philosophical framework is, in fact, obtrusive. Early in part 1 the speaker, like Hamlet, indulges his
philosophical bent:

> We are puppets, Man in his pride, and Beauty fair in her
>   flower;
> Do we move ourselves, or are moved by an unseen hand
>   at a game
> That pushes us off from the board, and others ever
>   succeed?

(1.126–28)

And in the end he embraces "the doom assign'd." The poem
foreshadows Maud's death in the description of her "Dead perfection" (1.83) and her "Passionless, pale, cold" wraith (1.91) as well
as the speaker's suicidal madness (1.53–56 and 1.639–42), thus
further eliciting an ironic perspective on the poem's events and its
protagonist. This perspective reinforces other sources of ideological ambivalence in the poem.

    Maud's ironies of situation, like its dramatic ironies, are nu-
merous. The poem's hero falls in love against his will; as a result, in
a country he hates for its competitiveness, he becomes competitive
with the "Lord" selected by Maud's brother as her suitor. He
similarly becomes contaminated by the "spirit of Cain" he derides

early in the poem, carrying that spirit to its extreme in the murder of "the Sultan." Ironically, by killing this enemy, the speaker indirectly kills his beloved, and the man who initially desires "a philosopher's life" and "a passionless peace" (1.150–51) turns finally to self-sacrifice in warfare as a way to improve the world.

Maud is, as I have noted, a monodrama in which our interactions with the hero on the level of ideology—and therefore our sympathies with and judgment of him—are constantly changing. These shift more radically than is common with most poems, according to the ideological predispositions of the reader. *Maud*'s extraordinary levels of ambivalence result, as well, from its complex ironies, many of them generated allusively. Not surprisingly, *Maud* confused many early readers and reviewers, to whom the poem seemed misnamed, having one too many vowels in the title, no matter *which* one.[24]

    Maud would appear to be a considerably less "muddy" poem if part 3 did not exist, that is, if the work concluded with the speaker's agony of madness, rather than his apparent recovery and his commitment to the war in the Crimea. Ending in this way, the poem's action would be wholly linear, the victimization of a speaker destroyed by his corrupt society progressive and uncomplicated by the apparent ideological reversals of part 3.

    If we are to reconcile Tennyson's commentary on *Maud*'s likeness to *Hamlet* with the contention that the hero may be seen, even in part 3 (pathetically and ironically) as a victim of his society, then a number of points about the ambivalence of Tennyson's art and his attitude toward war, particularly the Crimean War, need to be made. Throughout his remarks about *Maud* recorded in the *Memoir,* Tennyson is describing the speaker's self-concept. But that figure's self-sacrifice "to work for the good of mankind through the unselfishness born of a great passion," is nonetheless consistent with an ideological crux in much of Tennyson's poetry. Its clearest expressions appear in *The Idylls of the King* and the "Ode on the Death of the Duke of Wellington":

(ll. 203–8)   He that walks [the path of duty], only thirsting
                  For the right, and learns to deaden

Love of self, before his journey closes,
He shall find the stubborn thistle bursting
Into glossy purples, which outredden
All voluptuous garden-roses.

Having apparently transcended his obsession with self, the speaker in part 3 of *Maud* is about to complete the "long self-sacrifice of life"; indeed, that event is foreshadowed at the end of part 1, where, appropriately, he awaits Maud in her garden:

My heart would hear her and beat,
    Were it earth in an earthy bed;
My dust would hear her and beat,
    Had it lain for a century dead;
Would start and tremble under her feet,
    And blossom in purple and red.

(1.918–23)

The parallels between the floral death and resurrection imagery in these passages might cause us to view *Maud*'s speaker as a hero who is ennobled and saved, like the duke of Wellington (or King Arthur), by his selfless devotion to a larger cause and his anticipated destruction in its service.

But how can the hero be ennobled by involvement in a war that was clearly a debacle? From the viewpoint of a politically conservative reader, who, like many Victorians including Carlyle and Ruskin, might well be a critic of materialism *and* an imperialist, the answers to these questions might appear straightforward. Such a reader would have believed the Crimean War to be necessary and valuable because it was a war against tyranny and oppression, and thus a war that would serve in the progress of civilization (as King Arthur's early wars described in *The Idylls of the King* appear to do). Any individual who selflessly participated in such wars was on the "path of duty," if not to salvation, as were the Light Brigade (despite the fact that "Some one had blundered" [l. 12] in ordering their charge). "When can their glory fade?" (l. 50). Tennyson rhetorically asks in the last stanza of "The Charge of the Light Brigade." Like Wellington, Arthur, and the soldiers of the Light Brigade, *Maud*'s hero embodies the pattern of self-sacrifice and devotion to a transcendent cause essential to Victorian chivalric and imperial values.

As is clearest perhaps in Tennyson's poetry and the prose of Carlyle, these values contributed powerfully to a widespread perfectibilian ideology that included a fully developed theory of history.

For Tennyson, as for Carlyle, heroes who embody such values are, nonetheless, exceptions to the norm—models of future human perfection like Arthur Henry Hallam—who are discovered providentially during an era in Britain,

> When the poor are hovell'd and hustled together, each sex
>   like swine,
> When only the ledger lives, and when only not all men
>   lie. . . .
> And the vitriol madness flushes up in the ruffian's head,
> Till the filthy by-lane rings to the yell of the trampled
>   wife,
> And chalk and alum and plaster are sold to the poor for
>   bread,
> And the spirit of murder works in the very means of life.

(1.34–40)

This country where "nature is one with rapine" (1.123) has not changed by the conclusion of *Maud,* as Tennyson's remarks to Henry Van Dyke make clear. However, in this poem, as in *Locksley Hall, In Memoriam,* and even *Locksley Hall Sixty Years After,* the speaker looks to the future, not at all denying the present condition of England that he derides early in the poem. In the end he cleaves, not to the *nation* he has despised, but to "a cause that I felt to be pure and true" (3.31) (although from the antinational perspective he appears to be a pathetic tool in his nation's conduct of political wars, still alien and exploited). The speaker's imminent self-sacrifice, from his own perspective, serves "the right," the world's advance toward perfection:

> That an iron tyranny now should bend or cease,
> The glory of manhood stand on his ancient height,
> Nor Britain's one sole God be the millionaire:
> No more shall commerce be all in all.

(3.20–23)

The "iron tyranny" is most obviously that of Czar Nicholas I, but the phrase—particularly in light of the lines that follow it—is

ambiguous. Throughout his life the speaker has suffered at the
tyrannical hands of a materialistic and competitive society. Ironically, by serving this corrupt society that has been exploiting his
family and that will destroy him, he hopes to reform and redeem it.
Like Hamlet, he must become his nation's victim before he can
become its savior. The hero of *Maud,* in fact, enacts in his life the
general pattern of historical progress most clearly described (in the
form of a rhetorical question) in "Love and Duty" (1842):

> O, shall the braggart shout
> For some blind glimpse of freedom work itself
> Thro' madness, hated by the wise, to law,
> System, and empire?

(ll. 5–8)

Henry Kozicki has properly argued that the hero of *Maud* is his
society's "symbolic scapegoat," whose "private grief . . . finally
must be exorcised . . . through a firming of the will and a resolve
to historical involvement" and whose "ritual death of 'self' . . .
leads to resurrection" and to an "apocalyptic fire birth."[25]

In this reading, part 3 of *Maud* is neither superfluous nor
unprepared for. Rather, it is crucial to the ideological functions of
the poem as they derive from its intertextual operations—its appropriations of *Hamlet* and its subversive resonances of Spasmodic
poetry. As an early commentator on Spasmodicism, Jerome Buckley observed a central feature of Spasmodic heroes: they dependably yield "to a titanic egotism." His perception is supported by
nearly every recent critic who takes up their work.[26] For Tennyson
as he began to compose *Maud,* Dobell's *Balder* would have provided the most egregious example of the misguided pretensions of
Spasmodic heroes and of the social values they support. Balder
fully expects to become

> . . . the King of men, and on the inform
> And perishable substance of the Time
> Beget a better world.

He has firmly believed in his mission

> Up thro' my mystic years, since in that hour
> Of young and unforgotten extasy

I put my question to the universe,
And overhead the beech-trees murmured "Yes."[27]

Rather than suppressing the self in acts of unacknowledged heroism that advance the cause of "law, / System, and empire," such
self-aggrandizing would-be heroes must have appeared to Tennyson truly to have "taken the stamp" of their Epicurean age, where,
according to Carlyle, "The word *Soul* . . . seems to be synony-
mous with *Stomach*."[28] Despite his misadventures, the genuine
hero of Tennyson's poem resembles Hamlet, who contemplates
"self-slaughter" (1.2.132) even in his first soliloquy, scorning all
that the "unweeded garden" (1.2.135) of this world has to offer. In
the end *Maud*'s speaker clearly repudiates the cult of self that Balder
flamboyantly indulges. He does so in favor of a larger cause. Thus
in *Maud* the critique of self-interest as the driving force in a corrupt
society becomes, as well, an attack upon Spasmodicism, a literary
ideology that merely embodies and extends the false values of its
audience.

But *Maud* finds out direction through indirection. By means
of the formal design and thematic vacillations of this monodrama,
Tennyson is able to accomplish much beyond the deployment of
social and literary critiques. As we have seen, the difficulties with
this poem are many and complex. They are intertextual as well as
ideological and often result from the poem's deliberate engagement
with the particulars of the contemporary historical scene out of
which it emerges as a literary fabrication, so that—like all works
that draw attention to their own historicity—it is an event that is at
once fictive and factual or real, not only entering into dialogue with
contemporary events but also holding the potential to influence
history by altering the perceptions, values, and, presumably, the
actions of its readers. In short, the poem self-consciously enters
into history with the prospect of redirecting it. But any literary
work can do so only if it attains acceptance and readership, that is,
power in the world. Tennyson, of course, as a popular poet laureate, was uniquely in a position to accomplish such a goal, and he
was in this position in large part because of his ability to produce
ideologically ambivalent literary works that appealed to an un-
usually broad readership.[29]

In the case of *Maud* Tennyson generated a poem with, for many readers, baffling and conflicted ideological movements. Ostensibly the poem presents within it multiple ideologies through the monologue of a protagonist whose values appear to fluctuate and upon whom the reader's perspective is encouraged—by the speaker's emotional and ideological shifts—to change repeatedly in the course of the poem. Moreover, because of *Maud's* fabric of intertextual relations (visible to most educated readers in 1855)—to *Hamlet,* to the forms, moods, and style of Spasmodic poetry, and even to Tennyson's own recent political poems—the work compels an awareness of the inescapable interchange between political and literary ideologies. And through its various intertextual manipulations (especially of its Spasmodic and Shakespearian pre-texts), it interrogates the operations of that interchange, just as it interrogates the process of formulating and adhering to ideology. Depending upon the sensibility and ideological proclivities the reader of 1855 brought to *Maud,* it might be viewed as a poem that advocates either conservative or radical, or radically conservative, political values; a poem that presents a critique of the popular literary taste for Spasmodic poems, or one that embraces Spasmodic modes heartily; a poem that insists upon the literary value of contemporary events, or, through its use of *Hamlet* as a crucial palimpsest, one that denies such valuation. As Margaret Oliphant's representative commentary makes clear, the poem effectively draws attention to its own multivalence, the constellation of ostensibly contradictory voices, as well as political and social values, that its speaker—and the poem as a transvalued reflex of other, current and past, literary voices and values—embodies. Presenting an exemplary network of interacting intertexts and ideological stances, *Maud* becomes a metatext for the historical moment in which it appeared, one that may be seen to elude the political, social, and literary particulars of its composition only by means of self-consciously incorporating them.

IV

Dante Rossetti: Parody and Ideology

IN A RECENT ESSAY, Claus Uhlig comes to the problematic conclusion that many literary works, because of their deliberate intertextuality, concern themselves preeminently with their own histories or genealogies. "It is doubtlessly true, and all the more so since the Romantic era," he insists, "that the aging of poetic forms and genres constantly increases their self-consciousness as knowledge of their own historicity. Through this progressive self-reflection, whose sphere is intertextuality, literature is in the end transformed into metaliterature, mere references to its own history."[1] For Uhlig views of history and of the self in relation to history—especially our creations or works in relation to past works—are deeply ideological.[2] As has often been observed, it was during the nineteenth century that "the modern discipline of history first came fully into its own as a truly rigorous inquiry into the past."[3] Ultimately, however, because of "the very success of scientific history at reconstituting the past," the powerful awareness of the past itself became "burdensome and intimidating . . . revealing—in Tennyson's metaphor—all the models that could not be remodeled." In fact, the apocalyptic aims of the Romantic poets early in the century begin to reflect "the idea that history, simply by existing, exhausts possibilities, leaving its readers with a despairing sense of their own belatedness and impotence. And this despair in turn leads to anxious quests for novelty, to a hectic avant-gardism, and in the end to an inescapable fin de siècle ennui."[4]

As self-appointed heirs of the Romantics, the Pre-Raphaelite poets—Dante Rossetti foremost among them—display in their works an extraordinary degree of historical self-consciousness, as would seem appropriate to their concept of themselves as a transitional, literary avant-garde.[5] Once observed, the powerful effects of Rossetti's own historical self-consciousness upon his poetry compel us to look at his work in new ways. Many of his poems are deliberate intertexts, works that manipulate palimpsests parodically in order both to resist the social actuality which obsessed his contemporaries and to open up new tracks for future writers. This is a fundamentally Romantic, specifically Wordsworthian project.[6] There is a crucial difference, however, between Rossetti's project and that of Wordsworth—or Blake, Shelley, and Keats, for that matter. Whereas these historically hyperconscious Romantics were visibly dedicated to supplanting the ideologies of their literary precursors with their own literary and political ideologies, Rossetti attempts uniquely to employ the intertextual dimensions of his work to create the illusion of altogether eliding and superseding ideology, as it is commonly conceived. Moving beyond even Uhlig's formulation of the metaliterary implications of intertextuality, Rossetti appears virtually to embrace intertextuality *as* a coherent and self-sufficient ideology. The intertextual dimensions of his poetry enable him seemingly to marginalize "those modes of feeling, valuing, perceiving and believing which have some kind of relation to the maintenance and reproduction of social power,"[7] by refocusing all such modes of experience on the structure, history, and intrinsic qualities of literary textuality itself, propounding as a supreme value the creation and deciphering of texts that are highly ornamental, artistically complex, and layered. Since no text is autonomous, all texts being derivative (as are all creators of texts), this dialectical activity becomes for Rossetti the preeminent mode of self-definition, intellectual inquiry, social understanding, and spiritual self-generation.

In a brief preface to his translations of the early Italian poets (1861), Rossetti laments the deteriorating form in which thirteenth-century Italian poems have become available to nineteenth-century readers because of "clumsy transcription and pedantic superstructure." He insists that, "At this stage the task of talking much more about them in any language is hardly to be entered upon; and a translation . . . remains perhaps the most direct form of commentary."[8] Here Rossetti quite properly implies that a translation *is* an interpretation, but one which most closely echoes or contains an originary text. These remarks may, in fact, be seen as Rossetti's first comments in print to broach matters of literary appropriation, transvaluation, and intertextuality. That his first published volume consists entirely of translations suggests a useful starting place for any study of Rossetti's own poetic works, whose sources in the poetry of Dante, Petrarch, Milton, Poe, Keats, Shelley, and even the Gothic novelists have been thoroughly discussed by critics, but without helping us to grapple in genuinely productive ways with the unique difficulties presented by Rossetti's verse.

The more often we read certain poems by Rossetti, the more puzzling, uncertain, and ambiguous their tone, their purpose, and of course, therefore, their meaning seems to become. Such is the case with works that we sense are to some extent derivative, referring to earlier texts formally, imagistically, or ideologically. Some of Rossetti's most important poems, these works are often pervasively self-reflexive, and their original versions date from the late 1840s and early 1850s when, as David Riede has made clear, Rossetti was still intensively searching for "an idea of the world." During this period, "gradually, Rossetti was beginning to distill a personal style and voice from the multitudinous mass of literary and artistic precedents and from his own mixed ethnic heritage, but despite his uneasy balancing of traditions, he remained uncertain about his artistic direction and purpose. For this reason, in both his writing and his painting, his best works of the late 1840s and early 1850s are all attempts to explore or expound the relation of the artist to his art, to nature, to society."[9] A short list of these works would include the "Old and New Art" sonnets, "The Portrait," "Ave," "The Staff and the Scrip," "Sister Helen," "The Bride's Prelude," numerous other sonnets from *The House of Life,* "Jenny," "The Burden of Nineveh," and "The Blessed Damozel." In these poems, as in the bulk of Rossetti's paintings, stylistic mannerisms, tonal ambiguities, and echoes of form and conventions from certain of his literary precursors—Keats, Browning, Milton, and Dante especially—so obtrude that the intertextual effects upon the reader are disorienting and for some readers distracting. That is to say that the poem's ostensible subject matter and purpose seem to be subsumed and overpowered by such an extreme degree of artistic self-consciousness that the poetic project itself is surrounded by uncertainty.

We finish the last stanza of *The Portrait,* for instance, trying to unravel a constellation of interactive images and elaborate conceits that invite symbolic or even allegorical interpretation and that vaguely echo Poe, Browning, and Petrarchan tradition. By the poem's conclusion the speaker has fully demonstrated the depth of his passion for his dead beloved. He has done so while contemplating the portrait he had painted of her when alive and remembering the circumstances that led to its creation:

> Here with her face doth memory sit
> Meanwhile, and wait the day's decline,
>   Till other eyes shall look from it,
>   Eyes of the spirit's Palestine,
>   Even than the old gaze tenderer:
> While hopes and aims long lost with her
>   Stand round her image side by side
>   Like tombs of pilgrims that have died
> About the Holy Sepulchre.[10]

Once we have deciphered this stanza and the poem that it concludes, attention has shifted altogether from the ostensible subject of the poem (the prospect of salvation through the haunting memories of a dead beloved)—to the hermeneutic project itself. The problems of reading, interpreting, making sense of the elaborate ornamental surfaces of the poem have thrust themselves so far forward and required such "fundamental brainwork" of us, that we become finally more interested in surfaces, in techniques and their employment, than in the subject matter being presented. Issues of aesthetics—symbolism, form, style, tone, etc.—fully displace and supersede matters of substance—theme or philosophy or ideology. Rather than a "willing suspension of disbelief," Rossetti seems bent at every turn on enforcing disbelief and distraction upon the reader in ways that remind us of the new generation of radically self-conscious parodic novelists—Fowles, Barth, Borges, or Eco, for instance.

One simple explanation of the purpose and effect of Rossetti's deliberate destabilization and subversion of his own texts might fall properly into line with Jerome McGann's insistence (some twenty years ago) that Rossetti's procedures serve to reinforce his central aestheticism: literature's last gift, like love's, is merely literature itself.[11] Art and artistry must, therefore, like a beautiful woman, draw attention to themselves—their elaborate, complex, ornamental surfaces—in order to enthrall or seduce us. This explanation, however, does not finally do justice to the complex of responses that Rossetti's best poems evoke. The frequent reader of these texts finds them not only ornate and beautiful but also rich and deep in their allusiveness to other texts and to the entire literary enterprise. He finds them simultaneously sincere and parodic; derivative yet original; fraught with ineffable philosophic weight yet somehow hollow; ambiguous; ironic—and finally, elusive.

A general approach to Rossetti's poems that proves more adequate in explaining their complex operations than those of the past—biographical, new critical, or aestheticist—derives from recent expansions of our modes of critical thinking that have emerged from the concern among semioticians, deconstructionists, and new historical critics with all matters related to intertextuality and self-reflexiveness in literature. Rossetti's best known poem, "The Blessed Damozel," serves as an illuminating exemplary text.

As all readers of this inverted elegy know, it dramatizes the craving for reunion felt by two lovers separated by death. The central dialogue is between the full-bosomed Damozel—lamenting her separation while leaning earthward from the gold bar of heaven—and her distant beloved who thinks about her from below. The poem's pathos derives, for some readers, from the fact that for the Damozel the distance between the two is finally insuperable; however, her lover, whose voice and perspective gradually merge with that of the narrator, ironically claims to hear her voice, her words, her tears, but their communication is one-sided, and the Damozel remains a victim of Heaven's exquisite torture of separation, as her languorous suffering is exacerbated by witnessing the pairs of joyous lovers reuniting around her. As all readers of the poem also know, the lovers' dialogue is embedded in an elaborate setting and is at various levels fantastical: the narrator's cosmic vision seems so portentous, and at once detailed yet ambiguous, as to be fantastic; each lover fantasizes about the present circumstances of the other; and the Damozel fantasizes about the pair's future together after reunion in heaven.[12]

The reader of this poem is likely to scrutinize it with special attention, because a number of its features strike us as curious—hyperconscious, oddly derivative, even self-mocking. The more we contemplate the poem's possible purpose and meaning, the more unsettling and disorienting we find the work. As almost every commentator on the poem has noted, we are puzzled, for instance, from the very first stanzas by the unorthodox combination of the spiritual and the sensual or erotic. The former elements include an array of traditional religious symbols and an insistence upon medieval numerology, while the latter elements are introduced into the poem with images of the Damozel's gown "ungirt from clasp to hem," her hair "yellow like ripe corn," and her "bosom" pressing against the bar of heaven (*Poetical Works*, p. 1). Further, the attempt at cosmological mapping early in the poem is accomplished in such deliberately vague terms that it seems disorienting rather than helpful. That the "rampart of God's house" looks downward over absolute Space toward the solar system is clear enough from stanza 5. That Rossetti insistently refines upon this scheme in stanza 6, using redefinitions even more abstract than their originals (Space becomes a "flood of ether"), along with mixed metaphors, seems altogether to undercut the project of mapping the cosmos, however. We are no wiser afterwards than we were before. The language of stanza 7 is so trite and hyperbolic—invoking such phrases as "deathless love" and "heart-remembered names"—that it verges on the ironic, especially as the associations of spirituality that such terminology elicits are abruptly truncated in the next stanza's notorious description of the Damozel's palpably "warm" bosom. Such startling pseudoeroti-

cism, seemingly determined to explode all former theological concepts of heaven, culminates in mid poem when the Damozel describes the rebaptism of their love at the anticipated moment of
reunion: "As unto a stream we will step down, / And bathe there in
God's sight."

Unsettling descriptions and events punctuate the last third of
the poem as well. How are we to respond to the moment at which
the earth-bound lover, for the first time with certainty, perceives
the sound of the Damozel's voice in a continuation of what is
presumably "that bird's song" of stanza 11: "We two, we two, thou
says't?" he says. Somehow the source of this light chirrup seems
incommensurate with the lover's insistence (in an allusion to II
Corinthians 6:14) upon the eternal union of his and the Damozel's
souls. The presentation of the heavenly court in the next stanza also
seems overly literal. Indeed, the depiction of Mary and her five
handmaidens sitting round to pass judgment on the cases of lovers
is deflated by the scene's evocation of the historical courts of love
presided over by Eleanor of Acquitaine in late twelfth-century
France. This association is reinforced by the image of an audience
of angels playing citherns and citholes, as well as the poem's pervasive archaisms, including its title. The penultimate demystification
of the poem's issues comes with the damozel's plea "Only to live as
once on earth / With Love"—surely a radical literalization of
Keats's antitraditional notion of enjoying "ourselves here after by
having what we call happiness on Earth repeated in a finer tone."[13]
And the poem's final perplexing move—drawing our attention
away from its substance to the problem of narrative form—is the
last stanza's perspectival sleight of hand, in which the identity of the
omniscient narrator merges with that of the aggrieved lover. This
formal trick for some readers makes the conclusion seem as equivocal or hollow or contrived as it is full of pathos.

How then does the reader deal with this curious poem whose
tone seems to exist in some unexplored grey area—some void of
linguistic ether—between sincerity on the one hand and parody, as
it is traditionally understood, on the other? He may go so far as to
conclude that "The Blessed Damozel" is, in some rare and complex
fashion, a hoax; that it was written with tongue partially in cheek;

or that it awkwardly presents itself as at once serious and mocking and thus a novel kind of parody for the mid-nineteenth century, a work that is self-reflexive and self-parodic while densely allusive— echoing, imitating, or parodying a number of originary or enabling texts and traditions. That is to say, it is pervasively, complexly intertextual and dialogic. Given the extent to which tonal ambiguities, dialogism, and intertextuality are striking features of other major poems by Rossetti as well as "The Blessed Damozel," it is worth investigating, in theoretical as well as practical terms, the full implications of the parodic horizons in Rossetti's verse.

Some especially useful theoretical discussion of parody has appeared in recent years in the writing of Barthes, Genette, Riffaterre, and Bakhtin. But these theorists have done work that serves, finally, to marginalize, bracket, or in other ways delimit and deflate parody both as a literary genre (or subgenre) and as a medium for self-conscious ideological discourse. Linda Hutcheon's recent book, *A Theory of Parody,* however, largely succeeds in rehabilitating parody by cogently redefining it as a specific mode of discourse and by enlarging our notions of what constitutes parody and what literary parody can accomplish.[14] In doing so, she forcefully demonstrates the interrelations between parody and some central issues that emerge in recent semiotic, formalist, and new historical approaches to literature and literary theory.

   According to Hutcheon, in her own appropriation and reification of recent theorists, "a parodic text [is] defined as a formal synthesis, an incorporation of a backgrounded text into itself. But the textual doubling of parody (unlike pastiche, allusion, quotation, and so on) functions to mark difference. . . . on a pragmatic level parody [is] not limited to producing a ridiculous effect (*para* as 'counter' or 'against'), but . . . the equally strong suggestion of complicity and accord (*para* as 'beside') allow[s] for an opening up of the range of parody."[15] Thus, there exist "both comic and serious types of parody." Indeed, as Hutcheon points out, "even in the nineteenth century, when the ridiculing definition of parody was most current . . . reverence was often perceived as underlying the intention of parody."[16] Further, parody "is never a mode of parasitic symbiosis. On the formal level, it is always a paradoxical structure of contrasting synthesis, a kind of differential dependence of one text upon another." Parody, moreover, can involve a whole ethos or set of conventions rather than a single text: paradoxically, "parody's transgressions [or transvaluations of a text or a set of conventions] ultimately [are] authorized by the very norm it seeks to subvert. . . . In formal terms, it inscribes the mocked conventions onto itself thereby guaranteeing their continued existence." But, of course, "this paradox of legalized though unofficial subversion . . . posits, as a prerequisite to its very existence, a certain aesthetic institutionalization which entails the acknowledgment of recognizable, stable forms and conventions."[17] But the texts, conventions, traditions, or institutions encoded by an author in a parodic text require a sophisticated reader to recognize them and to decode the text, that is, to perceive the work at hand as parodic and dialogic, as transcontextual and transvaluative. Most works thus understood are also perceived finally as avant-garde. They engage in a form of what Barthes termed "double-directed" discourse, often "rework[ing] those discourses whose weight has become tyrannical." (For Rossetti, these would include the traditions of Dante and Milton.)

I would argue that these descriptions of parody powerfully illuminate the operations of many poems by Rossetti that clearly present themselves *as* avant-garde works. The dominant traditions with which they are in dialogue and which they attempt to transvalue are those of Petrarchism, Christianity, and Romanticism— especially in its exotic or supernatural and its medievalist guises.

In the case of "The Blessed Damozel" a unique equilibrium between preservation and subversion of originary texts, their conventions and values, is achieved. As I have already suggested, formally Rossetti's poem inverts the traditional conventions of the pastoral elegy; here it is primarily the dead beloved who grieves volubly for her lover who remains alive. The expected natural details of the genre's setting are also displaced: that is, they are either thoroughly etherealized or replaced with deliberately artificial props, such as the gold bar of heaven and its fountains of light. Symbolism full of potentially Christian meaning—such as the seven stars in the Damozel's hair and the three lilies in her hand—are drained of all such meaning and become merely ornamental.[18] Courtly and Petrarchan conventions, like the poem's pseudo-Dantean cosmology with its heavenly vistas, are thrust upon us with such literalness that they become at best disorienting and at worst absurd. The bizarre deployment of the supernatural here, too, displaces our usual conceptions of God, Heaven, angels, and the rituals conventionally associated with them. This heaven of lovers is a nontraditional fantasy, a bricolage of previous religious and literary conventions, images, values, and beliefs here appropriated and reformulated to authorize a new romantic ideology. This ideology is entirely aesthetic and insists that internalized sensory responses to experience alone constitute the spiritual. But such responses require a sense of loss or separation as a catalyst for their generation and thus seem to become wholly solipsistic and self-reflexive, as does the art which undertakes to represent them. In the world(s) of this poem, fantasy finally subsumes experience, and the most powerful fantasies emerge as much from previous art and literature as from experience itself. "The Blessed Damozel" read in this way must be seen finally as *seriously* parodic of its pretexts. The poem presents various dialogues—with medieval, Miltonic, Romantic, and Gothic precursors; with the traditional elegy; with the lovers who are themselves in dialogue. Finally, however, the poem appears to be in inconclusive dialogue with its own tentative values, images, and aspirations which emerge from its self-conscious reworkings of past artworks and their ideologies. Rather than asserting explicit positions on the amatory, religious, and philosophical questions it raises, the poem elides such questions in favor of emphasizing through its self-reflexivity the purely literary and aesthetic ones which emerge from its complexly dialogical operations.

Such inconclusiveness, equivocation, and ambiguity are common qualities of Rossetti's poems drafted early in his career, as might be seen from analysis of other important works. "The Burden of Nineveh," for instance, is an interior monologue triggered by archaeological events. The speaker contemplates their meaning upon leaving the British Museum, where he has just viewed the

Elgin Marbles, "the prize / Dead Greece vouchsafes to living eyes." As he makes "the swing-door spin" and issues from the building, workers are "hoisting in / A winged beast from Nineveh." By the end of the poem the speaker's thoughts have led him to an epiphanic historical vision:

> . . . on my sight . . . burst
> That future of the best or worst
> When some may question which was first,
> Of London or Nineveh.

(p. 28)

In the course of the poem other questions of historicity and ideology are contemplated explicitly, alongside implicit questions about parody and self-referentiality as qualities that inevitably inhere in every religious artifact and, indeed, every work of art. Ultimately, according to this poem that invokes and argues against Ruskin, art is only an illusory index of the culture which produced it. Art defiantly rejects its originary historical contexts and transgresses—by transcending and eliding—the ideological values of the culture from which it emerges.

Paradoxically, this activity can take place only by means of parodic procedures, which precisely define the texts—as well as their historical positions and their ideologies—that Rossetti's poem presents itself as supplanting. This set of simultaneous moves within the poem draws attention to the phenomenology of the text itself as layered artifact. Just as the "meaning" of the Assyrian Bull-god (and every artwork) depends upon the contexts, the historical and ideological vantage points from which it is read or observed, so the sequence of parodic strategies within the poem draws attention to the phenomenology of *this* text as an accretive fabrication: its "meaning" can be construed only by deciphering the text as palimpsest. The speaker concludes that,

> . . . it may chance indeed that when
> Man's age is hoary among men,—
> His centuries threescore and ten,—
> His furthest childhood shall seem then
> More clear than later times may be:

(pp. 29–30)

Who, finding in this desert place
This form, shall hold us for some race
That walked not in Christ's lowly ways,
But bowed its pride and vowed its praise
    Unto the god of Nineveh.

The smile rose first,—anon drew nigh
The thought: . . . Those heavy wings spread high,
So sure of flight, which do not fly;
That set gaze never on the sky;
    Those scriptured flanks it cannot see;
Its crown, a brow-contracting load;
Its planted feet which trust the sod: . . .
(So grew the image as I trod:)
O Nineveh, was this thy God,—
    Thine also, mighty Nineveh?

Like the phenomenon of the Bull-god, Rossetti's poem reconstitutes hermeneutics as a branch of archaeology. But also like the Assyrian artifact, this poem, which subsumes all of its pre-texts, appears self-sufficient and elusive: "From their dead Past thou livs't alone; / And still thy shadow is thine own." The Bull-god as text provides a commentary not only upon its progenitors and successors along with their respective contexts but also upon itself as an accommodation of all possible historical and ideological contexts. It is a "dead disbowelled mystery" with "human face," with "hoofs behind and hoofs before," and "flanks with dark runes fretted o'er."

    The parodied texts that Rossetti appropriates—the "fretted runes" Rossetti frets over—in his speaker's questions to the Bull-god include works by Shelley and Keats, who are echoed here, but also (and more generally) works by Ruskin and biblical books. By the time Rossetti began reshaping "The Burden of Nineveh" in 1856, Ruskin's absolutist and evangelical view that art is a clear embodiment of the historically specific spiritual and moral values of the culture which produced it had been fully elaborated in *The Stones of Venice*. Against that general position, Rossetti here argues a historically relativistic case. Similarly, references to the book of

Jonah and Christ's temptations by Satan (p. 27) serve—especially in light of the poem's conclusion—as an ironic commentary on the myopic absolutism and the ahistoricism of Christian "orthodoxy." They also serve, however, to insist on the much greater longevity of Christian texts (its art) than the historically limited spiritual beliefs that inspired them. These texts, again in a general way, are parodied here in the mock-prophetic tone and substance of the last three stanzas.

Rossetti's appropriations of Shelley's "Ozymandias" and Keats's "Ode on a Grecian Urn" are more direct and specific. His procedure with respect to these texts is deliberately self-parodic, as well: the author in his relation to these pre-texts behaves as the English have behaved in appropriating and assimilating into their own gigantic cultural monument (the British Museum) the works of art from many great civilizations that preceded the British Empire:

> And now,—they and their gods and thou
> All relics here together,—now
(p. 26)   Whose profit? whether bull or cow,
> Isis or Ibis, who or how,
>   Whether of Thebes of Nineveh?

At the same time Rossetti's use of Shelley and Keats is parodic in the sense of working with and extending the conventions as well as the apparent insights of their poems.

Near the end of "The Burden of Nineveh" Rossetti invokes the central image of "Ozymandias": the half-buried monument to the pharaoh, around which "the lone and level sands stretch far away." Rossetti's speaker retrospectively envisions "the burial-clouds of sand" which, centuries past, "Rose o'er" the Bull-god's eyes "And blinded him with destiny" (p. 29). Rossetti is in a position, however, to update Shelley's historically limited view of the "collossal Wreck" that is Ozymandias's monument. This artifact, too, or portions of it, might well be plundered and given new life as a historical "fact / Connected with [a] zealous tract" in the British collection, as Rossetti gives new life to Shelley's poem and enriches its central irony.

In stanza 3 of "The Burden of Nineveh" Rossetti similarly parodies Keats's "Ode on a Grecian Urn," appropriating a Romantic text that also concerns itself with the transcontextualization of an artifact from an ancient civilization and the hermeneutical problems that result. Rossetti borrows Keats's strategy of asking questions of the artifact and answering them in a way that only proliferates questions. At the same time Rossetti heightens the historical self-consciousness of this project by introducing into his stanzas parodic echoes of Keats's "Ode to Psyche" as well. Rossetti's historical questions—

> What song did the brown maidens sing,
> From purple mouths alternating,
(p. 22)   When that [rush-wrapping] was woven languidly?
> What vows, what rites, what prayers preferr'd,
> What songs has the strange image heard?

—echo not only the concluding questions of stanza 1 in "Ode on a Grecian Urn," but also Keats's catalogue of rituals and service belatedly needed for the proper worship of Psyche, who has no temple,

> Nor altar heap'd with flowers;
> Nor virgin-choir to make delicious moan
> Upon the midnight hours;
> No voice, no lute, no pipe, no incense sweet
> From chain-swung censer teeming;
> No shrine, no grove, no oracle, no heat
> Of pale-mouth'd prophet dreaming.[19]

The questions both poets ask can be answered only with precise and extensive historical knowledge which both poets refuse to supply, insisting that the present artifact supersedes such concerns, as well as all cultural works and rituals that have enabled its production. This text annuls and supplants such absences (to which it paradoxically draws attention) by its exclusive presence.

With its parodies of the Bible, Shelley, and Keats, the "burden" of Rossetti's "Nineveh" thus becomes a weight of critical and self-critical meaning that elides traditional ideologies; it is also a refrain, as an inevitable and recontextualized reenactment of historically layered creative moments and *their* patterns of meaning. This poem tells us not only of the burdens of the past as they are appropriated by the present but of the fact that all parodies as artistic reenactments are burdensome: weighted with critical commentary on all historical eras, all relevant works of art, all ideologies of all writers and readers, including the present ones.

In such poems as "The Blessed Damozel" and "The Burden of Nineveh," begun early in his career, Rossetti was searching not only for an "idea of the world," as David Riede has argued, and a coherent system of aesthetic values; he was also searching with extreme caution for a secure idea of a discrete self, as well as an idea of the self in relation to others.[20] The latter part of this quest, in the early versions of his poems, focuses almost exclusively upon explorations of the amatory self and the artistic self, that is, the self in its highest or quintessential synchronic relations with society individualized in the form of a lover; and the self in its supreme, because creative, diachronic relations with the great creative selves of the past. While the quest for love reveals psychological compulsion, the quest for position displays a willed ambition to demonstrate unique talent.

In the 1848 sonnets included among the three "Old and New Art" poems of the *House of Life,* "Not as These" grapples with the young artist's yearning to distinguish himself from contemporaries and precursors alike. It insists in the end, however, that artistic greatness in the future can be achieved, not by looking to one's contemporaries, but by confronting the "great Past":

(p. 193)
> Unto the lights of the great Past, new-lit
>   Fair for the Future's track, look thou instead,—
>   Say thou instead, "I am not as *these* are."

The implication here is unmistakable: the track to the future is in every sense *over* that of the past. In order to *become* the future the prospective artist must reillumine the works of his great precursors; that is, he must appropriate, transvalue, and transcontextualize them. The same point is made, albeit abstractly, in the final sonnet of this subsequence, "The Husbandman." Here the possibility is raised of regenerating in oneself those whom God "Called . . . to labour in his vineyard first." For,

Which of ye knoweth *he* is not that last
Who may be first by faith and will?—yea, his
The hand which after the appointed days
And hours shall give a Future to their Past?

(p. 194)

These poems suggest what Rossetti's translations in 1861 and other early works such as "The Blessed Damozel" and "The Burden of Nineveh" confirm: that as early as 1848 Rossetti had formulated at least the outlines of an avant-garde program to achieve success and importance as an artist. And that program was deeply intertextual and dialogic, requiring parodic reworkings of those earlier poets and poetic ethos he reverenced most. This program is visible even in a poem as ostensibly self-referential, ahistorical, and nonideological as "The Portrait."

In this poem Browning's "My Last Duchess" is the pre-text being simultaneously displaced and admired. On a grander scale, however, Rossetti's work sets out obliquely to destabilize and subvert the entire Dantean ethos, especially the orthodox Christian conventions of belief associated with Dante, Petrarch, and their imitators. In form, theme, and characterization, Rossetti's poem presents itself as a sequel to Browning's, which it deliberately echoes from the first stanza. A monologic meditation rather than a dramatic monologue, "The Portrait" presents a speaker whose character is the obverse of the duke of Ferrara's: rather than merely an admirer of art, he is an artist for whom the portrait serves as a potential mode of communion with his dead beloved, not her replacement and a controllable improvement upon the original. Before her death the artist's beloved herself constituted the ideal, while her portrait is "Less than her shadow on the grass / Or than her image in the stream." This speaker is, moreover, a genuine lover rather than one concerned with wives as "objects," symbols of wealth, power, and social station. While Browning's duke is a thoroughgoing materialist, Rossetti's artist-lover is obsessed with the ephemeral and spiritual dimensions of his relationship: having "shrined" his beloved's face "Mid mystic trees," he anticipates the day when his soul shall

. . . stand rapt and awed,
When, by the new birth borne abroad
Throughout the music of the suns,
It enters in her soul at once
And knows the silence there for God!

(p. 132)

Ultimately, Browning's duke is concerned with marriage vows as a means to increased wealth and power, while for Rossetti's painter the twice-spoken words of love—"whose silence wastes and kills"—though "disavowed" by fate, are merely precursors to permanent, visually communicated vows.

In these ways, then, Rossetti's poem responds directly to Browning's, presenting the positive amatory *and* aesthetic values absent from "My Last Duchess." Like all true parodies, Rossetti's is thus authorized by and dependent upon its pre-text, but it also supersedes it. At the same time, "The Portrait" appropriates and supersedes the Petrarchan and Dantean conventions of love's spiritualizing influence which inform the value system of the poem and to which it adheres. That is, after unquestionably accepting both the Dantean language and situation that serve to apotheosize a dead beloved as an agent of salvation, Rossetti displaces them from their originary Christian contexts by presenting the moment of the speaker's own apotheosis and reunion with her in a parodic sexual image of penetration. The "knowledge" of God that he hopes to attain in uniting with his beloved's soul is *transcendently* carnal. Yet, such parodic qualities upon which the full "meaning" of Rossetti's poem depends are ambiguously encoded and require decoding by a sophisticated reader. They are embedded in variously vague, abstract, or merely generalized language and metaphors that allow "innocent" readings of the text, thus appearing to elide ideological commitment.

From such a perspective the parodic qualities of Rossetti's early poems, including "The Portrait," "The Blessed Damozel," and "The Burden of Nineveh," seem to be largely self-protective. Through their reliance upon great and familiar literary precursors, his poems accrue authority. Through their self-reflexivity and circularity they preempt any judgment that might easily be passed on matters of ideology. Moreover, through their transvaluation and transcontextualization of the forms, conventions, imagery, and typological structures of originary texts, Rossetti's poems locate their existence at the boundaries of the avant-garde and of ideological commitment. They simultaneously assert and elide values which might, presented differently, be seen to confront and displace the fundamental values embodied in the historically specific texts and traditions Rossetti parodies. Such a visible subversion of the ideological dispositions of his pre-texts, however, would make Rossetti's poem, like those of his precursors, subject to imprisonment by history. To elude such a fate Rossetti employs intertextual strategies to generate poems that present themselves as avant-garde intertexts, whose deep consciousness of historicity itself is deployed to defuse any delimiting ideological or historical critique.

But despite initial appearances, Rossetti's poems do embody a historically specific ideology. As I have suggested, the tentative and oblique repudiation, subversion, and devaluation of conventional ideological statement in Rossetti's work lead to a reconstitution of ideology in exclusively aesthetic terms. Through the processes of allusion, parody, and self-parody by which "new art" is generated, Rossetti's poems individually exalt purely aesthetic valuation above political or social or religious valuation. Art is represented as the unique source of fulfillment, permanence, and transcendence in life. Thus, as a unified body of work, Rossetti's productions do bear a definable "relation to the maintenance and reproduction of social power." They actively participate in the competitive, historically localized phenomenon of poetic supersessions. In doing so they reinforce the aesthetic ideology they inscribe and (revising Shelley and Wordsworth) relocate the structures of immutable worldly and spiritual power in the exclusive habitations of the artist's studio and the poet's study.

V

In the Shadow of E. B. B.:
Christina Rossetti and
Ideological Estrangement

THE YEAR AFTER Christina Rossetti's death Andrew Lang contrasted her poetic accomplishments with those of Elizabeth Barrett Browning, adding his views to what in late Victorian England was already something of a critical tradition. Ironically for feminist admirers of Rossetti today, Lang begins his eulogy with a statement that demonstrates his captivity to patriarchal domestic and amatory ideologies that both Rossetti and Browning—in very different ways—had interrogated in their poetry. "We are now deprived of the greatest English poet of the sex which is made to inspire poetry, rather than to create it," Lang lamented. "Except Mrs. Browning, we have no one to be named with Miss Rossetti in all the roll-call of our literary history. . . . [Yet] for the quality of conscious art, and for music and colour of words in regular composition, Miss Rossetti seems . . . unmatched. The faults of Mrs. Browning she did not follow."[1] By 1895 such comparisons between the two Victorian "poetesses" were commonplace because, at least in the eyes of male reviewers and critics, only these two among a score of serious female poets had achieved genuine artistic stature. In these straw contests for recognition Rossetti was often declared the victor.[2]

Rossetti's brother Dante Gabriel, who was her mentor and regularly provided critiques of her poetry before publication, would have approved Lang's decision. When reading poems intended for his sister's second volume he had complained of the "falsetto muscularity" of some pieces in "the Barrett-Browning style."[3] Often reluctantly, Rossetti usually took her brother's advice in these matters and, to his satisfaction, succeeded in effacing all evidence of "falsetto muscularity" in her work. The result was that, though brief arguments about the relative stature of Rossetti and Browning often appear in the pages of Victorian periodicals, their poems and the authorial self-images their poetry projects are usually acknowledged to be worlds apart. Browning was notorious for engaging social and political topics considered unsuitable to women poets, while Rossetti was canonized long before her death as a kind of poet and saint substantially different from the figure of "woman and poet" Browning sets up as a model in *Aurora Leigh*. These writers appeared to Victorian audiences so very different from one another largely because of the hundreds of devotional poems Rossetti published. These, along with her six volumes of devotional prose, caused her more secular poetry to be read (often correctly) in terms of her religious values. Rossetti's first biographer, Mackenzie Bell, who knew her work as well as anyone at the turn of the century, is representative in his view that "hardly any, if any, trace of the influence of Elizabeth Barrett Browning is discernible in Christina Rossetti's work."[4]

Rossetti herself might well have disagreed with Bell and certainly would have contested Lang's assertion of her artistic superiority over Browning. During her lifetime Rossetti had, in fact, already done as much privately. In a characteristically modest letter reacting to Patchett Martin's published opinion that she was the "greater literary artist," Rossetti concluded definitively: "Yet all said, I doubt whether the woman is born, or for many a long day, if ever, will be born, who will balance not to say outweigh Mrs. Browning."[5] As this comment and others in her letters make clear, Rossetti profoundly admired Browning, as both woman and artist. That admiration was in part evoked by Browning's sallies into traditionally masculine fields of interest and by the impressive quantity of her work. She had attained a level of productivity that Rossetti usually associated with male poets. In a letter to Gabriel she laments her own restricted poetic scope and energies, which contrast with those of Browning: "It is impossible [for me] to go on singing out-loud to [my] one-stringed lyre. It is not in me, and therefore it will never come out of me, to turn to politics or philanthropy with Mrs. Browning: such many-sidedness I leave to a greater than I, and, having said my say, may well sit silent. . . . at the worst I suppose a few posthumous groans may be found amongst my remains. Here is a great discovery, 'Women are not Men.' "[6] These remarks are fascinating for several reasons, not the least of which is Rossetti's apparent masculinist perceptions of Browning, who struggled so visibly throughout her career to be received as a *serious female* poet. Despite her strong admiration, Rossetti views Browning as a kind of artistic cross-dresser. Further, Rossetti's apparent resignation to the customary feminine role of silent passivity—often echoed in her poems—positions her, by contrast with the outspoken Browning it would seem, as an ideological conformist to prescribed gender roles. Perplexingly, however, such acquiescence is called into question everywhere in her work (prose, as well as poetry). Even in this letter her ostensibly trite observation that "women are not men" resists her brother's attempts to influence her and appears self-subverting. The stubborn assertiveness of the rhetoric in this passage, like so many in Rossetti's correspondence, suggests that she has, at least internally, transformed what is normally accepted as a position of powerlessness into a repository of power. Reading it, we feel close to the source of Rossetti's strength as a woman and poet, and that strength, in opposition to Elizabeth Barrett Browning's, lies, not in assertive outspokenness, but rather in a baffling and defiant, sometimes ostensibly self-contradictory, sometimes masochistic, and sometimes riddling, silence.

Such is the case, for example, in the concluding poem of her great sonnet of sonnets, the *Monna Innominata* (1881), a work prefaced by an odd and elusive dedication of sorts to Elizabeth Barrett Browning, the outspoken "happy" lover of the *Sonnets from the Portuguese*. After thirteen initially playful but increasingly anguished sonnets spoken by an unknown female troubadour (with high-Victorian values and discursive practices), the speaker repudiates her earthly beloved in favor of God and hopes for an ultimate reunion with him in the "flowering land / Of love" where they shall stand as "happy equals." For now, she concludes with a lament:

Youth and beauty gone, what doth remain?
  The longing of a heart pent up forlorn,
    A silent heart whose silence loves and longs;
    The silence of a heart which sang its songs
  While youth and beauty made a summer morn,
Silence of love that cannot sing again.[7]

This speaker defiantly renounces in this world what is an unquestionably powerful erotic love, in favor of an idealized spiritual
passion in the afterlife. Her adoption of the traditional role of
silence, after speaking with impassioned (and artful) eloquence,
generates within the reader a sense of frustration, perhaps even
anger. Her choice simply makes no sense in terms of the erotic
compulsions that drive most of us. Even more baffling is the extent
to which the movement of this sequence deliberately resists, and
indeed sets out to subvert, the domestic and amatory ideology, as
well as the gender roles, ostensibly propounded in the parallel
sequence of sonnets by Browning admiringly invoked in Rossetti's
headnote.[8] The obvious explanation of the speaker's choice and of
Rossetti's rhetorical strategy in the *Monna Innominata,* it would
appear, derives from her pervasive religious values, which shun all
affairs of this world as vanity. Rossetti's best poems, for the most
part, usually enter that world discursively and reject it. Her force as
a poet, according to any simple analysis of her work, derives from
her traditionary Christian stance of *vanitas mundi.* But this explanation, as I shall later argue, is incomplete. After all, Browning—not
to mention other eminent Victorian "poetesses," from Adelaide
Proctor to Dora Greenwell and Jean Ingelow—were considered by
their contemporaries as appropriately theistic and devout, and the
gestures of their poems repeatedly invite this perspective. The
ostensible difference between the religiosity of these women poets
and that of Rossetti is one of degree. Browning in fact published a
good deal of religious poetry, including such works as "The Seraphim," *A Drama of Exile,* and a number of hymns.

    The year after designating Browning the "Great Poetess of
our . . . day and nation" in her epigraph to the *Monna Innominata*

(Poems, 2:86), Rossetti was asked to write a life of Browning for John Ingram's *Eminent Women* series. In the event she did not write the book, because Robert Browning apparently refused to endorse the project, but her response to Ingram tells us yet more about her perspective on the single female precursor whose stature and work proved enabling for her own career: "I should write with enthusiasm of that great poetess and (I believe) lovable woman, whom I was never, however, so fortunate as to meet."[9] Such comments as these, along with echoes and implicit ideological challenges to Browning that inform Rossetti's poetry, suggest that she had Browning in mind even at the very beginning of her public career, when she submitted six poems to William Edmondstoune Aytoun at *Blackwood's* on August 1, 1854. In her letter to Aytoun she anticipates Browning's *Aurora Leigh* (1856), who insists, "I too have my vocation,—work to do."[10] Rossetti tries to anticipate any misapprehension that her aspirations to be received as a serious woman poet are radical or arrogant. She explains, "I hope that I shall not be misunderstood as guilty of egotism or foolish vanity when I say that my love for what is good in the works of others teaches me that there is something above the despicable in mine; that poetry is with me, not a mechanism but an impulse and a reality, and that I know my aims in writing to be pure, and directed to that which is true and right."[11] In 1854 no other woman poet was taken as seriously, by men and women alike, as Elizabeth Barrett Browning, who had, in fact, been a contender for the post of poet laureate only four years earlier. Rossetti, at twenty-three, with only a handful of published poems, was implicitly making the comparisons that commentators decades later would hit upon. Unlike Elizabeth Barrett Browning, who had lamented, "I look everywhere for grandmothers and see none,"[12] Rossetti could look to at least one conspicuous figure of the generation preceding her own as a literary *mother*.

For the most part, Rossetti did not write "political and philanthropic" poems, as Browning did. But she did appropriate a number of Browning's thematic concerns and poetic strategies. Like Browning, Rossetti often transposes the traditional forms, as well as the courtly, medievalist, and amatory subject matter, of the ballad and sonnet to serve uniquely Victorian ideological ends. Most often, however, these radically diverge from the purposes served by such transpositions in the work of Browning. For instance, in a number of poems—including "The Iniquity of the Fathers," "An Apple-Gathering," "The Convent Threshold," and even "Goblin Market"—Rossetti explores the issues surrounding "fallen" women, issues that culminated in Browning's poetry with the depiction of Marian Erle in *Aurora Leigh*. Like Browning, Rossetti refused to condemn the victims of men's sexual energies, but unlike her precursor, she denied the value of their reentry into the world of social relations. In "The Lowest Room" Rossetti appears also to challenge the conclusions about professional aspirations and possibilities for women presented by Browning in early poems about Queen Victoria and Felicia Hemans, as well as the later *Aurora Leigh*. In several poems, too, but especially "Eve," Rossetti echoes Browning's concern in *A Drama of Exile* to reinterpret the events of the Fall from Eve's viewpoint, but once again Rossetti does so to a significantly different end than Browning. Yet another deeply ideological concern for both poets was motherhood. Although never a mother Rossetti, the devoted daughter, was preoccupied with motherhood as a source of both rich emotions and female power. On the cultural authority and supreme importance of mothers, the work of Browning and Rossetti is in full agreement.

In poems by Rossetti and Browning that traverse such common formal, thematic, or sociological ground, the sharp ideological divergences between them are, at first, difficult to define, even when Rossetti's work most visibly declares its intertextual relations with that of Browning. Our inability to arrive at such definitions is in part the result of early feminism's totalizing tendencies in appropriating both writers. We have been guilty of ignoring important but subtle ideological subcultures in Victorian England. Thus, one recent critic can make an almost unqualified argument for Browning's feminist dispositions, while another asserts her thorough captivity to patriarchal ideological norms. The evidence does, in fact, seem highly contradictory, arguing for a more moderate case: that a "conservative feminism" dominates Browning's work.[13] But some subtler and more historically accurate assessment of Browning's views on the cultural role of women is essential if we are genuinely to understand the ideological operations of her work. Similarly varied and opposed perceptions of Rossetti have complicated the critical scene in the last few years, and for the same reasons.[14] Commentators have not been adequately wary of the influence of their own cultural values when attempting to understand the work of either poet, nor have they been adequately conscientious in recovering specific historical contexts and ideologies that inform these important poets' work. The generalized view often put forward oversimplifies the particular value systems and cultural perspectives at work in poems by Browning and Rossetti in ways that compel us to misconstrue them.

Approaching key poems by Rossetti intertextually, that is, as revisionist appropriations of work by Browning, allows us to perceive some ideological fine distinctions operating in poetry by women during the second half of the nineteenth century. These distinctions identify crucial but varied sources of genuine power for women during an era that commentators, a century later, regularly and simplistically castigate for disempowering women, even though a female monarch was, during the lives of both poets, a focus of enormous political power in the world's richest, strongest, and most influential nation.

Victorian Women and Power in Poetry

The year after Victoria's ascension to the throne Elizabeth Barrett published her first book of poems to receive anything like general recognition. She was thirty-two, not quite old enough to be the new queen's mother and still young enough to pursue poetic fame. Not surprisingly, *The Seraphim and Other Poems* contains works that discuss both the new queen and poetic ambition. These poems share a concern with the attainment of power in the world by women. Such power is perceived as a direct extension of female subjectivity as it was defined by Victorian ideological norms. That is, the power of the female poet and the power of the queen, presented in both cases as real and considerable, attach to ideals of female sympathy, honesty, sensitivity, and spirituality. These char-

acteristics reinforce worldly power but also assure heavenly rewards for *the burden* of wielding it in this life.

The poems I refer to are Barrett's elegy on the death of Felicia
Hemans, which envisions her sister poetess Laetitia Landon
mourning Hemans's death, and the fascinating pair of poems, "The
Young Queen" and "Victoria's Tears." "Felicia Hemans" quietly
and accurately celebrates the accomplishment of Hemans and presents her as a model for "L. E. L.":

> Perhaps she shuddered while the world's cold hand her
>   brow was wreathing,
> But never wronged that mystic breath which breathed in
>   all her breathing,
> Which drew, from rocky earth and man, abstraction high
>   and moving,
> Beauty, if not the beautiful, and love, if not the loving.

(Works, 2:83)

Barrett clearly believes that Hemans's power as a poet derives from
generally Romantic and specifically Wordsworthian literary projects, and her accomplishment in that movement (made visible and
successful by male poets) will immortalize her. In the poem's last
two stanzas the elegiac turn positions Hemans, "crowned and
living," in heaven and pronounces an oddly admonitory benediction on Landon, advocating a feminine pose idealized by Victorians, but one that, Barrett insists, yields permanent influence in
this world, as well as apotheosis in the next:

> May thine own England say for thee what now for Her it
>   sayeth—
> "Albeit softly in our ears her silver song was ringing,
> The foot-fall of her parting soul is softer than her
>   singing."

(Works, 2:83)

In commemorating Hemans's achievement Barrett appears merely
to reinforce accepted stereotypes of woman's supreme sensitivity
and her angelic nature, which generates "silver song." From these
qualities derives her popularity and power in the world, as well as
her heavenly reward, and these she hopes will crown Landon's
career, as they have that of Hemans.

"The Young Queen" begins with three stanzas lamenting the death of William IV and freezing the moment of transition between monarchs. While "all things express / All glory's nothingness" in the face of the king's death, the "youthful Queen" can remember only "what has been— / Her childhood's rest by loving heart, and sport on grassy sod" (*Works,* 2:107). This projected moment of Wordsworthian reminiscence gives way to admonitions that the queen "call on God" for support, because

A nation looks to thee

For steadfast sympathy:

Make room within thy bright clear eyes for all its
gathered tears.

(*Works,*
2:108)

Abruptly, this young woman has become mother of a nation and must act according to the domestic ideals of Victorian motherhood.

As students of Victorian history and literature are well aware, throughout Victoria's reign a widely propagated and generally accepted domestic ideology dominated middle-class culture and powerfully influenced both the upper and lower classes as well. Henry Mayhew provided a typical description of the ideal middle-class Victorian home as "a kind of social sanctuary." He elaborates, "[The family dwelling is] a spot sacred to peace and goodwill, where love alone is to rule, and harmony to prevail, and whence every enemy is to be excluded. . . . whence all the cares and jealousies of life are excluded, where . . . the honest love of children yields a rich compensation for the hollow friendship of men, and where the gracious trustfulness and honied consolation of woman, makes ample atonement for the petty suspicions and heartlessness of strangers."[15] This ideology clearly emphasized woman's composite role as man's spiritual comforter, the bearer of his children, and "sweet orderer and arranger" of his household (according to Ruskin in "Of Queen's Gardens"). The ideal of motherhood, including all of these functions, accrued enormous mythical and iconic power in Victorian England.[16] As Lynda Nead has observed, "motherhood was regarded as the most valuable and natural component of woman's mission; it was woman's main reason for being and her chief source of pleasure. Maternal love was constructed as the apex of feminine purity and as an unattainable model for all other human relationships." Further, by means of all the apparatuses of culture—from science to literature and the other arts—this "specific historical construction of femininity was made to seem natural and universal."[17] We must understand as well that this ideology was, insofar as it prescribed *women's* role, amatory as well as domestic. In her enormously popular book *The Daughters of England,* for instance, Sarah Stickney Ellis explained that "To love is woman's *nature*—to be beloved, is the consequence of her having properly exercised and controlled that nature. To love is woman's *duty*—to be beloved, is her reward."[18] This domestic and amatory ideology is clearly at the heart of "Victoria's Tears." Victoria's reward for renouncing prematurely the Wordsworthian joys of childhood is, as the last stanza insists, both earthly and heavenly: the "grateful isles" she now commands by means of her feminine "sympathy" and spirituality ("bright clear eyes")

> Shall give thee back their smiles,
> And as thy mother joys in thee, in them shalt *thou* rejoice;
> Rejoice to meekly bow
> A somewhat paler brow,
> While the King of kings shall bless thee by the British people's voice!

(*Works,* 2:108)

Notable in this poem is the ease with which the familiar Victorian ideology that designates woman as the repository of domestic and spiritual values is transposed to the sphere of worldly power traditionally accepted as prohibited to women. The basis of Browning's apparent advocacy here that the domestic sphere may be expanded into the world of politics can, however, also be discovered in Victorian conduct books. A commentator on the roles of women less well known than Sarah Stickney Ellis, but equally representative in her views, is Mrs. Roe. She agrees with Ellis and Ruskin that woman's mission is, ultimately, "to superintend and arrange those things which form the physical comforts of the home, and administer to the temporal wants of those who look to her to supply them." But she adds significantly to these stereotypical functions. It is also woman's "duty to adorn that home with the refinements of intellectual culture, to make herself a suitable companion to her husband, a mother competent to train her children, and a mistress fit to rule and guide her household."[19] Ruling and guiding are thus by no means foreign to woman's domestic role as it was commonly defined.[20] In "Victoria's Tears" Browning simply transposes the domestic ideology to a much larger sphere: the kingdom becomes Victoria's household. The principles of command and control remain unchanged and derive from the unique subjectivity of the female in her acculturated role as spiritual guide and mother. A faith in the power of that subjectivity, unusual because so starkly visible, operates in "Victoria's Tears," whose five stanzas all conclude with variations upon the refrain, "She wept, to wear a crown!" Victoria's childhood is suddenly forced to yield (not unlike the mythicized Virgin's at the Annunciation) to the supreme responsibilities, but also the supreme power, required of a mother to the nation.

Victoria's tears in this poem signal the advent of an enhanced and expanded mythology of female purity, sensitivity, and spirituality that carries power with it in precisely the same way that Christian mythologies carry with them real power in the world. Commitment to transcendent idealities and supreme moral values, according to the myth that is demonstrably validated in reality, yields supremacy in the mundane spheres of human activity as well:

> The tyrant's sceptre cannot move,
>   As those pure tears have moved!
> The nature in thine eyes we see,
>   That tyrants cannot own—
> The love that guardeth liberties!

(*Works,* 2:109)

The crucial distinction between this "natural," "pure," loving, and prospectively triumphant monarch, on the one hand, and "tyrants" of the past, on the other, has curiously less to do with the nation Victoria now governs and the liberties it guarantees its people than with the *kind* of power Victoria can deploy as a woman who has the liberty to cry and thus to "move" her own and, presumably, other

nations. And that power has explicitly divine origins and divine
rewards:

> God bless thee, weeping Queen,
> With blessing more divine!
> And fill with happier love than earth's
> That tender heart of thine!
> That when the thrones of earth shall be
> As low as graves brought down,
> A pierced Hand may give to thee
> The crown which angels shout to see!
> Thou wilt not *weep,*
> To wear that heavenly crown!

(Works,
2:110)

Skeptical twentieth-century commentators who would perceive
this poem as a combination of sentimentality and illusory but commonplace Victorian notions of woman's (emotionally and spiritu-
ally superior) nature thus miss a crucial feature of nineteenth-
century gender ideology: middle-class idealizations of women
created an arena of real power for them in the domestic sphere that
could be extended or transposed, sometimes with subversive sub-
tlety and cleverness, to political, or, for that matter, poetic, spheres
of activity. As a young and virtually unknown poet, Barrett seizes
the opportunity to proclaim in a now privileged feminine discourse
the new queen's uniquely female power in the world. Barrett's
project serves not only to reinforce the authority of the adolescent
monarch, however, but also, reciprocally, to authorize her own
prospective stature in the literary world. Assuming the traditional
role of visionary poet and proclaiming in public verse the power of
the queen, Barrett empowers herself as well—all the while retaining the stance of self-effacement required of women by the Victorian domestic ideology.

Despite evidence of "falsetto muscularity," Browning—and
Rossetti after her—repeatedly insist upon differentiating the roles
and potential of women from those of men in all spheres of activity.
Aurora Leigh at first appears to deny such distinctions. In book 5,
for instance, Aurora bewails the degrading necessity of a male
muse for female poets, the heroine finally repudiating "This vile

woman's way / of trailing garments" and refusing to "traffic with the personal thought / In art's pure temple." She dedicates herself to "Art for art, / And good for God Himself, the essential Good," as if a man, and determines to "keep our aims sublime, our eyes erect." She concludes, however, by acknowledging the greater likelihood that in this project her "woman-hands" may "shake and fail," where (implicitly) those of a man would not (*Works*, 5:3).

In this she, and her female creator, seem unexceptional Victorians. Deirdre David has properly observed that Browning modeled "her poetic and intellectual career upon traditionally male lines, yet the work most fully expressing her aesthetic and political beliefs [*Aurora Leigh*] is the poetic narrative of a woman writer whose experience is rendered through bold imagery associated with female experience." Ultimately, however, all of Browning's poetic efforts demonstrate how "the 'art' of the woman poet performs a 'service' for a patriarchal vision. . . . Woman's talent is made the attendant of conservative male ideals."[21] David's position, like that of feminist critics who argue the antithetical case that Browning deliberately defied the constraints a patriarchal culture imposed upon Victorian women, rests upon a view of the situation of Victorian women that allows only two contradictory perspectives on the ideological options available to them. In fact, as the work of Browning and Rossetti demonstrates, other nonconforming strategies for female self-realization and the realization of what must be seen as genuine power for women and influence for their work emerged in Victorian England.

Such power seldom took the specifically economic, social, or political forms late twentieth-century commentators typically fetishize as a result of ideological dispositions that limit our perceptions of what constitutes "power" or independence or efficacy in the world. In this respect, we may be more captive to limited and limiting cultural norms than were bright and inventive Victorian women like Browning and Rossetti, each of whom discovered different strategies for exposing, reappraising, and, to a significant degree, circumventing ideologies powerfully felt as constraining. Rossetti's strategy was, I shall argue, to adopt a position of ideological estrangement authorized by her strict religious beliefs. Browning's was to parade her poetic and intellectual strengths as visibly as possible before a reading public compelled to become aware that, while not crossing the boundaries of ideological normalcy—as George Eliot did in her private life or as Harriet Martineau did in her publications—she was reassessing those boundaries in a manner that would allow for their future expansion. Both poets thus appear to uphold the fundamental gender roles commonly thought of as patriarchal, and they operate within them. At the same time both relentlessly interrogate those roles along with the social, aesthetic, and intellectual values that support them. Such simultaneous acquiescence and interrogation perplexes recent commentators, who contradict one another in fairly pitched battles, alternately presenting each author as a prospectively radical feminist or a "servant of the patriarchy" (David's phrase).

Browning fully accepted the Victorian domestic ideology that exalted women as ministering angels—pure, compassionate, spiritual—but her effective strategy in exploiting that ideology was to reposition it in the public sphere, as I have begun to argue. She wrote poems on politics, social issues, serious religious controversies, and women's literary ambitions that never relinquish, but instead deliberately employ, Victorian ideals of female subjectivity. Dante Rossetti's accusations of "falsetto muscularity" result, not from any attempt on Browning's part to adopt a masculine persona, but rather from her energetic redeployment of ideals of femininity in areas of concern normally off limits to Victorian women. She is, in short, fiercely committed to radically expanding the "domestic" sphere of women's influence to the world at large.

Surprisingly, Browning's project to extend the boundaries of feminine influence through her poetry, like so much else in her work, is indebted to Wordsworth. Aurora Leigh's important pronouncements on the function of poetry in the modern world (in book 5) are in fact a literalized transposition of Wordsworth's descriptions of the proper operations of poetry and the true vocation of the poet. The power of Wordsworth's influence on Browning has long been acknowledged.[22] Browning herself paid homage to him in her *Essay on Mind* (1826) and in her sonnet "On a Portrait of Wordsworth by B. R. Haydon" (1844). But that influence culminates in her masterwork when her poet-heroine pronounces upon the contemporaneity of her own poetry:

Nay, if there's room for poets in this world

. . . . .

Their sole work is to represent the age,
Their age, not Charlemagne's, this live, throbbing age,
That brawls, cheats, maddens, calculates, aspires,
(*Works*, 5:7)   And spends more passion, more heroic heat,
Betwixt the mirrors of its drawing rooms,
Than Roland with his knights, at Roncesvalles.
To flinch from modern varnish, coat or flounce,
Cry out for togas and the picturesque,
Is fatal,—foolish too.

Although this passage may appear distant indeed from Wordsworth's critique (in his Preface to the second edition of the *Lyrical
Ballads*) of the degraded tastes of his own contemporaries, Browning's insistence here upon realism in poetry reinscribes Wordsworth's apotheosis of the commonplace: "situations from common
life" and the "language really used by men." If her reader thinks
that the Romneys and Marian Erles of her epic are unpoetic, she
insists through *Aurora Leigh* that

King Arthur's self
(*Works*, 5:7)   Was commonplace to Lady Guenever;
And Camelot to minstrels seemed as flat
As Regent street to poets.

The true "artist's part" to her is to transfix "with a special,
central power"

The flat experience of the common man,
And turning outward, with a sudden wrench,
(*Works*,   Half agony, half ecstasy, the thing
5:12)   He feels the inmost: never felt the less
Because he sings it.

Here and elsewhere in her work Browning implicitly invokes the
blessing of Wordsworth as her preeminent literary forefather in
order to appropriate the grand, transcendental enterprise of his
poetry defined in the "Prospectus" to the *Excursion*:

> Paradise, and groves
> Elysian, Fortunate Fields—like those of old
> Sought in the Atlantic Main—why should they be
> A history only of departed things,
> Or a mere fiction of what never was?
> For the discerning intellect of Man,
> When wedded to this goodly universe
> In love and holy passion, shall find these
> A simple produce of the common day.[23]

Wishing to feminize and in every sense realize the poetic ambition Wordsworth expresses in the "Prospectus," she literalizes his project of creating a Paradise on earth and reads "common" as "ordinary." But that effort will yield transcendent dividends:

> We [poets] staggering 'neath our burden as mere men,
> Being called to stand up straight as demi-gods,
> Support the intolerable strain and stress
> Of the universal, and send clearly up
> With voices broken by the human sob,
> Our poems to find rhymes among the stars!

(*Works,* 5:13)

Aurora Leigh, like Wordsworth, believes in the heroic mission and potential of the poet, but she goes well beyond her Romantic precursor in extending to women the sublime capacity to transfigure the commonplace. To Browning's articulate claims for the power of poetry and for the potential heroism of women outside the domestic sphere, and to Browning's corollary insistence on the value of "the world" as the exclusive subject matter of poetry, Christina Rossetti responds in much of her work.

"The Lowest Room" is perhaps Rossetti's fullest poetic discussion of the Victorian domestic ideology, the constraints it imposes upon women, and the propriety of challenges to it. It is a poem that has been criticized for advocating acquiescence under the guise of Christian devotion and "hope deferred": in the end the speaker, whose "sluggish pulse" has been stirred by reading Homer and who feels ashamed of her unambitious, "aimless" domestic life, resigns herself to "the lowest place" and looks to the Apocalypse for fulfillment, "When all deep secrets shall be shown, / And many last be first." In doing so she implies the answer to the central question of the long dialogue with her sister that constitutes the "action" of the poem: "Why should not you, why should not I / Attain heroic strength?" (*Poems*, 1:203) In effect, the question is answered through the character and actions of the unnamed sister herself, an "intuitively wise," quietly Christian, and supremely domestic young woman who becomes, during the twenty years that elapse between the first half of the poem and the last, a stereotypical Victorian "Angel in the House."

Though not published until 1864, "The Lowest Room" is dated September 30, 1856, in manuscript, approximately a month before the publication of *Aurora Leigh*. This historical fact seems at first extraordinary, since Rossetti's poem appears to be a direct response to issues that emerge in book 5 of Browning's epic novel-poem. Those issues include not only the possibility of female "heroism," in opposition to traditional domestic roles for women, but also the more popular controversy over the value of the present age compared to distant "golden ages." While insisting that poets "represent the[ir] age" rather than an idealized past, Aurora Leigh also debunks the heroic past:

> I could never deem . . .
> That Homer's heroes measured twelve feet high.
> They were but men!—his Helen's hair turned grey
> *(Works, 5:5)* Like any plain Miss Smith's, who wears a front;
> And Hector's infant whimpered at a plume
> As yours last Friday at a turkey-cock.
> All men are possible heroes: every age,
> Heroic in proportions.

In argument with her sister who adopts the view propounded here, Rossetti's heroine, by contrast, remains skeptical:

> "Ah well, be those the days of dross;
> *(Poems,*   This, if you will, the age of gold:
> 1:202–3)   Yet had those days a spark of warmth,
>   While these are somewhat cold—

"Are somewhat mean and cold and slow,
    Are stunted from heroic growth:
We gain but little when we prove
    The worthlessness of both."

At issue in Rossetti's poem, however, are not finally the virtues or
deficiencies of the present world in contrast to the past, but rather
the nature of genuinely heroic and virtuous behavior for an educated and aspiring young Victorian woman. This is, of course, a
fundamental concern in *Aurora Leigh,* as well, but it is prefigured in
a good deal of Browning's earlier poetry, as we have seen.

    Although, given its date of composition, "The Lowest Room"
cannot be a response to *Aurora Leigh,* we *can* specify the single poem
by Browning that it deliberately challenges. "Hector in the Garden" appeared in her *Poems of 1850.* It is a dramatic monologue in
which the speaker recalls discovering, at nine years old, "A huge
giant wrought of spade" in her garden. She dubs him "Hector, son
of Priam!" (*Works,* 1:195) and manufactures his arms from daffodils
and daisies, speculating that he might in fact rise up to face and
terrify her. This fantasy she describes as one of "my childhood's
bright romances," but it has an allegorical significance and a powerful influence upon her later life that she now rehearses for her
(presumably) nine-year-old auditor, Canidian. The garden mound
where Hector appears, for instance, is described as laurel covered;
yet, in "arming" Hector she employs the stereotypical feminine
ability to arrange flowers. This is a talent Rossetti particularly
attributes to her heroine's sister in "The Lowest Room"—"she
made her choice of flowers / Intuitively wise." But Browning's
speaker, who is demonstrably a poet, is now determined to employ
her memories and her unique abilities as a woman ambitiously, in
the arena normally reserved for Hectors. In the end she invokes
"God's patience through my soul" to serve a distinctly unfeminine
purpose:

That no dreamer, no neglecter
    Of the present's work unsped,
I may wake up and be doing,
Life's heroic ends pursuing,

(*Works,*
1:196)

> Though my past is dead as Hector,
> And though Hector is twice dead.

This is precisely the sort of ambition Rossetti's poem, through its sisterly dialogue, cautions against. Such aspirations reveal "A selfish, souring discontent / Pride-born, the devil's sin" (*Poems,* 1:204). In place of such prospectively unwomanly and un-Christian ambitions Rossetti presents two separate but ideologically compatible alternatives. The first is illustrated in the adult life of the speaker's sister, who has become the ideal domestic embodiment of Victorian womanhood: she is "a stately wife," "loved and loving" with a "husband honourable, brave" and "next to him one like herself, / One daughter golden-curled" (*Poems,* 1:206). She "thrives" in this role, however, *only* because she is one "who learn[s] of Christ." This "happy" sister is, nonetheless, overshadowed by the "unhappy" speaker, whose lot in life is to "live alone" and "watch." Having learned with difficulty that "lifelong lesson of the past," she is "content to take the lowest place." But this stance is ultimately not just one of superior Christian devotion, it is one that is deliberately estranged both from the activities of the masculine world to which Browning's speaker appears committed and from the domestic ideology which the younger sister in Rossetti's poem clearly embraces:[24]

   . . . I sat alone and watched;

      My lot in life, to live alone

  In mine own world of interests,

    Much felt but little shown.

(*Poems,*
1:207)

The position of power in which the speaking voice of most poetry by Rossetti situates itself is precisely this prophetic and monitory one of estrangement from worldly ideologies. Rossetti uses it consistently to challenge the values of her contemporaries: those like Browning who insist upon the value and power in the world of unsequestered femininity, as well as those women of the middle classes who view their domestic "angelic" role preeminently as a source of material, rather than spiritual, well-being. Significantly, Rossetti's alienated stance is one available only to *women* in her era, and the power that developed from it was also uniquely available to Victorian women.

Eve, The World, and the Politics of Motherhood

Jerome McGann has begun to explore how ideological estrangement operates in Rossetti's poetry. Surprisingly, he is the first critic to do so. His arguments that her work "moves . . . aggressively against every current of worldliness" and that its frequent "surreality is an indictment of worldly language and worlded attachments, whether personal or social" is powerfully illustrated in her sonnet "The World":[25]

> By day she wooes me, soft, exceeding fair:
>   But all night as the moon so changeth she;
>   Loathsome and foul with hideous leprosy
> And subtle serpents gliding in her hair.
> By day she wooes me to the outer air,
>   Ripe fruits, sweet flowers, and full satiety:
>   But thro' the night, a beast she grins at me,
> A very monster void of love and prayer.
> By day she stands a lie: by night she stands
>   In all the naked horror of the truth
> With pushing horns and clawed and clutching hands.
> Is this a friend indeed; that I should sell
>   My soul to her, give her my life and youth,
> Till my feet, cloven too, take hold on hell?

(Poems, 1:76–77)

That the world is here portrayed *by* a woman poet as a seductive and sinister femme fatale is striking. Is this depiction, a modern reader with historicist inclinations might well ask, largely a product of the cultural power that attached to the image of the fallen woman in Victorian England (which Rossetti's brother, for instance, interrogates in his notorious poem "Jenny")? Alternatively, is Rossetti revising traditional satanic mythologies (including Milton's), feminizing Lucifer? Or more plausibly, does the sonnet simply function as a radical allegorization of the world as Sin (again borrowing from the tradition Milton refurbishes)? With any of these perspectives, two conclusions are impossible to avoid. The first is that Rossetti's work (insofar as this poem is representative) distances itself so greatly both from the materialist, progressivist, and domestic ideologies of her age and from stances (like Browning's) that would extend those ideologies, that we are compelled to read her often defiantly ahistorical poetry in its particular historical contexts in order to fathom its critical power. Rossetti, as McGann has observed, is radically alienated not only from the dominant systems of value in Victorian England but also from "most currently accessible forms of thought which would raise up a critique" of them.[26] The second conclusion "The World" forces upon us complements the first: this self-consciously postlapsarian poem that ostensibly flaunts woman as the embodiment of evil appropriates, refashions, and conflates Christian mythologies in such a way as to recall and implicitly focus attention upon the figure of Eve, the poem's presiding absent presence, who was the first woman to defy rigid patriarchal ideologies and reduce the world to a house of sin and temptation.

But like most of Rossetti's fallen women, her Eve figures are usually extraordinarily sympathetic.[27] This is the case as well in Browning's long response to *Paradise Lost, a Drama of Exile,* published some twenty years before Rossetti wrote her own, much briefer, "Eve." In nearly twenty-three hundred lines of verse Browning attempts an entirely different project from that of Milton, according to the important Preface to her drama. "Milton is too high, and I am too low, to render it necessary for me to disavow any rash emulation of his divine faculty on his own ground," she explains. Even her subject is not really the same. The focus of her poem, unlike Milton's, "was the new and strange experience of the fallen humanity, as it went forth from Paradise into the wilderness; with a peculiar reference to Eve's alloted [*sic*] grief, which, considering that self-sacrifice belonged to her womanhood, and the consciousness of originating the Fall to her offence,—appeared to me imperfectly apprehended hitherto, and more expressible by a woman than a man" (*Works,* 2:143–44). Browning wishes to recreate Milton's Eve as a sympathetic figure, but in the event her success is limited. The male characters—Adam, Christ, and Lucifer himself—are the centers of rhetorical power and dominance in this poem that serves ultimately, like "Victoria's Tears," to confirm and reinforce the Victorian domestic ideology, while, paradoxically, demonstrating the efficacy of female poetry on a traditionally masculinist topos.

The ideological crux of Browning's poem appears near the end of it. After Christ has reprimanded the elements and especially the animal world for harshness in blaming Eve for their newly fallen condition, he commands Adam to "Bless the woman." Adam's blessing, significantly, is couched in a series of imperatives idealizing womanhood in familiar Victorian terms:

> Henceforward, arise, aspire
> To all the calms and magnanimities,
> The lofty uses and the noble ends,
> The sanctified devotion and full work,
> To which thou art elect for evermore,
> First woman, wife, and mother!

(Works, 2:211)

Shortly, Adam pronounces upon the (equally familiar) domestic roles of women:

> Rise, woman, rise
> To thy peculiar and best altitudes
> Of doing good and of enduring ill,
> Of comforting for ill, and teaching good,
> And reconciling all that ill and good
> Unto the patience of a constant hope,—
> Rise with thy daughters! If sin came by thee,
> And by sin, death,—the ransom-righteousness,
> The heavenly life and compensative rest
> Shall come by means of thee.

(Works, 2:211–12)

The ideology Browning's poem supports, like the divine plan Eve's actions ultimately serve, is patriarchal. Eve eagerly submits to the role Adam prescribes for her:

> I accept
> For me and for my daughters this high part
> Which lowly shall be counted. Noble work

(Works, 2:213)

> Shall hold me in the place of garden-rest,
> And in the place of Eden's lost delight
> Worthy endurance of permitted pain.

We cannot, however, ignore the fact that this ideology empowers women in specific ways that transcend the activities of getting and spending (of economics and politics) in the fallen world. According to the myth that Browning's ambitious poem reinscribes, mankind can be "ransomed" *only* through the agency of women. Upon their "righteousness," goodness, compassion, and patience depends the fate of all men and women. For women like Browning who appear to subscribe to such transcendental views of gender roles, women's power *in the world,* especially as mothers, must have seemed not only genuine but supreme. This poem and its composition must therefore be understood as an assertion of such power. While to modern feminist readers *A Drama of Exile* may appear self-subverting in its submission to the patriarchy, this work, like so many of Browning's poems, nonetheless privileges the female voice in radical ways and is an enabling demonstration that women can take command of the mythologies that have traditionally determined their cultural status and constraints.

This demonstration is convincing in part because of the poem's formal virtuosity. It is more Shelleyan than Miltonic in the diversity of its verse forms and the complexity of its dramatic structure. But the emotional force of the work emerges, not from technical displays, but from Browning's facility with character depiction. Lucifer, however, not Eve, dominates this poem. His rhetorical tours de force, it would appear, are designed to compete with those of Milton's Satan. Lucifer's final speech, for instance, is an energetic malediction upon Adam and Eve. It is Spasmodic both in its passion and in its resistance to the poet's control:

> May your tears fall hot
> On all the hissing scorns o' the creatures here, —
> And yet rejoice! Increase and multiply
> Ye in your generations, in all plagues,
> Corruptions, melancholies, poverties,
> And hideous forms of life and fears of death, —
>   . . . . .

(*Works,* 2:198)

Rejoice,—because ye have not, set in you,
This hate which shall pursue you—this fire-hate
Which glares without, because it burns within—
Which kills from ashes—this potential hate,
Wherein I, angel, in antagonism
To God and his reflex beatitudes,
Moan ever . . .
And gasp for space amid the Infinite,
And toss for rest amid the Desertness,
Self-orphaned by my will, and self-elect
To kingship of resistant agony
Toward the Good round me—hating good and love,
And willing to hate good and to hate love,
And willing to will on so evermore.

Like Satan in Milton's epic, Browning's impassioned Lucifer presides over the first two-thirds of her drama, and his final imprecations echo those already pronounced upon Adam and Eve by the animals and natural elements. I quote them at length because they provide a revealing contrast to Rossetti's economical and highly effective presentation of Satan in the brief closing stanza of her seventy-line poem.

Rossetti's "Eve" presents itself as a kind of minimalist sequel to *A Drama of Exile* that succinctly achieves Browning's stated goal: to focus on "Eve's allotted grief, . . . more expressible by a woman than a man." More than this, the unpretentious form, tonal simplicity, and characteristically Rossettian, childlike diction of the poem generate a subtle parody of Browning's far more ambitious and finally unwieldy work. "Eve" successfully demonstrates the power of Rossetti's "poetics of conciseness,"[28] especially when her verse situates itself outside of worldly ideologies in order prophetically to renounce and subvert them. The intertextual operations of her poem subtly rebuke the pride that underlies Browning's attempt not only to extend and reinforce such ideologies but also to compete with Milton. One effect of Rossetti's poem is, in fact, to suggest that Browning's prefatory repudiation of any such intent is disingenuous.

"Eve" has a symmetrical, two-part structure, the first thirty-five lines spoken by a grieving Eve, the last by the wholly sympathetic narrator. Mankind's ejection from Eden is long past in this poem. The occasion of Eve's lament is the murder of Abel, but as if to recall the situation of exiled Eve in Browning's work, Rossetti now positions Eve as an exile from her home outside Eden:

> "While I sit at the door
> Sick to gaze within
> Mine eye weepeth sore
> For sorrow and sin:
> As a tree my sin stands
> To darken all lands;
> Death is the fruit it bore."

(Poems, 1:156)

Eve feels alienated in the world which she, in a sense, created, but Rossetti's strategy in depicting her estrangement evokes compassion, as does her retrospective wish that Adam, "my brother," had "said me nay." Then only she "might have pined away; / I, but none other" (*Poems*, 1:157). Rossetti's desexualization of the relationship between Adam and Eve in the poem is subversive. It recalls Milton's insistence on sexual desire as the motivation for Adam's collusion in the Fall, while further dividing the responsibility for its repercussions equally between Adam and Eve. Without Adam's choice to join Eve, death and its visible sign in the corpse she now looks upon could never have been conceived. In her anguish, nonetheless, Eve accepts full responsibility for the event:[29]

> "I, Eve, sad mother
> Of all who must live,
> I, not another,
> Plucked bitterest fruit to give
> My friend, husband, lover;—
> O wanton eyes, run over;
> Who but I should grieve?—"

(Poems, 1:157)

The poem's second half, presenting reactions to Eve's grief from "Each pitious beast" in the fallen world around her, responds to the angry "Second Spirit" of Browning's drama, the "spirit of harmless beasts," who castigates Adam and Eve for having brought on them "undeserved perdition" and asks, "Why have ye done this thing? What did we do / That we should fall from bliss as ye from duty?" (*Works,* 2:88). Rossetti focuses especially on the "birds, with viewless wings of harmonies" (*Works,* 2:187). Unlike these creatures in Browning's poem, Rossetti's eagles, larks, ravens, and conies wholly sympathize with Eve's distress (*Poems,* 1:158). Nonetheless, just as the accusations of Browning's unsympathetic creatures culminate in Lucifer's curses, the caring gestures of Rossetti's compassionate beasts are truncated by Satan's appearance in the brief but powerful final stanza of her poem:

> Only the serpent in the dust
> Wriggling and crawling,
> Grinned an evil grin and thrust
> His tongue out with its fork.

(*Poems,* 1:158)

Our attention thus focuses, finally, on the original liar responsible for Eve's profound misery, but Rossetti's strategy also subtly reminds us of mankind's promised destiny and Eve's eventual apotheosis: her seed shall bruise his head.

In her prose works, Rossetti produced other significant commentaries on Eve that serve as a gloss on this poem, while providing clear statements of her perspective on the position of women in Victorian culture, and her view turns out to be far more radical than Browning's. In a passage from *Letter and Spirit* Rossetti describes Eve as the type of all women and, more specifically, of all mothers. Surprisingly, she envisions Eve, "that first and typical woman, as indulging quite innocently sundry refined tastes and aspirations, a castle-building spirit (if so it may be called), a feminine boldness and directness of aim combined with a no less feminine guessiness [*sic*] as to means. Her very virtues may have opened the door to temptation. By birthright gracious and accessible, she lends an ear to all petitions from all petitioners. She desires to instruct ignorance, to rectify misapprehension: 'unto the pure all things are pure.'" This Eve is more of a saint than a sinner, a victim of her desirable feminine qualities: innocence, idealism, "boldness and directness," compassion. Rossetti declares that such "tenderness of spirit seems . . . lovely in the great first mother of mankind." In this view, Eve retained her innocence, it would appear, even after the Fall: "she offered Adam a share of her own good fortune." That she was "talked . . . over to [Satan's] side"[30] serves more to condemn the world in which she found herself vulnerable than to expose her own moral deficiencies. In *The Face of the Deep*, Rossetti designates Eve's seminal failings; they are "disbelief and disobedience" rather than pride. The logical extension of Rossetti's perspective is that, once removed from this world (at the judgment) Eve, "the beloved first mother of us all," will "stand before the Throne" at the foot of God. (And, she poignantly adds, "Who that has loved and revered her own immediate dear mother, will not echo the hope?")[31] Clearly, for Rossetti, Eve is a name to conjure with, and the image it brings to mind is hardly the traditional one afflicted with pride but rather one that embodies the ideal of motherhood. Genuine attempts to realize this ideal for women, according to Rossetti, uniquely justify their participation, and even their pursuit of power, alongside men, *in the world.*

Rossetti makes clear her general view of the social relations between the sexes in *The Face of the Deep,* and that view might at first appear conventional. She figures the social body, "whose right hand is man, whose left woman; in one sense equal, in another sense unequal. The right hand is labourer, acquirer, achiever: the left hand helps, but has little independence, and is more apt at carrying than at executing. The right hand runs the risks, fights the battles: the left hand abides in comparative quiet and safety; except (a material exception) that in the *mutual* relationship of the twain it is in some ways far more liable to undergo than to inflict hurt, to be cut (for instance) than to cut."[32] Read carefully, this passage reveals a thoroughly un-Victorian attitude toward domestic relations, implicitly deidealizing marriage, which is at best for Rossetti a necessary evil for those who are compelled to cooperate in the social organism. In an important letter to Augusta Webster, who had solicited Rossetti's support for the suffrage movement, she expands upon this view, assuring Webster that it derives directly from the Bible. "Does it not appear as if the Bible was based upon an understood unalterable distinction between men and women, their position, duties, privileges. . . . not merely under the Old but also under the New Dispensation. [There is] no doubt that the highest functions are not *in this world* open to both sexes: and if not all, then a selection must be made and a line drawn somewhere."[33] Rossetti can espouse these beliefs in the sure knowledge of one consolation and inspiration for every daughter of Eve: that in the afterlife, she "will be made equal with men and angels; arrayed in all human virtues, and decked with all communicable Divine graces."[34] For the most part, Rossetti sees women in conventional worldly relationships to men as passive receptors and guardians, a domestic watch of sorts. Their roles most often involve victimization and suffering. In notes on Genesis (never published during her lifetime) Rossetti underscores this view: "There seems to be a sense in which from the Fall downwards the penalty of death has been laid on man and of life on woman. To Eve: 'I will greatly multiply thy sorrow and thy conception; in sorrow thou shalt bring forth children.' . . . [F]rom the father alone is derived the stock and essence of the child; the mother, transmitting her own humanity, contributing no more than the nourishment, development, style so to say. The father active, the mother receptive."[35]

As these passages from her prose and as many of her poems make clear, Rossetti saw little opportunity for genuine fulfillment in any of the roles prescribed for women during her era.[36] "A Triad," for instance, like the *Monna Innominata* sonnets, starkly challenges the sentimental ideals of love and marriage that Elizabeth Barrett Browning had reinforced in the *Sonnets from the Portuguese* and even in *Aurora Leigh*. Rossetti comments upon the three stations available to contemporary women: the fallen woman "shame[s] herself in love"; the "famished" spinster "die[s] for love"; and the "sluggish wife" grows "gross in soulless love" (*Poems,* 1:29). Although this social vision is replicated everywhere in Rossetti's poetry, motherhood provides a space for at least partial escape from unfulfillment. As a biblically dictated and socially necessary vocation for those women who succumb to the fierce ideological pressures upon them, motherhood can be empowering and rewarding—as is clear from "The Lowest Room" as well as

"Goblin Market," for instance—but only if it is pursued with an active awareness of the spiritual (that is, Christian) responsibilities it entails.

In an extraordinary passage from the letter to Webster, Rossetti demonstrates a fairly ingenuous faith that men will protect women's "rights" without the need for women to enter the world of politics. But that this might not be the case leads her to a radical position, based largely on her idealization of mothers as guardians of their children against all prospective predators. If "female rights are sure to be overborne for lack of female voting influence," she confesses,

> then . . . I feel disposed to shoot ahead of my instructresses, and to assert that female M. P.'s are only right and reasonable. Also I take exceptions at the exclusion of married women from the suffrage,—for who so apt as Mothers—all previous arguments allowed for the moment—to protect the interests of themselves and of their offspring? I do think if anything ever does sweep away the barrier of sex, and make the female not a giantess or a heroine but at once and full grown a hero and giant, it is that mighty maternal love which makes little birds and little beasts as well as little women matches for very big adversaries.[37]

Under special circumstances, Rossetti appears resigned to the entry of women into the masculinist world that she otherwise wholly renounces, and in this she echoes Browning. But it is crucial to remember that the pursuit of "Life's heroic ends" for women like Browning's speaker in "Hector in the Garden" and for Aurora Leigh does not depend upon exceptional circumstances. It is, rather, a matter of principle, pride, ambition, and faith in the value of activity in the world that men dominate.

Rossetti's idealization of mothers exclusively in the spiritualized domestic sphere serves to correct Browning's adventurous extension of maternal activity, often as a trope, into the male world.[38] "Victoria's Tears" is a touchstone for Browning's large project of reappraising the restricted cultural situation of women, but even poems like "Mother and Poet" and "Parting Lovers" that express compassion for women constrained within the domestic

sphere, whose sons, husbands, and lovers are lost (or prospectively
lost) to battle, protest against such sequestration:

> Some women bear children in strength,
> And bite back the cry of their pain in self-scorn;
> But the birth-pangs of nations will wring us at length
> Into wail such as this—and we sit on forlorn
> When the man-child is born.

("Mother
and Poet,"
Works, 6:75)

Even more disturbing to Rossetti than such protestations would
have been Browning's literal extrapolation of Tennyson's metaphor of the "Mother-Age" (from "Locksley Hall") in a key passage
from book 5 of *Aurora Leigh*. Here Browning's heroine advocates
the writing of epic poetry on contemporary subjects:

> Never flinch,
> But still, unscrupulously epic, catch
> Upon the burning lava of a song,
> The full-veined, heaving, double-breasted Age:
> That, when the next shall come, the men of that
> May touch the impress with reverent hand, and say
> "Behold,—behold the paps we all have sucked!
> This bosom seems to beat still, or at least
> It sets ours beating. This is living art,
> Which thus presents, and thus records true life."

(*Works*, 5:7–
8)

Such "true life" of the

> . . . throbbing age,
> That brawls, cheats, maddens, calculates, aspires,
> And spends . . . passion . . . [and] heroic heat,
> Betwixt the mirrors of its drawing-rooms

(*Works*, 5:7)

constitutes "The World" that Rossetti in her poetry earnestly and
repeatedly renounces for its vanities. Using the quintessential act of
motherhood to figure a female epic poet's ambition to render this
world would have distressed Christina Rossetti. Equally dismay-
ing was Browning's celebration, in the *Sonnets from the Portuguese,*
of an active collusion with the amatory ideologies of that world.

Poets in Love

That Rossetti's responses to the work of Barrett Browning were conflicted is clear from her headnote to the *Monna Innominata* sonnets, as well as from her involvement in a slight controversy that arose over its intended meaning. It is worth reprinting the note in full:

> *Beatrice, immortalized by "altissimo poeta . . . contanto aman-te"; Laura, celebrated by a great tho' an inferior bard,—have alike paid the exceptional penalty of exceptional honour, and have come down to us resplendent with charms, but (at least, to my apprehension) scant of attractiveness.*
>
> *These heroines of world-wide fame were preceded by a bevy of unnamed ladies "donne innominate" sung by a school of less conspicuous poets; and in that land and that period which gave simultaneous birth to Catholics, to Albigenses, and to Troubadours, one can imagine many a lady as sharing her lover's poetic aptitude, while the barrier between them might be one held sacred by both, yet not such as to render mutual love incompatible with mutual honour.*
>
> *Had such a lady spoken for herself, the portrait left us might have appeared more tender, if less dignified than any drawn even by a devoted friend. Or had the Great Poetess of our own day and nation only been unhappy instead of happy, her circumstances would have invited her to bequeath to us, in lieu of the "Portuguese Sonnets," an inimitable "donna innominata" drawn not from fancy but from feeling, and worthy to occupy a niche beside Beatrice and Laura.*

(*Poems,* 2:86)

This preface has remarkable implications, both for Rossetti's aesthetic values and for the intertextual relations between her work and Browning's. Published exactly two decades after Browning's death, Rossetti's sonnet sequence demonstrates a simultaneous allegiance to her precursor and quiet compulsion to correct what Rossetti perceived as the mistaken directions of her poetry. Only by 1881 did she feel adequately removed from the shadow of Browning's reputation to discuss the work of the "Great Poetess" publicly.

One aspect of that discussion is its direct and forceful challenge to
Browning's by then well-known insistence on the need for contemporary poets to deal with contemporary issues and employ contemporary settings, to "represent . . . Their age, not Charlemagne's"
(*Works,* 5:7). The passage also suggests that Browning's very "happiness" in love constituted a concession to the dominant and, for
women (at least from Rossetti's point of view), often disempowering amatory ideology of their day, in the end preventing her sonnets
from entering into successful competition with the work of the
great male poets of the past whom Browning elsewhere openly
challenges. [39]

These perceptions are substantiated by a letter to William
Michael Rossetti in which Christina responded to Hall Caine's
review of *A Pageant and Other Poems,* which had appeared in *The
Academy.* According to Rossetti, he "misapprehended my reference
to the *Portuguese Sonnets.*" She explains,

> *Surely not only what I meant to say but what I do say is, not that
> the Lady of [Browning's] sonnets is surpassable, but that a
> "Donna innominata" by the same hand [Browning's] might well
> have been unsurpassable. The Lady in question [the speaker in*
> Sonnets from the Portuguese], *as she actually stands, I was not
> regarding as an "innominata" at all—because the latter type,
> according to the traditional figures I had in view, is surrounded by
> unlike circumstances. I rather wonder that no one (so far as I
> know) ever hit on my semi-historical argument before for such
> treatment,—it seems to me so full of poetic suggestiveness.* [40]

Like the wholesale renunciations of "the world" elsewhere in her
poetry, Rossetti's special interest in distancing her sequence historically allows her to present, from the unique perspective of a
woman, a critique of the amatory ideology at the heart of Western
culture. The power of this ideology born in the twelfth century had
reached its apogee in Victorian England. Designating the contemporary intertext of her work as the *Sonnets from the Portuguese,* a
work that merely uses Victorian language and conventions to reinscribe the ideology of its troubadour, Petrarchan, and Dantean
palimpsests, enhances the critical force of Rossetti's poem. The

Monna Innominata itself deploys its persona at first to seduce the susceptible reader who subscribes to that ideology by presenting the familiar figure of an enamored woman who is also a projection of a far less familiar figure, an excellent poet. This poet reveres her beloved as "my heart's heart" who is "to me / More than myself" (*Poems*, 2:88). Her identity is, in traditional fashion, submerged in that of the man she loves until the larger sonnet's "turn" in the ninth poem, which begins the process of repudiating and subverting the traditional ideology of love that Browning had embraced in the *Sonnets from the Portuguese*. "Ready to spend and be spent for your sake," the speaker acknowledges "all / That might have been and now can never be" (*Poems*, 2:90–91). By the penultimate sonnet, the speaker has renounced all possibility of fulfilling her love in this world and surrenders herself and her beloved to the transcendent love of God, the unique source of genuine fulfillment and one that wholly devalues the kind of amatory experience celebrated by poets in love from the troubadours through Barrett Browning:

> Searching my heart for all that touches you,
>   I find there only love and love's goodwill
> Helpless to help and impotent to do,
>   Of understanding dull, of sight most dim;
>   And therefore I commend you back to Him
> Whose love your love's capacity can fill.

(*Poems*, 2:92–93)

Ultimately, as we have seen, Rossetti's female troubadour positions herself critically and inscrutably in the sphere of female silence beyond worldly vanities. She will "not bind fresh roses in my hair" or "seek for blossoms anywhere, / Except such common flowers as blow with corn" (*Poems*, 2:93).

This position generates considerable cultural power for the female poet, and that power is consolidated in the double distance from "the world" and its seductions that Rossetti creates by means of her headnote to the sequence. The *Monna Innominata*, that is, presents a historically distant female speaker who finally repudiates commonly accepted patriarchal amatory ideologies (as well as the worldly poetic modes that propagate them). But this figure is self-consciously projected by a contemporary poet deliberately in pursuit of a "semi-historical argument" that will distance her from the illusory seductions of "happy" love in her own era.

By contrast with Rossetti's speaker and the stance Rossetti herself adopts in the metacommentary of her headnote to the *Monna Innominata*, Browning had, in her *Sonnets from the Portuguese,* generated a paradigm of the sentimental and patriarchal amatory ideology of mid-Victorian England. Her poet-speaker presents herself as inferior and subservient to her beloved, while literally transformed by his adoration into the conventional Angel of domestic existence:

(no. 10, *Works,* 3:231–32)

> . . . in thy sight
> I stand transfigured, glorified aright,
> With conscience of the new rays that proceed
> Out of my face toward thine.

The conventional language of heavenly apotheosis and transfiguration punctuates these sonnets, but is, ironically, belied again and again by the speaker's desire for fulfillment of her erotic love in this world. At last convinced by her beloved's devotion to her (by sonnet twenty-three), she renounces all renunciatory impulses:

(no. 23, *Works,* 3:238)

> As brighter ladies do not count it strange,
> For love, to give up acres and degree,
> I yield the grave for thy sake, and exchange
> My near sweet view of Heaven, for earth with thee.

Similarly, a refusal to "fashion into speech / The love I bear" expressed in the early sonnets soon gives way to insistent poetic celebrations of her love. The "silence of my womanhood" and its accompanying "dauntless, voiceless fortitude" is replaced by her dedication to generating "perfect strains" that may "float / 'Neath master-hands" (no. 32, *Works,* 3:243), suggesting that woman's voice can be discovered only through affairs of the heart. That voice is, significantly, no longer controlled by woman. Thus, Browning's speaker "happily" relinquishes her identity, her independence, even her silent spiritual heart, to the manipulations of a man, and she willingly submits to him. In a coy but ideologically disingenuous role reversal, *he* is transposed as an "angel . . . in the world" (no. 42, *Works*, 3:247). That world is, when viewed through the lens of love, a "new Heaven" which the "patient angel" who articulates these poems hopes to enter (no. 39, *Works*, 3:246).[41]

The *Sonnets from the Portuguese* reinforce a well-known statement made by Elizabeth Barrett in a letter to Robert Browning concerning the differences between the sexes. In it she acknowledges that women possess "minds of quicker movement, but less power and depth" than men, further explaining that "there is a natural inferiority of mind in women—of the intellect . . . the history of art and of genius testifies to this fact openly."[42] As a woman poet, nonetheless, she felt compelled to venture outside the traditionally sequestered domestic sphere of women into the world whose domination by men she accepted. She genuinely hoped to gain some power in that world, to realize some possibilities for female "heroism." By contrast, Christina Rossetti insisted, more carefully and evasively, only on "distinctions" between men and women, and those limited to *this* world, where, she acknowledges, at least the subordination of wife to husband, is proper. But Rossetti keeps her eyes steadily upon another world, the afterlife, a "flowering land / Of love" where sexual equality will be attained (*Poems*, 2:89). Reading Rossetti, we are in danger of complete misunderstanding if we forget that, as a devout and strict, indeed obsessive, Anglo-Catholic, she consistently repudiated and thus devalorized "the world." Her repeated ideological challenges to Browning derive from this stance of estrangement from the particular values, especially masculinist and patriarchal values, that Browning consistently reinforces by attempting to enter the field of their operations and lay claim to them in the name of women.

Deirdre David has concluded that in all of Browning's poetry, "she aligns herself with a poetic tradition celebrating a privileged relationship of the poet to God and figuring the poet as enjoined by that relationship to be active in the world."[43] We should now begin to see the extent to which Browning's perception of woman's relationship to God, to man, and to the world was ideologically opposed to Rossetti's. Constitutionally quiet, patient, and polite,

Rossetti nonetheless attempted, through the subtle intertextual operations of her poetry, to correct the misguided directions of her singular precursor's work, but also to demonstrate the genuine admiration she felt for the only seriously accomplished woman poet and foremother she could identify, in Victorian England, as a model to be remodeled.

VI

·•◦◦◦•·

Art is Enough: Morris,
Keats, and Pre-Raphaelite
Amatory Ideologies

The Problem

ONE OF WILLIAM MORRIS's least read, least valued, and least understood long poems is *Love Is Enough,* published in December of
1872. E. P. Thompson, still the most incisive commentator on
Morris and his work, has insisted that "the poem . . . is unworthy
of Morris, and may be dismissed."[1] *Love Is Enough* is ignored,
however, at the risk of blinding ourselves to the complex intertextual relations among works by the Pre-Raphaelite poets, and between them and their Romantic precursors, especially Keats. Not
only is the poem pivotal in the development of Morris's aesthetic
values and political ideology (which fuse after 1875), but, like
Arnold's *Empedocles,* it is also a paradigm of the subtle, often
opaque relations between poetry and politics in Victorian England.

Love Is Enough was composed between mid-September of
1871 and the late spring of 1872, arguably the most difficult period
in Morris's life. On July 6, 1871, Morris had left London for his first
trip to Iceland.[2] He was gone exactly two months, returning home
on September 6.[3] The journey took place a month after he had
established joint tenancy with Dante Rossetti at Kelmscott Manor
and some seven months after the fourth and last volume of *The
Earthly Paradise* had appeared. The reviews, beginning with the
publication of the first volume in 1868, had been laudatory and
continued during the winter and spring of 1871 in an effusive vein.[4]
The poem had, in fact, served to position Morris alongside Tennyson and Browning as one of the most popular poets in England.

The trip to Iceland enabled Morris to rethink the directions his poetry had taken in *The Earthly Paradise,* in his translation with Eirikr Magnusson of the *Volsunga Saga,* and in the lyric poetry he'd written between 1868 and 1870.[5] Almost immediately upon his return, Morris was hard at work on *Love Is Enough,* a poem very different in form, style, and thematic direction from the narratives of *The Earthly Paradise.* On October 2 Rossetti was writing to their mutual friend William Bell Scott that "M. has set to work *with a will* on a sort of masque. . . . The poem is, I think, at a higher point of execution perhaps than anything that he has done—having a passionate lyric quality such as one found in his earliest work, and of course much more mature balance in carrying out. It will be a very fine work" (my italics).[6] Two and one-half weeks later Morris himself explained to Charles Eliot Norton that the trip to Iceland "has been of great service to me: I was getting nervous & depressed and very much wanted a rest, and I don't think anything would have given me so complete a one—I came back extremely well and tough, and set to work at once on a new poem (which has nothing whatever to do with Iceland). . . . [I am] very much excited about it."[7] But *Love Is Enough* proved to be a crisis poem for Morris, one whose writing was tortured rather than "easy," as had been most of his previous poetry.[8] On February 13, 1872, Morris explained to his friend Louisa Baldwin, "I have been in trouble with my own work, which I couldn't make to march for a long time; but I think I have now brought it out of the maze of rewriting and despondency, though it is not exactly finished."[9] If the unusual three-month hiatus in Morris's correspondence is any indication, the completion of *Love Is Enough* was problematic indeed, blocking much of Morris's other, normally fluent, writing.

From such a struggle by an accomplished and acclaimed poet and from the remarks about *Love Is Enough* made by Rossetti, who was no mean judge of poetry, we would expect this work to be something of a masterpiece in the way of a highly conflicted artistic effort. But its reception upon publication in 1872, and since, has been at best tepid, at worst acerbic. Coventry Patmore, for instance, described the poem privately as "one of those things which, as Lord Dundreary says, 'No fellow can be expected to understand.'" George Meredith was more caustic: "I have looked at

Morris's poem . . . *Love Is Enough*. I looked away. The look was enough. Our public seems to possess the fearful art of insensibly castrating its favourites."[10] Published reviews (not nearly so widespread as those of *The Earthly Paradise*) were more respectfully equivocal, some admiring the "conception and . . . seriousness" of the effort, the "concentration and fullness of thought," the necessity for the reader to "live in the poem, not to dream of it." But the praise was notably qualified: Morris is castigated for losing "something of his easy mastery in abandoning the ruder form of the heroic couplet which he inherited from Chaucer." The poem is criticized for its "obscurity. . . . [It is] a little too vague and shadowy," despite its "singular originality." And at least one critic made the significant observation that the "long anapestic stanzas with double rhymes . . . have an echo here and there of Mr. Swinburne—perhaps inevitable, but hardly welcome. . . . indeed there are whole paragraphs that only want rhymes to remind us of Mr. Swinburne."[11]

The poem is seldom discussed by modern critics, who, apparently, discover the same difficulties and defects in *Love Is Enough* that disturbed earlier readers. The work is of greatest interest to biographers of Morris, who see the restlessness of King Pharamond, the poem's hero, and his pursuit of an ethereal ideal beloved as a clear revelation of Morris's own amatory dissatisfactions. Even the most enthusiastic recent admirer of this poem with the intriguing subtitle, *The Freeing of Pharamond,* insists that it exposes a very important stage in Morris's poetic development because it "takes us closest to the pain and heroic self-awareness of [his] most crucial years."[12] The biographers are far less generous. Philip Henderson describes *Love Is Enough* as "rarefied" and entirely without vigor, "more pale and wan than *The Earthly Paradise*."[13] And E. P. Thompson is relentless in his condemnation: "The technical intricacies of the poem's structure . . . are largely mechanical. The characters . . . are mere shadows of the shadows in *The Earthly Paradise*. The long lines with their facile rhythm . . . have . . . a deadly langour of feeling and emptiness of thought. . . . The narrative itself is a sort of shadow . . . and the poetry of mood, divorced from any particularities of events, situations or relationships, relapses again and again into either rhetoric or cliché. It is a poem which might as well be forgotten—the lowest ebb of Morris's creative life."[14]

Surprisingly, Morris himself was quite satisfied with his difficult poem, despite both public and private criticisms. Yet complacency was uncharacteristic of him. Even with the strong reception of *The Earthly Paradise,* for instance, he acknowledged to Swinburne that "I am rather painfully conscious myself that the book would have done me more credit if there had been nothing in it but the [Lovers of] Gudrun, though I don't think the others quite the worst things I have done—yet they are all too long and flabby—damn it!—."[15] About *Love Is Enough,* however, Morris felt differently. Late in life he described the poem positively as "a fantastic little book."[16] According to Mackail, Morris "felt that this new poem was both tentative and difficult," but "its failure to make any impression on a large audience was received by him with perfect equanimity. It was *a thing he had done to please himself,* and he thought highly of it, but he did not expect it to please other people to anything like the same degree."[17]

Presumably, then, *Love Is Enough* had a private significance for Morris which most commentators take to be biographical, that is, unconnected with public, or even more narrowly poetic, events of the period 1870–72, during which the poem must have been germinating and was eventually written. Certainly it is possible that *Love Is Enough* is an escapist reaction to Morris's unsatisfactory homelife, his awareness that rather than fulfilling his ideal of a love relationship, his wife had turned her attentions to his close friend, Rossetti, leaving him at once frustrated and alien. Yet, as analysis of the poem reveals, *Love Is Enough* is a deeply intertextual work—like all of Morris's longer poems and most of his lyrics as well. But it is more "obscure" and "shadowy"—one might say, after Harold Bloom, more repressed—in its allusions and appropriations than his poems that openly depend on Mallorian, Froissartian, Chaucerian, Germanic, Greek, or Icelandic pre-texts. Although by no means a great poem, *Love Is Enough* is a highly wrought work highly valued by an extremely popular and influential Victorian poet who was capable of great work. It is also a powerfully ideo-

logical poem by a poet who curiously renounced political engagement for the first half of his career but who, like his own hero in
The Pilgrims of Hope (1885), became "born again" (Morris's phrase)
into the sphere of political and especially literary political activity at
mid-life. Such a curious bifurcation in a poet's work encourages a
close analysis of contexts surrounding the production of a major
poetic effort generated shortly before the period of conversion,
especially when such contexts involve explosive events on several
fronts.

The significance of this poem as a work of ideological crisis
lies primarily in its intertextual operations. *Love Is Enough* is in
every sense a dialogical poem, incorporating intratextual dialogues
between Pharamond and an allegorized figure of Love; between
Pharamond and his foster father, Oliver; and between the hero and
his beloved, Azalais; but also implicitly among the four pairs of
lovers who appear in the poem. *Love Is Enough* establishes intertextual dialogues as well—with the work of Keats, Rossetti, and
Swinburne. These concern the possibilities of achieving amatory
fulfillment in this world, on the one hand, and the conflict between
love and worldly power, on the other. Through these dialogues,
the poem becomes for Morris a social act of poetic retrenchment
and revisionism (including self-revision). It is his attempt to trans-
ume the elegiac Pre-Raphaelite ideology of love (founded in part on
the 1819 poems of Keats), especially as that ideology had attained
extraordinary public visibility in Rossetti's controversial *Poems* of
1870 and as it constituted the thematic foundation of Swinburne's
1869 "Prelude" to *Tristram of Lyonesse*.[18] Morris himself had projected this same ideology in his early *Defence of Guenevere* poems
(1858) and more recently in the narratives of *The Earthly Paradise*.
Love Is Enough, however, presents an optimistic amatory ideology
that derives predominantly from early, rather than later, Keats, that
is, from the essentially optimistic attitude toward love expressed in
Endymion, whose amatory values are largely solipsistic and ethereal.

But the thematic thrust and the action of *Love Is Enough* have a
secondary function that is also derived intertextually. As will become clear in the discussion of the poem that follows, King Phara-

mond is "freed" in his pursuit of an amatory ideal (that is also an aesthetic ideal) precisely by renouncing politics—his responsibility and involvement in the public world. Morris had, of course, since his earliest available statements on the subject, abjured political involvement and had continued to do so as the "idle dreamer" of *The Earthly Paradise*. But, as I shall argue, in 1871 events on the Continent, along with the radical new political poetry of Swinburne, impelled Morris in *Love Is Enough* to repudiate with special urgency the deployment of art for political purposes. The events of the spring of 1871, nonetheless, retained a compelling influence on his ideological dispositions; in 1885 with *The Pilgrims of Hope,* the only significant longer poem written late in his life, Morris returned to the political crisis and upheaval of the Paris Commune—whose significance he could scarcely acknowledge at the time—for the setting of his poem's climactic events.

The Poem

The form Morris chose for *Love Is Enough* is unique in his work. Rossetti's description of it as a masque comes close to Morris's own designation of the poem (in its Argument) as "a Morality." The structure of the play complicates its ostensibly simple theme dramatized by the quest of Pharamond, "whom nothing but love might satisfy, who left all to seek love, & having found it, found this also, that he had enough, though he lacked all else."[19] The action of the poem is related largely through dialogues between Pharamond and his foster father, Oliver, but also between lovers in three pairs—Giles and Joan, the emperor and empress, and Pharamond and Azalais. In addition, the actors who play the leading roles (we are told by Giles and Joan) are wholly fulfilled in love, like the characters they play and like the other two pairs of lovers. Beyond this scheme of thematic replication through framing, Morris designs his "morality" self-consciously as a metadrama by introducing between scenes of dialogue the allegorical figure of Love, who comments on Pharamond's progress in his service, often generalizing from Pharamond's sufferings, frustrations, and, finally, fulfillment. Love eventually represents himself as a god figure guiding all lovers to an eternity of bliss in the House of Love after the world's apocalyptic "last fight that swalloweth up the sea" (*Works*, 9:80). In a further metadramatic move, Morris introduces between scenes eight lyrical interludes designated as "The Music." All of these begin with a refrain taken from the poem's title and its simple theme, "Love Is Enough."

The poem's setting is vaguely medieval. This "morality," presented on the day of the emperor and empress's nuptials, is introduced by a town mayor, and witnessed by Giles and Joan, who comment on its action along with the play's relevance to their own love relationship.

The action is introduced as Master Oliver discusses with a "Councillor" recent unsuccessful attempts to wrest Pharamond from an extended state of despondency and distraction. Such activities as hunting, sailing, and tourneying have failed to restore him. Subsequently, Pharamond relates to his beloved "fosterer" that his malaise has resulted from ephemeral dream visions of a beloved, the first of which occurred after a battle that signaled the beginning of his rise to power five years earlier:

> . . . slumber came o'er me in the first of the sunrise;
> Then as there lay my body rapt away was my spirit,
> And a cold and thick mist for a while was about me,
> And when that cleared away, lo, the mountain-walled
> country.

(*Works*, 9:27)
> . . . . .
>
> By the withy-wrought gate of a garden I found me
> 'Neath the goodly green boughs of the apple full-
> blossomed;
> And fulfilled of great pleasure I was as I entered
> The fair place of flowers, and wherefore I knew not.
> Then lo, mid the birds' song a woman's voice singing.

With this reversal of events and images central to Keats's "La Belle Dame sans Merci," Pharamond follows the voice and discovers "the unknown desire / Of my soul . . . wrought in shape of a woman," a Rossettian anima. She resembles a "twin sister" (*Works*, 9:29). As in Endymion's first dream vision of Cynthia, Pharamond approaches union with the beloved only to be awakened abruptly,

"As bodiless there I stretched hands toward her beauty, / And voiceless cried out, as the cold mists swept o'er me." But the interruption is preceded by a wholly Keatsian moment of suspended eroticism:

> Now her singing had ceased, though yet heaved her
>   bosom
> As with lips lightly parted and eyes of one seeking
> She stood face to face with the Love that she knew not,
> The love that she longed for and waited unwitting;
> She moved not, I breathed not—

(*Works*, 9:29)

Pharamond's determined quest for the beloved begins because his visions of her diminish in direct proportion as his worldly successes and power increase: "Then waned my sweet vision midst glory's fulfilment, / And still with its waning, hot waxed my desire" (*Works*, 9:31). When challenged, nonetheless, Pharamond insists upon the reality of his "dreams," such as one in which

> . . . I heard her sweet breath and her feet falling near me,
> And the rustle of her raiment as she sought through the
>   darkness
> Sought, I knew not for what, till her arms clung about
>   me
> With a cry that was hers, that was mine as I wakened.

(*Works*, 9:41)

Unlike other dreams that "lied to the body of bliss beyond telling," in these dreams of his beloved

> . . . my soul was not sleeping,
> It knew that she touched not this body that trembled
> At the thought of her body sore trembling to see me;
> It lied of no bliss as desire swept it onward.

(*Works*, 9:41)

With Love as his unseen guide and Oliver as his companion, Pharamond wanders abroad, pursuing the beloved of his dreams for more than three years, his quest periodically reinspired by fleeting intimations of the beloved's yearning for him.

After a long illness, in despair and wishing to die, Pharamond encounters Azalais, who is guided to him by "The Music." This climactic scene presents a pastoral and subdued revision of the moment of union between Shelley's Prometheus and Asia. Love prepares for it with a benediction:

> Sleep then, O Pharamond, till her kiss shall awake thee,
> For, lo, here comes the sun o'er the tops of the
>   mountains,
> And she with his light in her hair comes before him.
>   . . . . .
> Breathe gently between them, O breeze of the morning!
> Wind round them unthought of, sweet scent of the
>   blossoms!
> Treasure up every minute of this tide of their meeting,
> O flower-bedecked Earth! with such tales of my triumph
> Is your life still renewed, and spring comes back for ever
> From that forge of all glory that brought forth my
>   blessing.
> O welcome, Love's darling! Shall this day ever darken,
> Whose dawn I have dight for thy longing triumphant?

(*Works,* 58–59)

Here is Morris's "Triumph of Love," a determined challenge, if not to Shelley's *Triumph of Life,* then certainly to Swinburne's amatory pessimism in "The Triumph of Time" and to the elegiac tone of all his love poems and most of Rossetti's. The lovers' moment of union is signalled as Pharamond exclaims to Azalais,

> —Ah, unending, unchanging desire fulfils me!
> I cry out for thy comfort as thou clingest about me.
> O joy hard to bear, but for memory of sorrow,
> But for pity of past days whose bitter is sweet now.

(*Works,* 62)

Immediately,"The Music" glosses this scene as a moment of apocalyptic rebirth. "New-born" through the agency of Love, "all doubt of desire, / All blindness, are ended" and the lovers' "forehead[s] are sealed with his seal" (*Works,* 9:63).

Love himself next presents a generalized commentary on this realization of Pharamond's dreams and fulfillment of his desire. Typically, Love's speech is deployed here to distance readers from the emotional experience that has been presented dramatically and to freeze it aesthetically, as Keats characteristically does. It becomes a thing of beauty that is a joy forever. Having recounted Pharamond's commitment to accompany Oliver on his return to their kingdom before rejoining Azalais, Love—acknowledging the universal Romantic yearning for "something evermore about to be"— raises the question all lovers eventually face: "our one desire / Fulfilled at last, what next shall feed the fire?" (*Works*, 9:64). But this is a rhetorical question designed to refocus audience attention on art as a vehicle of ideology. Love explains that he asks this question "not . . . to make my altar cold,"

(*Works*, 9:64–65)

> Rather that ye, my happy ones, should hold
> Enough of memory and enough of fear
> Within your hearts to keep its flame full clear;
> Rather that ye, still dearer to my heart,
> Whom words call hapless, yet should praise your part,
> Wherein the morning and the evening sun
> Are bright about a story never done;
> That those for chastening, these for joy should cling
> About the marvels that my minstrels sing.

Clearly, minstrels' tales teach values and behavior, in this case the supreme value of love which should be pursued at all costs, whether or not success is assured.

The optimism of the poem's climactic union of Pharamond and Azalais is reinforced rather than undermined, as some critics insist, by his return to his kingdom, which has been usurped by King Theobald during his absence. Once home, Pharamond recalls his accomplishments as warrior and king, wishing to be the subject of a "song . . . that . . . / May grow to [my name's] remembrance." But he places special emphasis on the conclusion to his imagined "song": "So, like Enoch of old, I was not, for God took me" (*Works*, 9:67). The God to whom he refers is, of course, Love. Now replaced in his people's attentions by his usurper, Pharamond describes himself as "freed." "Fresh waxeth my manhood," he announces, as he turns to political comments on the new regime. He views Theobald's entourage with equanimity, feeling compassion for a "dead-alive" and "blind" king who "feared for no pain and craved for no pleasure!" (*Works*, 9:73). His own past days of power and glory are "grown a dream of the dream ye have won me" (*Works*, 9:72), although the new dream of realized love is troubled by fears that his safe return to Azalais may be obstacled. Such fears are alleviated for the audience, however, in Love's last long monologue, where earlier apocalyptic image patterns are re-appropriated to assure all lovers and prospective lovers that

(*Works*,   The world thou lovest, e'en my world it is,
9:79)   Thy faithful hands yet reach out for my bliss,
          Thou seest me in the night and in the day
          Thou canst not dream that I can go astray.

Love here reveals that the suffering and frustrations of lovers will earn them a room in the House of Love which is perpetually built with "your bitter sighs . . . as toil-helping melodies," and "in the mortar of our gem-built wall / Your tears were mingled mid the rise and fall / Of golden trowels" (*Works*, 9:80). Like Keats's image of life as a "Mansion of many apartments," The House of Love has "many mansions" and shall be the place of all lovers' ultimate nup-tials: "Of me a wedding-garment shall ye gain / . . . A wedding-garment, and a glorious seat / Within my household" (*Works*, 9:78). Morris here exploits biblical imagery of apocalypse and resurrec-tion, but he does so, as we shall see, to different effects than Rossetti and Swinburne in their revisionist appropriations of simi-lar biblical texts. Morris transvalues these to support a wholly optimistic amatory ideology.

The final pages of *Love Is Enough* establish a symmetry with its opening scene and are taken up with metadramatic framing com-mentary. Joan and Giles and the empress and emperor "praise . . . Tales of old time, whereby alone / The fairness of the world is shown" (*Works*, 9:83). Joan is eager to invite the actors, who are also lovers, to her home, hoping, with Giles, "To learn love's meaning more and more" (*Works*, 9:85). And the empress conceives love as a "toil-girthed garden of desire" whose "changeless sweetness" serves as a stay "amid the turmoil" and "the rugged fields we needs must stumble o'er"—transparent metaphors for the dangers and hardships of active political life. Significantly, Joan concludes the poem with an invocation to Love:

(*Works,*
9:89)
> —O Love, go with us as we go,
> And from the might of thy fair hand
> Cast wide about the blooming land
> The seed of such-like tales as this!

This poetic seed, it is clear, presents a radical antithesis to that in Shelley's "Ode to the West Wind." Morris's germinal "tale" preserves the social and political world as it is, while transforming lovers' perceptions of it by inducing a new understanding of their God's beneficent potency in human affairs.

I rehearse the action of *Love Is Enough* in such detail because it is an unfamiliar work to many, even to some students of Morris, but also because when it is read, it is commonly misunderstood, viewed as a poem whose discussion of love extends the pessimism of tales in *The Earthly Paradise*. Carole Silver, for instance, finds unconvincing the poem's insistence that love requires the "death of the old self and the birth of the new." Instead, she asserts, "the undermeaning," that death and love are indistinguishable, dominates: "Pharamond and Azalais find each other only after each has faced—but not triumphed over—the yearning for oblivion. The separation that follows their temporary union is perhaps caused by the fact that neither can move beyond death to love."[20] In fact, the explicitly Keatsian connection between death and love that the poem establishes occupies only a brief portion of the poem, the dialogue between Pharamond and Love immediately before Azalais joins Pharamond. Thinking he has found death in his first direct confrontation with the figure of Love, Pharamond deliriously exclaims, "Be thou God, be thou Death, yet I love thee and dread not." And when Love asks him, "while thou livedst what thing wert thou loving?" Pharamond responds: "A dream and a lie—and my death—and I love it" (*Works,* 9:55). But the rhetorical purpose of Love's taunting equivocation in this scene is precisely that of Keats's imaginative dissolution into an impercipient state of being at first projected as the nightingale in his famous ode: it serves ultimately to awaken Pharamond, as Keats's persona is awakened, from a fanciful yearning for "easeful death" misperceived as simultaneous oblivion and fulfillment. But, explicitly rejecting the late Keatsian uncertainty of the "Ode to a Nightingale" and implicitly repudiating as an inadequate fulfillment the resigned sensualism of the "Ode on Melancholy," Morris presents Pharamond's escape from death as an awakening to the incontestable reality of his perfect, fulfilled love. At the end of his final monologue Pharamond insists on his rebirth into what Love has earlier designated the "bower . . . of *Earthly* Bliss" (my italics). He bears "witness to Love." Despite all inevitable changes the world cycles through, "Each long year of love" still "lieth in wait with his sweet tale untold,"

. . . and the first scarce beginneth,
Wherein I have hearkened to the word God hath
   whispered,
Why the fair world was fashioned mid wonders
   uncounted.

(*Works,*
9:75)

Here Pharamond confirms Love's earlier celebration of "the very sweetness of rewarded love," which asserts that

These lovers tread a bower they may not miss,
Whose door my servant keepeth, Earthly Bliss:
There in a little while shall they abide,
Nor each from each their wounds of wandering hide,
But kiss them, each on each, and find it sweet.

(*Works,*
9:48)

The Precursor

We have already glimpsed a number of passages in which various Keatsian texts emerge as palimpsests beneath Morris's reinscription of his favorite Romantic poet's early amatory ideals. Shortly, I will focus on key passages from *Love Is Enough* to show how Morris quietly corrects the emphasis on the later Keats in works by Rossetti and Swinburne, as well as his own poems, before 1872. He does so by invoking the visionary mode, along with the fundamental values, of *Endymion* and eschewing the "realism" of Keats's later work.[21] A brief review of Pre-Raphaelite appropriations of Keats will prove helpful along the way.

Soon after the publication of the first volume of *The Earthly Paradise* (1868), Morris received an appreciative letter from Keats's old friend Charles Cowden-Clarke, who speculates, "I am sure that you would not have had a more devoted admirer, and Brother in the faith of Love and Beauty, than in my beloved friend and schoolfellow, John Keats."[22] Morris responded that he was "delighted to have been able to give pleasure to . . . the friend of Keats, for whom I have such boundless admiration, and whom I venture to call one of my masters."[23] At that point in Morris's poetic development, it is clearly the mature Keats of the 1819 poems to whom he is most indebted.

Reviewing Morris's work to 1868, Walter Pater does not name Keats as Morris's most important Romantic precursor, but the values and atmosphere he discovers in Morris's recent poetry are those of the "Ode on Melancholy," "La Belle Dame sans Merci," "The Eve of St. Agnes," "Isabella," and "To Autumn." Characteristic of Morris's poems, he explains in a famous passage, is "the continual suggestion, pensive or passionate, of the shortness of life; this is contrasted with the bloom of the world and gives new seduction to it; the sense of death and the desire of beauty; the desire of beauty quickened by the sense of death." This poetry, Pater asserts "assum[es] artistic beauty of form to be an end in itself."[24] In its elegiac aestheticism and in its focus on the (mis)fortunes of love in this world (if in little else), this poetry is—and two years later would be designated as—Rossettian.

It is crucial here to distinguish between the qualities of Keats's later poems (as implicitly described by Pater) and those of *Endymion,* the only early poem that attained prominence among the Victorians. In Keats's poems of 1819, the closest we come to the permanent attainment of fulfillment in a love relationship is the equivocally satisfying union of Porphyro and Madelaine in "The Eve of St. Agnes." At the poem's climax Madelaine has demonstrated a clear preference for her dream of Porphyro (from which he has awakened her) over his reality. Yet these lovers must finally flee together "into the storm" of the real world, passing by "be-nightmared" drunks, while the reader is left with images of the pain of death (Angela) and its absolute finality (the beadsman). By contrast, *Endymion* is the narrative of a dream of ideal love that becomes a reality: Endymion's beloved goddess, Cynthia, is trans-formed into an accessible and human Indian maiden. In the end, through the agency of their love, Endymion is "spiritualized" by "some unlooked-for change," just as Cynthia has been humanized. The two "vanish far away" into a blissful, but presumably real, pastoral world.

The fate of these two lovers resembles the life that Pharamond anticipates for himself and Azalais: "In the land where my love . . . abideth / The poor land and kingless of the shepherding people, / There is peace there" (*Works,* 9:70). Significantly, it is a fate dis-tinctly unlike that of lovers in poems published up to 1872 by Rossetti, Swinburne, and Morris himself.

The primacy of Keats's influence on Rossetti's poetry is as-serted by most commentators. Oswald Doughty insists upon it: "despite Shelley's hold upon his early enthusiasms, and the fre-quent evidence of Shelley's influence upon his poetic thought, subjects, and emotional attitudes, despite also his enthusiasm for Browning, the poets whom . . . Rossetti most resembles are Ten-nyson and, above all, Keats."[25] In his sonnet on Keats Rossetti especially laments his precursor's "love found vain,"[26] and under that rubric Rossetti's transvaluations of Keats become most vis-ible.[27] Still, Rossetti most often reconstitutes the amatory ideology of such poems as "La Belle Dame sans Merci" and "Lamia" eth-ereally. Rossetti's bereft abandoned lovers—in "The Blessed Dam-ozel," "The Portrait," "The Stream's Secret," and the Willowood sonnets from *The House of Life,* for instance—are alone and palely loitering in this world not only because an ostensibly real beloved has died but also and more conspicuously because they know that the mystical ideal of love they envision is impossible to realize in the world. The "One Hope" concluding the 1870 sonnets toward *The House of Life* is at best a wan hope, all that remains of a love that has generated only "vain desire . . . and vain regret," and it is a hope for a better experience of love, not in this world, but—as in so many of Rossetti's poems—in an afterlife.[28] In this respect, the amatory ideology developed in the 1870 *Poems* and that Morris had to confront, as it were, in systematized form when preparing the review of this volume Rossetti insisted he write was a revisionist fusion of values from Keats *and* Shelley. As David Riede has observed, "Rossetti's treatment of love and his freedom to indulge in sensual description certainly owe much to the precedent of Keats, but his characteristically self-absorbed approach to ideal love has more in common with the work of . . . Shelley."[29]

Reviewing Rossetti's *Poems* was a task Morris did not relish,[30] as is clear from a remark that concludes his letter of April 25, 1870, to Aglaia Coronio: "I have done my review, just this moment— ugh!—"[31] Morris was understandably cautious in responding to Rossetti's conflation of Keatsian melancholy sensualism and Shelleyan etherealism. Morris finds himself repeatedly compelled to employ oxymorons to describe Rossetti's poetry, when he is not reduced to virtual incoherence: "No poem in this book," he explains, "is without the circle of [a] realizing mysticism, which deals wonderingly with all real things that can have poetic life given them by passion, and refuses to have to do with any invisible things that in the wide scope of its imagination cannot be made perfectly distinct and poetically real." "The Blessed Damozel" he describes as "a palpable dream, in which the heaven that exists as if for the sake of the beloved is as real as the earthly things about the lover, while these are scarcely less strange or less pervaded with a sense of his passion, than the things his imagination has made." Most of all Morris claims to admire Rossetti's "deep mysticism of thought, which . . . is both great in degree and passionate in kind."[32]

In this review, which predates by six months Buchanan's explosive attack on Rossetti in "The Fleshly School of Poetry," Morris primarily addresses issues of technique, atmosphere, and craft in Rossetti's work. He says little about its frequent thematic focus on obstacled, disappointed, or frustrated love. In connection with "The Blessed Damozel," he does elaborate the volume's dominant subject matter: "wild longing, and the shame of life, and despair of separation, and the worship of love." With regard to "Love's Nocturn" and "The Stream's Secret," however, we learn only that the first is "obscure with more than the obscurity of the dreamy subject" and that the latter is "wonderfully finished, and has very high musical qualities, and a certain stateliness of movement."[33] Morris's refusal to engage the elegiac amatory values of Rossetti's poems, as most reviewers did, is telling: although he appreciated the "realizing mysticism" and "palpable" dreaminess of these works, Morris found Rossetti's Shelleyan transvaluation of late Keatsian assumptions about love unpalatable, as his letter to Algaia Coronio suggests, and baffling, as the vague circumlocutions of his review demonstrate. But the elegiac amatory values of Keats's 1819 poems, as we have begun to see, also come under attack eighteen months later in *Love Is Enough*. These values Rossetti shared with Swinburne.

Although Swinburne, in his critical remarks about Keats, is concerned with him as a nature poet rather than a poet of love, he valued him very highly indeed. With Morris and Rossetti at Oxford in 1857, Swinburne was under the spell of Keats. As Morris explained, "Our clique was much influenced by Keats, who was a poet who represented semblances, as opposed to Shelley who had no eyes" (*Works*, 22:xxxi). For Swinburne the treatment of nature, however, remained "that especial field of work where all the giants and all the gods of art would fail to stand against [Keats] for an hour." And for his work in this field Swinburne's praise is unstinting:

> Keats, of all men born [was] ablest to hold his own with nature, and translate her gods into verbal incarnation; Keats, . . . was at once the lyrist and the lyre of that nature, the priest and the altar of those gods; more than all other poets receptive and passive of her influences and forces, and more than all other poets able and active to turn them all to a divine use, to transfigure them without transformation, to attune all colours and attemper all harmonies; [his] power upon these things, [his] gift of transfusion and expression, places him apart from all.[34]

Yet in Swinburne's canon Keats, a poetic "Giant" is superseded by Shelley, a "God." As Terry Meyers has made clear, for Swinburne Keats is unable "to join in a holistic unity the . . . spiritual . . . and the physical. It is only Shelley among the English Romantic lyrists . . . who fulfills one of Swinburne's most central critical demands, the ability to perceive in sensation the spiritual power behind it, and the ability to express in sound the reality and the unity of both."[35] Still, Swinburne is surely the most intertextually protean of Victorian poets, and frequent verbal echoes of Keats do appear in his work. Not unexpectedly, these echoes most often emerge in passages of sensual or erotic description. Further, as with Rossetti, it is the later Keats whom Swinburne echoes, and he does so thematically as well as verbally. In his essay on Keats, Swinburne castigates all Keats's work before 1819: "The *Ode to a Nightingale,* one of the final masterpieces, . . . is immediately preceded in all editions now current by some of the most vulgar and fulsome doggerel ever whimpered by a vapid and effeminate rhymester in the sickly stage of whelphood."[36]

The Keatsian emphasis on "beauty that must die," on the transitoriness of love, emerges implicitly in "The Eve of St. Agnes" and explicitly in "La Belle Dame sans Merci," as well as in the odes "To Melancholy and "On a Grecian Urn." It is also at the heart of all Swinburne's amatory poetry—from the pathos of *Atalanta in Calydon* and "The Triumph of Time," whose speaker's "whole life's love goes down in a day,"[37] to the apocalyptic depiction of love's inevitable decay in "A Forsaken Garden" and the heroic portrayal of those who die in Love's service in *Tristram of Lyonesse.* The melancholy, elegiac mood of these works is perfectly consonant with that of Morris's love poems before 1872. In some of those works, Morris is in fact bent upon extrapolating, through reinscription, the amatory ideology of earlier poems by Swinburne.

The narratives of *The Earthly Paradise,* for instance, are framed by two tales—"Atalanta's Race" and "The Hill of Venus"—topoi Swinburne had already treated in major poems, *Atalanta in Calydon* and *Laus Veneris.* And "The Lovers of Gudrun," which was, according to their correspondence, the favorite of both Morris and Swinburne, treats "the seed and fruit of bitter love" (*Works,* 5:250). Its heroine is, as Carole Silver has observed, a belle dame sans merci, like Swinburne's Venus: "less . . . a living woman than . . . a powerful force which destroys all who desire her. Cold and passive, . . . ambivalent and egocentric . . . [she is a type] of fatal beauty who personif[ies] the destructive aspects of earthly love." She is, like all of Swinburne's femme fatales from Mary Stuart and Atalanta through Venus and Iseult, "fated to be fatal, causing love even when [she does] not share it, causing destruction even when [she does] not intend it."[38] In this poem, as in so many by Swinburne that appropriate Keats's equation of death with love, rejection by the beloved generates a powerful death wish.

Yet hardly a greater distance can be imagined than between Morris's Gudrun and his Azalais, or between Pharamond's beloved and the belle dame of his last original long poem before *Love Is Enough,* Venus—who is "a curse unto the sons of men" (*Works,* 5:385). It is the distance between Keats's heartless Melancholy, whose might shall make trophies of all lovers' hearts, and his Cynthia (as the Indian maiden), who is, as it were, the fairy godmother of beloved women, granting all Endymion's wishes and satisfying all his desires.

In *Love Is Enough* Morris's reaction against Pre-Raphaelite adaptations of the late Keatsian elegiac view of love all three poets had previously shared is both surprising and anomalous. Morris's last long poem before his political conversion, *Sigurd the Volsung* (1875) is an epic tale "Of utter love defeated utterly, / Of Grief too strong to give Love time to die!" (*Works,* 7:290). And even *The Pilgrims of Hope* is largely elegiac in tone. *Love Is Enough* must be understood therefore as the product of particular pressures at work upon Morris from 1870 to 1872, pressures that led him at least temporarily to repudiate the amatory ideology of his former work— identical in its pessimism to that of Rossetti and Swinburne—in a return to Keats's *Endymion* as the originary source of regenerative erotic values. Such retrenchment was, as we shall see, compelled not only by the literary exemplars of despondency, if not despair, surrounding him but also by his new awareness of a prospectively chaotic political world that threatened the very survival of art.

The ideological pre-text for the conception of *Love Is Enough* is found in the famous "pleasure thermometer" passage of *Endymion.* Here Endymion explains to Peona the sources of true happiness in the world, the attainment of which he defines as "fellowship with essence." After detailing the relations between sensual pleasure and the achievement of spiritual transcendence, Endymion proceeds to describe love as the supreme among self-destroying "enthralments." "Its influence," he claims, "genders a novel sense,"

> At which we start and fret; till in the end,
> Melting into its radiance, we blend,
> Mingle, and so become a part of it,—
> Nor with aught else can our souls interknit
> So wingedly.

"So delicious is the unsating food," he continues,

> That men, who might have tower'd in the van
> Of all the congregated world, to fan
> And winnow from the coming step of time
> All chaff of custom . . .
> Have been content to let occasion die,
> Whilst they did sleep in love's elysium.

Endymion further acknowledges that he has "ever thought that [love] might bless / The world with benefits unknowingly."[39] *Love Is Enough* retrieves this essentialist amatory ideology, while parodically revising other isolated pre-texts from Keats and from the work of Morris's fellow Pre-Raphaelite poets.

The Pre-texts

Love Is Enough inscribes a network of structural, thematic, and stylistic echoes of Keats, Rossetti, and Swinburne beyond those already noted. Most obviously, the poem revises the Keatsian debate about dreaming that occupies poems from *Sleep and Poetry* through *The Fall of Hyperion*. Ultimately, Morris deconstructs all Keatsian distinctions between dream and reality: in the end, Pharamond is represented as "no dreamer weak" of the sort castigated in *The Fall of Hyperion,* but rather a strong dreamer like Endymion, whose dreams properly intuit what is possible, available, and valuable in reality, especially to one whose fate love presides over.

Just as Oliver, Pharamond's devoted foster father and counselor, is the counterpart of Peona, Endymion's loving sister, for instance, he, too, presents a skeptical perspective at first on the value and validity of dreams. After Pharamond rehearses his first dreams of Azalais, Oliver muses privately that his king is "mid evil sunken." Pharamond realizes that, "thou deemest me mad," but insists, "a dream thou mayst call it, / But not such a dream as thou know'st of" (*Works*, 9:28). Although Oliver does not wish to distress Pharamond more than he is already disturbed by the fading of his dreams and the apparent inaccessibility of his ideal, Oliver is only gradually willing to believe in Pharamond's dreams and aid him in the quest to realize them. Like Peona, who is similarly gentle with Endymion, but who nonetheless, chides, "Why pierce high-fronted honour to the quick / For nothing but a dream?" (*Keats*, p. 125), Oliver has worked unsuccessfully to rescue Pharamond from the influence of his visions. Like Endymion's, they have been "such . . . / That never tongue . . . / Could figure out and to conception bring" (*Keats*, pp. 119–20). The most important effect of dreams upon these heroes, however, is social and political: both relinquish illusions of the value commonly attributed to leadership, and they privilege love in its place. Pharamond's lines (discussed earlier) renouncing political activity and its value in the world, in fact, replicate Endymion's radical stance against pursuing "the world's praises." Midway through Book 1 Endymion explains to Peona,

(*Keats*, p. 127)

> "Now, if this earthly love has power to make
> Men's being mortal, immortal; to shake
> Ambition from their memories, and brim
> Their measure of content; what merest whim,
> Seems all this poor endeavor after fame,
> To one, who keeps within his steadfast aim
> A love immortal."

Keatsian resonances early in *Love Is Enough* make clear the poem's validation of this amatory ideology and its repudiation of Keats's later insistence on the illusory and delusory effects of the "fancy" that "cannot cheat so well / As she is fam'd to do." ("Ode to a Nightingale," *Keats*, p. 372). Morris's argument is established early in the poem's second framing dialogue, when the empress acknowledges the emperor as the fulfillment of the dream she "dreamed . . . throughout the day" (*Works*, 9:6). This poem insists upon the identity of reality and "dreamland"—in the framing dialogues, as well as in the tale itself and Love's commentary upon it—precisely because all central characters (except Oliver) are dominated by "earthly love . . . immortal" and fulfilled in a way that those to whom such experience is alien can imagine only as "dream." The empress concludes:

> Nay, dreamland has no clocks the wise ones say,
> And while our hands move at the break of day
> We dream of years: and I am dreaming still
> And need no change my cup of joy to fill.

(*Works*, 9:9)

Unlike Keats's dreamers of 1819 who awake to cold, drear realities, those in *Love Is Enough* have discovered that dreams constitute reality for those who are fully alive to Love's power. To project this vision forcefully at the climax of the poem's action Morris presents a revisionist parody of the truly evil dream of Keats's famous knight at arms. Just as that dream in "La Belle Dame sans Merci" follows the union of the knight and his epipsyche, so Love's monologue serves as an immediate commentary on the scene in which Pharamond and Azalais's love is consummated:

> —Ah, Well-beloved, I fell asleep e'en now,
> And in my sleep some enemy did show
> Sad ghosts of bitter things, and names unknown
> For things I know—a maze with shame bestrown
> And ruin and death; til e'en myself did seem
> A wandering curse amidst a hopeless dream.
> —Yet see! I live, no older than of old,
> What tales soe'er of changing Time has told.

(*Works*, 9:66)

One such pessimistic "tale" clearly is rehearsed in "La Belle Dame sans Merci." Earlier in *Love Is Enough* a similar Keatsian parody, this time of "To Autumn," appears in the third "Music," providing an initial pattern for such revisionist moves. Speaking of Love, as all these lyric interludes do, the poem concludes,

But this is the harvest and the garnering season,
    And the leaf and the blossom in the ripe fruit are
        blended.

(*Works*,
9:21)
It sprang without sowing, it grew without heeding,
    Ye knew not its name and ye knew not its measure,
    Ye noted it not mid your hope and your pleasure;
There was pain in its blossom, despair in its seeding,
    But daylong your bosom now nurseth its treasure.

Unlike "To Autumn," this passage insists upon the nondelusory permanence of love's treasure; as the rest of *Love Is Enough* confirms, it is an eternal harvest. Such parodic strikes against the arguments of Keats's later poetry are the basis in *Love Is Enough* for subversive resonances of Rossetti and Swinburne as well.

In his poem Morris echoes phrases and also appropriates a number of prominent techniques from Rossetti's *Poems* of 1870. Complexly, he reworks as the "House of Love" the proleptic title for Rossetti's sonnet sequence, *The House of Life,* a title itself derived from Keats's notion of life as a mansion of many apartments. But "the House of Love" is, in fact, Rossetti's own phrase from "Stillborn Love" (1870), there used to designate the dwelling place of the hour of love, a child "which might have been yet might not be, / Which man's and woman's heart conceived and bore / Yet whereof life was barren." Only in an imagined afterlife do the parents of that hour become "wedded souls" whose child now "leaped to them and in their faces yearned" (Doughty, p. 118). Morris's strategic repositioning of the House of Love in the context of his poem celebrating amatory fulfillment offers a critique of Rossetti's timorous anxieties and his pessimism in the face of love. Clearly the entire conception and design of Morris's poem undercuts the elegiac directions of Rossetti's sonnet sequence.

Similarly, Morris parodies the frequent use of strategic allegorizations in Rossetti's sonnets where Love appears, after "Death-in-Love" (sonnet 23), as only an equivocally beneficent deity. Desolate without his beloved, for instance, the speaker at the close of the Willowood sonnets feels "Love's face / Pressed on my neck with moan of pity and grace" (Doughty, p. 118). Rossetti's poetic obsession with obstacled, disappointed, and failed love and his fantasies of deferred fulfillment may well even have inspired a commentary by Love in Morris's poem just before Pharamond's quest begins. After promising that Azalais "shall . . . know some day / The love that in [Pharamond's] lonely longing lay," Love insists that he keeps his promises:

> . . . love lies alone
> In loving hearts like fire within the stone:
> Then strikes my hand, and lo, the flax ablaze!
> —Those tales of empty striving, and lost days
> Folk tell of sometimes—never lit my fire
> Such ruin as this; but Pride and Vain-desire,
> My counterfeits and foes, have done the deed.
> Beware, Beloved! for they sow the weed
> Where I the wheat: they meddle where I leave,
> Take what I scorn, cast by what I receive,
> Sunder my yoke, yoke that I would dissever,
> Pull down the house my hands would build for ever.

(Works, 9:38)

The final allusion especially functions to reproach Rossetti for worshiping false gods, Pride and Vain-desire.

A room in the House of Love is, in Morris's poem, the posthumous reward promised to Love's faithful worshipers who, unlike Azalais and Pharamond, do not secure a place in the House of Earthly Bliss. Morris appropriates Rossetti's vision of a heaven for lovers, but only as a last resort—and, ideologically, a source of reassurance—for those, *unlike* the characters in his play, whose love remains unfulfilled in life. These unhappy couples, according to Rossetti, "Together tread at last the immortal strand / With eyes where burning memory lights love home" ("Stillborn Love," Doughty, p. 118). One such lover, the bereaved figure in "The Woodspurge" cannot even utter his grief: his "lips, drawn in, said not Alas!" Morris alludes to this desolate lover, whose "hair was over in the grass" (Doughty, p. 134), in Love's final monologue, where he speaks of his servants who "deemed me dead." But he denies his absence from their lives:

(*Works,*
9:77)

> My tears have dropped anigh the hapless head
> Deep buried in the grass and crying out
> For heaven to fall, and end despair or doubt:
> Lo, for such days I speak and say, believe
> That from these hands reward ye shall receive.

Resurrected, they will gain "A wedding-garment, and a glorious seat / Within my household" (*Works,* 9:78). With only one exception, "Across my threshold naked all must pass," but the exception is significantly described in an ironic allusion to "Jenny," whose speaker is baffled when contemplating the essential identity of the whore and the Victorian angel in the house: "Of the same lump . . . / For honour and dishonour made, / Two sister vessels" (Doughty, p. 68). Morris's allegorized Love tells his audience to "Fear not; no vessel to dishonour born / Is in my house" (*Works,* 9:78), which Morris has, with the revisionist ideology of his poem, reconstructed and purified of Rossettian equivocations.

As we have seen, *Love Is Enough* echoes a number of pre-texts from Rossetti's 1870 *Poems,* but Morris also recalls from beginning to end of his poem a single work by Swinburne, the "Prelude" to *Tristram of Lyonesse,* first published in 1869 (long before Swinburne's epic was completed). There is little doubt that Morris was familiar with the "Prelude," since, as their letters confirm, these friends exchanged all their works. As Swinburne proceeded with his long poem in later years, he in fact consulted Morris about sources and analogues.[40]

Written in heroic couplets, Swinburne's "Prelude" justifies his choice of the story of Tristram and Iseult from among all great tragic lovers immortalized in verse. It begins by celebrating Love as "the first and last of all things made," the "spirit that for temporal veil has on / The souls of all men woven in unison." Swinburne's Love, like Morris's, is the transcendent, generative spiritual force operating in the world through the experiences of lovers, whose lives it is the function of poets to memorialize: the "heat of lamping song" has

> Made for all these their sweet particular air
> To shine in, their own beams and names to bear,

Their ways to wander and their wards to keep,
Till story and song and glory and all things sleep.[41]

Midway through the "Prelude" Swinburne catalogues the "sweet shining signs of women's names" through whom Love fills "the days up of his dateless year." Here the poet cites the tales of Helen, Hero, Alcyone, Iseult, Rosamond, Dido, Juliet, Cleopatra, Francesca, Thisbe, Angelica, and finally Guenevere, each symbolizing a month "wherethrough the year sees move, / Full of the sun, the sun-god which is love" (*Poems*, 4:9). From these Swinburne chooses to resuscitate Iseult and her beloved Tristram in his commemorative "lamping song," despite the "many . . . feet gone before me." Confessing only that he "has the heart to follow" in the tracks of his precursors, Swinburne is determined to "blow my living breath / Between dead lips forgotten even of death" (*Poems*, 4:12).

Echoing even the introductory strategy of Swinburne's planned poem, Morris includes acknowledgment in Love's first monologue that "in the heaven from whence my dreams go forth / Are stored the signs that make the world of worth." These signs are the names of great lovers, including half the figures cited by Swinburne. Morris diverges from Swinburne, as we might expect, in his choice of Medea, Ariadne, Brynhild, and Gudrun, but his procedure is precisely the same and, like Swinburne, he features the names of Guenevere and Iseult. The list of celebrated lovers in Morris's poem is, however, designed to distinguish the purpose of this work—and, by implication, its amatory ideology—from that of elegists like Swinburne. "Nought shall be your need / Of tears compassionate," Love instructs the audience, for his concern here is decidedly not with the "crown of love" that is "woven of bitter death and deathless fame, / Bethorned with woe, and fruited thick with shame" (*Works*, 9:12). In a framing maneuver toward the end of his poem, Morris returns to his own earlier insistence that this is a tale of fulfillment and attainment of "Earthly Bliss," of "faithful hearts who overcome." Yet Love is careful to remind his audience that even those lovers who "at the last fail" do not fail "to be mine." In a move that strategically designates Morris's amatory ideology as comprehensive of the more limited elegiac projects of other

"minstrels," he implicitly refers to Swinburne's unfinished poem.
All tragic hearts, Love explains,

> In diverse ways . . . drink the fateful wine
> Those twain drank mid the lulling of the storm
> Upon the Irish Sea, when love grown warm
> Kindled and blazed, and lit the days to come,
> The hope and joy and death that led them home.
> —In diverse ways; yet having drunk, be sure
> The flame thus lighted ever shall endure,
> So my feet trod the grapes whereby it glowed.

(Works,
9:80)

The Politics

Most readers would doubtless find *Love Is Enough* a thoroughly
apolitical work. Yet, by now it should be clear that in a number of
ways it is decidedly political. For one thing, the poem is, as we have
seen, highly self-conscious in matters of form, stylistic variety, and
allusions to pre-texts; indeed, its "literariness" might be seen as the
poem's secondary subject, after love. More powerfully even than
Morris's earlier poems, this one would appear to support Walter
Pater's claim that his work "assume[s] artistic beauty of form to be
an end in itself."[42] But here whatever beauty the poem accomplishes is defined by the ideology it serves. Aesthetic success is
coterminous with an ideal of erotic fulfillment. It is precisely this
feature of *Love Is Enough* that has discouraged readers from Meredith to E. P. Thompson, who find it "obscure," "shadowy," and
"dreamy." The poem deliberately presents itself, in fact, as doubly
dream-bound: a self-conscious retreat into the idealities of love
within the idealities of art. But such a strenuous denial of the value
of activity in the "real" world is a political move in its own right,
subversive in its repudiation of the values normally held in that
world. Indeed, an artistic work that advocates the "freeing" of its
hero from the half-life of political activity and responsibility condemns those who pursue such involvement, as Pharamond's deri-
sive comments on the life of the new king, Theobald, make clear.

  But beyond this, as I have argued, *Love Is Enough* also advocates a particularized system of values upon which to base action

and behavior in the world. Visible in its intertextual operations, the poem's ideology is specifically derived from second and third generation Romanticism, invoking a return to early Keatsian ideals and revising those central to Pre-Raphaelite love poetry before 1872. Thus, for all Morris's claims to be an "idle singer of an empty day," his work visibly participates in the larger late-Romantic project that employs, in the form of "aestheticism" and as a basic ideological strategy, the politics of renunciation. If *Love Is Enough* is designed to inspire fidelity to an ideal of erotic love frequently challenged in daily life (not to mention political life), then it serves to extend the imperative with which *The Earthly Paradise* opens:

(*Works*, 3:3)

Forget six counties overhung with smoke,
Forget the snorting steam and piston stroke,
Forget the spreading of the hideous town;
And dream.

Going well beyond this subversive invitation, *Love Is Enough* argues that the dream of love *is* an authentic and attainable reality, indeed the only one that offers true fulfillment in life.

Perhaps surprisingly, this ideology dominates *The Pilgrims of Hope* as well as *Love Is Enough*. The poem of 1885, whose climactic action takes place in the highly charged political atmosphere of Paris during the spring of 1871, serves in unexpected ways as the sequel to Morris's "apolitical" poem of 1871, whose narrator, the allegorized figure of Love, appears at *its* climax "clad as a pilgrim."

Like *Love Is Enough, The Pilgrims of Hope* is a dramatic poem. Appropriately, however, Morris chose to write it in a form conventionally used in Victorian England to present topical subject matter. *The Pilgrims of Hope* is made up of thirteen dramatic monologues of varying lengths, introduced by Morris's Shelleyan parody, "The Song of the March Wind." If only in its social criticism, its overt advocacy of a political ideology, and its form, the poem resembles Tennyson's *Maud* more than it does Morris's own earlier work. The monologues tell the story of a rural couple who move to London, have a child "of very love . . . born" (*Works*, 24:380), and who themselves are shortly "born again" into political radicalism, specifically the version of communism dominant in England and

France in 1870–71. Because of his political activity, Richard (the main speaker in the sequence) loses his position as an artisan and is jailed after participating in a fracas at a political rally. Afterwards, he becomes close friends with Arthur, who joins the couple in their political activities, begins and sustains an affair with Richard's wife, and eventually provides for their son while the ménage embarks for France to aid the Paris Communards in their spring usurpation and resistance. There Richard's wife and Arthur are killed. Richard returns to England and recounts these events to an anonymous listener. Clinging "to the love of the past and the love of the day to be," Richard has come "to look to my son, and myself to get stout and strong, / That two men there might be hereafter to battle against the wrong" (*Works,* 24:408). This poem, in its subordination of love to political ideology and activity, is clearly the antithesis of *Love Is Enough,* a corrective, it would seem to the escapist naïveté of the earlier poem, but one which does not disavow, but rather reinforces, the amatory ideology of that poem, extending it—with the maintenance of Richard's at first idealized and later unembittered love for his wife—into the arena of political action.

Understanding the intertextual operations of *Love Is Enough* and its ideological relationship to *The Pilgrims of Hope* may alter the way we understand the process of Morris's political conversion in the mid-1870s and its significance to his literary activities. That his conversion involved a radical shift in priorities and the causes to which he devoted his energies is a commonplace. As all students of Morris are aware, the change became visible in his work by 1877. He played an essential role in forming The Society for the Protection of Ancient Buildings, and later in the same year, he contributed money, energy, and his voice to the Eastern Question Association. As Mackail was the first to observe, "almost without knowing it, Morris was now beginning to take a part in public action and political life."[43] His doing so would seem to reverse the position he took (albeit as a poetic persona) in *The Earthly Paradise* as the "idle dreamer of an empty day" and certainly the escapist stance he implicitly adopted in *Love Is Enough*. Both of those works reinforce assertions he had made as early as July 1856 in a well-known letter to Cormell Price. Insisting on his exclusive valuation of "love and work, these two things only," he explains, "I can't enter into politico-social subjects with any interest, for on the whole I see that things are in a muddle, and I have no power or vocation to set them right in ever so little degree. My work is the embodiment of dreams in one form or another."[44] By 1879, however, he was leading public protests (against the restoration of St. Marks in Venice), and by 1883 he had joined the Democratic Federation and become an extremely active socialist. Two years later, with *The Pilgrims of Hope,* he would look back to the spring of 1871 and its aftermath to find in the Paris Commune "a model for socialist society,"[45] implicitly correcting the limited vision of his escapist poetic reaction against such an ideal in *Love Is Enough.*

As I began by recounting, just over a month after the collapse of the Paris Commune, Morris left for Iceland, for him the geographical equivalent of dreamland. By then he was certainly familiar with the tumultuous events on the Continent. Despite the absence in his correspondence and surviving papers of any "contemporary references . . . to the Paris Commune," as E. P. Thompson argues, Morris "cannot have been unaware of these things. About the true course of events in the Commune he was unlikely to have had any clear understanding, in the chorus of fear and vilification of the bourgeois press: but if (as was likely) he read the [May 1871] *Fortnightly Review* he would not have missed Frederick Harrison's courageous defence of the Communards."[46] That Morris became interested in the Commune only after reading Karl Marx is possible but unlikely. As early as the seventh letter of *Fors Clavigera,* dated July 1, 1871, Ruskin—Morris's acknowledged mentor—had discussed "the fighting in Paris" and the "Parisian notion of Communism." And, since 1870, the war in Europe had been much on the minds of Rossetti and Swinburne. Rossetti repeatedly complained about the effect of "continental events." Because of them, he lamented to William Bell Scott late in 1870, "this year's art . . . has assumed a very unusual aspect."[47] In the same year Swinburne was, by contrast, ebullient. After the establishment of the Third Republic on September 4, he wrote to William Michael Rossetti that he was inspired to "go out and kiss everybody I meet. . . . I am nine tenths out of my mind with joy and pride in Paris."[48] These events must have seemed especially propitious to Swinburne, who was completing *Songs before Sunrise,* his volume of radically republican political poems.

This work was issued in late January of 1871, exactly two months before the establishment of the Commune and four months before its collapse. As was his routine, Swinburne doubtless had Andrew Chatto forward a copy of his new book to Morris, but for Swinburne and Morris both, whatever prescience Swinburne's poems might have displayed was overshadowed by one final event of the May fighting: the burning of the Louvre by the Communards. Swinburne's response (June 1, to William Michael Rossetti) was characteristically vitriolic: "So far from objecting to the infliction of death on the incindiaries of the Louvre I should wish to have . . . a law passed throughout the world authorising any citizen of any nation to take their lives with impunity and assurance of national thanks—to shoot them down wherever met like dogs."[49] Surely Thompson is right to speculate that with Morris, too, this event "must have fallen as a heavy blow." Yet, Morris seems "to have suppressed, half-consciously, the effect of these events and writings [about them] upon his mind."[50] The eventual product of this apparent suppression was *Love Is Enough,* a politically reactionary poem.

Contributing to Morris's reaction, presumably, were inescapable reminders of the Commune in his immediate circle soon after his return from Iceland and throughout the period in which he was, with difficulty, writing *Love Is Enough.* In the same letter to William Bell Scott in which Rossetti discusses *Love Is Enough* (the new poem Morris had set to work on "with a will"), he also mentions "a letter [in the *Pall Mall Gazette*] about a Communalist Benevolent Society" which "interested me, as they seem really, poor fellows, to be helping each other in a very bad plight."[51] In mid-December Rossetti mentions to John Tupper that an artist and a friend of his who had been a Communard has taken refuge in London. Such refugees, it seems, were not only the subject of letters and conversation, but also guests in Rossetti and Morris's circle. In 1872, Swinburne writes to the liberal politician James Stanfield on behalf of his "friend M. Andrieux," who had given "his support in principle to the [Commune] against the government of Versailles: though not less *in*capable of the absurdities and anarchies than of the subsequent atrocities which dishonoured the worst among the adherents of the Commune."[52] Swinburne had met Andrieux during a gathering at Madox Brown's that included William Michael Rossetti and Henry Wallis, among others.

Love Is Enough, positioned in these contexts, may now be seen as a defiant rejection of all varieties of political activism—from those distressingly visible in the rise and fall of the Commune to literary political endeavors like those of Swinburne's *Songs before Sunrise* whose success or failure in the world is less measurable. Such pursuits are supplanted in Morris's poem by early Keatsian ideals of fulfilled love and by art, which serves to memorialize and instruct in love's preeminent value, not only in individual lives but also as a force in human history. As is the case with nearly all of Morris's creative work, here love and art are inseparable necessities of life if we are to discover any beauty in it. As Morris insists in his essay "The Beauty of Life," "that beauty, which is what is meant by *art* . . . is, I contend, no mere accident to human life, which people can take or leave as they choose, but a positive necessity of life, if we are to live as nature meant us to" (*Works,* 22:53). Norman Kelvin understands Morris properly, as few critics do, on this point. For Morris, he explains, "the 'wanting' of art and the gratifying of the want is as *primary* as pleasure-seeking in sex is for Freud. The desire for art is in no sense . . . a sublimation of a drive for sexual or any other gratification."[53] Indeed, the desire for art and for erotic love are, with Morris, equally powerful psychological impulses. He realized only by the mid-seventies, however, that their gratification in a "fallen" social world required political action. This is so because "time . . . has delivered up art to be the exclusive privilege of a few, and has taken from the people their birthright; while both wronged and wrongers have been wholly unconscious of what they were doing" (*Works,* 22:57). "Reforms" are necessary because of the "evils [men] live amongst," having "degraded themselves into something less than men" (*Works,* 22:62). Thus, just as *Love Is Enough* serves as a corrective to what Morris in 1871 retrospectively perceived as the misguided, because elegiac, amatory ideology of his earlier poetry, so by 1885 *The Pilgrims of Hope* serves as a revisionist apologia for his blindness—in that major work from the year of the Paris Commune— to the insufficiency of either love or art without a political regeneration of society that would guarantee the survival of both.

With his return, in *Love Is Enough,* to early Keatsian ideals of love and art (as a thing of beauty that is a joy forever), Morris ironically failed to recognize the political critique embedded in his pre-text. As David Bromwich has demonstrated, Keats's "Cockney couplets" in *Endymion* convey ideology through style, repudiating both the conservative closed couplet of Augustans like Pope and the (by 1817) politically retrograde blank verse of Wordsworth. Beyond this, Keats includes in his poem overt attacks—like the one that begins book 3—on capitalist oppressors, "who lord it o'er their fellow-men / With most prevailing tinsel" (*Keats,* p. 163). The substance of such attacks is, nonetheless, echoed throughout Morris's later writings.[54] Morris's conservative reaction against the amatory and political ideologies of his fellow Pre-Raphaelite poets in 1871 thus turns out as well to be an unwitting subversion of the political gestures inscribed by the precursor whose supposed counterideology he was attempting to subsume within his own poem. Eventually, however, Morris did assimilate the full political as well as the amatory ideology of the early Keats, who—in his faith that love "might bless / The world with benefits unknowingly"—is born again in 1885 as a pilgrim of hope.

VII

Swinburne, Wordsworth, and the Politics of Mortality

> Hence in a season of calm weather
> Though inland far we be,
> Our Souls have sight of that immortal sea
> Which brought us hither,
> Can in a moment travel thither,
> And see the Children sport upon the shore,
> And hear the mighty waters rolling evermore.[1]

These familiar lines conclude the pivotal ninth stanza of Wordsworth's "Ode: Intimations of Immortality from Recollections of Early Childhood." By the time of Wordsworth's death forty-six years after the poem had been completed, the mythos of human immortality this work constructed—delineating man's passages from preexistence to incarnation to a posthumous return to the originary spiritual matrix—had become a cultural commonplace in Victorian England. The mythos constitutes a thematic foundation and a body of transcendental assumptions in Victorian literary texts as diverse as *Aurora Leigh* and *David Copperfield;* Tennyson's "The Two Voices" and "In Memoriam"; Browning's "Cleon" and "Asolando"; and Arnold's *Empedocles,* "The Scholar-Gypsy," and "Thyrsis," among literally hundreds of other works in all genres. As Lawrence Kramer has observed, such works dependably appropriate "the Romantic dialectic in which the self seeks imaginative compensation for the loss of its capacity to experience the world as a radiant plenitude," and they often replicate "the language, structure, or imagery of the Ode." It is "as if the Ode constituted a pattern of experience rather than a pattern of representation."[2]

To the extent that Wordsworth's Ode thus generated a mode of perceiving experience that became something of a cultural compulsion for many of his contemporaries and, judging from the evidence of literature, for nearly all Victorian readers, it is a poem of extraordinary ideological power, instructing its audience that nature beneficently helps man to perceive the certainty of spiritual immortality. Despite the poem's ostensible "pantheism," by mid-century it generally served to reinforce traditional Christian beliefs in the immortality of the soul, especially as later generations read it with the knowledge of Wordsworth's undeniable Anglican ortho-doxy. Nonetheless, as Wordsworth himself acknowledged in his headnote to the poem, the process of interrogating the material world in order to transcend it (a process culminating in the poem's elaborate sea imagery), is one of wish fulfillment: "Nothing was more difficult for me in childhood than to admit the notion of death as a state applicable to my own being." The pattern of experience presented here ultimately sanctions the solipsism, the "abyss of idealism," Wordsworth found frightening in his youth but difficult of access by his adult years when the Ode was written. He explains that, as a child, "I was often unable to think of external things as having external existence, and I communed with all that I saw as something not apart from, but inherent in, my own immaterial nature. Many times while going to school . . . I grasped at a wall or tree to recall myself from this abyss of idealism to the reality. At that time I was afraid of such processes. In later periods of life I have deplored . . . a subjugation of an opposite character."[3] The Ode is thus a deliberately, albeit abstractly, political poem, a conscious revolt—carried out in a medium that bridges the gulf between material and immaterial worlds—against "subjugation" by nature, by finitude and mortality.[4]

One of the later Romantics who was unable to escape the cultural power of Wordsworth's Ode was Swinburne. Thirty years ago Cecil Lang properly insisted that "Swinburne was much more nearly a Wordsworthian, and not merely in the descriptive mode, than he himself realized or than his critics have acknowledged."[5] Supremely self-conscious about matters of literary precedents, debts, and obligations, Swinburne generated his own myth of immortality opposed to Wordsworth's, one reified uniquely from histories of poetic achievement and succession. As the mythicized poet Thalassius (1880), for instance, he rehearses the process of his own immortalization. Through the ministrations of Apollo, he becomes "no more a singer, but a song" that will emerge permanently from "the dawnless dark of death." Swinburne's vision of his own posthumous future as one attainable by all great poets is reinforced (elsewhere) in the example of Sappho, who by virtue of her nature poetry, has arisen from "thick darkness and the insuperable sea" of death. Her "songs once heard," she predicts in her monologue, will "cleave to men's lives":

> Blossom of branches, and on each high hill
> Clear air and wind, and under in clamorous vales
> Fierce noises of the fiery nightingales,
> Buds burning in the sudden spring like fire,
> The wan washed sand and the waves' vain desire,
> Sails seen like blown white flowers at sea, and words
> That bring tears swiftest, and long notes of birds
> Violently singing till the whole world sings—
> I Sappho shall be one with all these things,
> With all high things for ever.[6]

And in his famous elegy on the death of Baudelaire, what remains of this passionate and sorrowful French poet after his death, according to Swinburne, is only the *Fleurs du mal.* Because his songs will survive through "all time's changes," death cannot estrange Swinburne's

Poems,
:54)

> . . . spirit from communion of thy song—
> These memories and these melodies that throng
> Veiled porches of a Muse funereal—
> These I salute, these touch, these clasp and fold
> As though a hand were in my hand to hold.

Swinburne emphatically denies any other form of immortal being for his revered friend and poet: "Our dreams pursue our dead and do not find" (*Poems,* 3:53).

As perhaps the most elegiac among a host of elegiac Victorian poets, Swinburne was obsessed with the finality of death, along with its Keatsian easefulness. In clear reaction against Wordsworthian, as well as Christian, fictions of immortality, poem after poem insists that death is oblivion: "there is no God found stronger than death; and death is a sleep" ("Hymn to Proserpine," 1866, *Poems*, 1:73). This belief, presented variously, informs nearly all his poetry, even his political works. And in a forceful and repeated, usually climactic, strategy of revisionist subversion, death is often figured in these poems using Wordsworth's central metaphor of immortality, the sea. "The Triumph of Time" (1866) is Swinburne's first full-dress response to Wordsworth's Ode, as even the title suggests. Its suicidal speaker, disappointed in love, deconstructs Wordsworth's Romantic trope by reviving and valorizing the originary Hellenic myth that Wordsworth appears, with deliberate obtuseness, to have ignored. But Swinburne's appropriation revises even the myth of Aphrodite, conflating that goddess with Proserpine. (Presumably the association resulted from the love of both figures for Adonis.) Death yields liberation from the agonies of life and a fantasized, surrogate fulfillment of desires life has denied:

> I will go back to the great sweet mother,
> Mother and lover of men, the sea.
> I will go down to her, I and none other,
> Close with her, kiss her and mix her with me;

(*Poems*, 1:42)

> Cling to her, strive with her, hold her fast:
> O fair white mother, in days long past
> Born without sister, born without brother,
> Set free my soul as thy soul is free.

At the most abstract level, Swinburne, like Wordsworth, politicizes his sea trope. For him, too, it signals liberation from materiality. But that liberation carries with it no hope of reincarnation and no language of orthodoxy to recall Wordsworth's insistence that

(*Wordsworth*, p. 460)

> . . . trailing clouds of glory do we come
> From God, who is our home:
> Heaven lies about us in our infancy!

For Swinburne such poetic compromises with what, in remarks or Wordsworth written in 1867, he described as "inveterate and invincible Philistinism" presented a formidable misuse and misunderstanding of the relations among nature, art, and man (as both a spiritual and material being). For him Wordsworth's Ode served to propagate "the good and evil influence of that great poet, perverse theorist, and incomplete man,"[7] an influence in whose field of force even such independent thinkers and poets as Matthew Arnold appeared to be captive.

Throughout his career, Swinburne felt compelled to challenge Wordsworth's power over Victorian audiences, as is clear from the intertextual operations of his poetry and the explicit commentaries on Wordsworth in his essays. Analysis of Swinburne's attempts to subvert Wordsworth's mythos of immortality, in particular, helps to explain the preoccupation with death and with sea imagery in his poetry, but it also clarifies the crucial relationship in his work between politics and the issue of mortality. In addition, his poems, which often enact a poetic mythology in which death truly becomes the mother of beauty, provide a set of Victorian texts especially illuminated by recent theoretical discussions of the relations between aesthetics and ideology.[8]

Swinburne on Wordsworth

Swinburne had begun reading Wordsworth before he was twelve. At that age, with his family and Elizabeth Missing Sewell, he made a pilgrimage to Rydal Mount, where "the aged Wordsworth received them with great civility," according to Sewell's account. Wordsworth "was so very nice to Algernon . . . that I could have cried, as Algernon did when we went away. . . . Lady Jane [Swinburne] said . . . how he had looked forward to [the visit] as he was already acquainted with [Wordsworth's] writings. . . . Some observation was made about Algernon's not forgetting his visit, and Wordsworth's words were, 'He did not think Algernon would forget him.'"[9] The visit turned out to be memorable in unexpected, sometimes ironic ways: in later years Swinburne not only recalled the visit,[10] but also often reread and discussed Wordsworth, sometimes derisively as the "scholar of Rydal" (*Works,* 15:84). Swinburne's epistolary references to Wordsworth begin to help us understand the extraordinary intertextual relations between

the work of two highly influential poets in the Romantic tradition.[11] Commentary on Wordsworth in Swinburne's essays extends that understanding, while only analysis of representative
Wordsworthian poems by Swinburne can fully demystify the ideological operations of Wordsworthian intertexts, especially the Intimations Ode, in his work.

Swinburne's letters begin to explain what he admired and
what he disliked in the poetry and ideology of his monumental
Romantic precursor. It is clear, for instance, that Swinburne often
did not admire commonly revered poems by the laureate (although
he did praise "Tintern Abbey" and "Resolution and Independence"). Apparently for the first time, at nineteen, Swinburne read
The Prelude (more than six years after its publication), commenting
that he "should be sorry to do it again, fine as many passages are"
(*Letters,* 1:10). He also disparaged *The Excursion,* "The Ruined
Cottage," and "The Thorn" (*Works,* 14:231–32, 220, 226). But he
rates often obscure poems of pure description or of simple, humanitarian sympathy (such as "The Convict") and dramatic poems far
more highly than the overtly philosophical works (*Letters,* 5:147–
48). Especially in his later years, Swinburne reveled in poems that
demonstrate Wordsworth's "wholesome and happy and grateful
delight in Nature" (*Letters,* 6:94). By contrast, he facetiously cites
the "unwholesome" Intimations Ode with some frequency. He
does so in connection with his child friend, Bertie Mason, to
whose "little breast," he explains, "I think it may be said that
'years'—eleven years—have brought the comparatively 'philosophic mind'" (*Letters,* 5:107). (Facetiousness aside, Swinburne
was, in his reverence for children, clearly even more indebted to
Wordsworthian mythologies than many child-worshiping Victorians.)

Far more complexly, Swinburne regularly castigates Wordsworth's work in manic satirical remarks. In 1876, for instance, an
attack upon himself and the Rossettis by a priest writing in the
Contemporary Review precipitates a euphoric, free-associated fantasy that Swinburne records in a long letter to William Michael
Rossetti. With the Eastern Question much on Swinburne's mind at
the time, this "Bulgaro-Galilean" critic evokes his ideological

wrath and inspires, as the foundation of an alternate religious system, visions of a Bulgarian reincarnation of Swinburne's revered Marquis de Sade—one Sadyk Pasha, the "living evidence . . . of the Incarnation and Resurrection of the Flesh." He concludes the elaborate spoof: "I only wonder that the pages of the Christian and Bulgarian Spectator have not anticipated my own feeble and inadequate profession of faith—of a faith most mercifully cheered and fortified by this 'Intimation of Immortality'—how far beyond any of those vouchsafed to and commemorated by Wordsworth!" (*Letters,* 3:205). Six years earlier, he had written to Rossetti in a similar but more ebullient vein, of his "discovery" that book eight of Wordsworth's *Excursion* alludes—with the appearance of "two blooming boys" before the Wanderer—to the Marquis de Sade, of whom the " 'gray-haired Wanderer' was a portrait from the life." Because of this discovery Swinburne projects "a fundamental study on Wordsworth and de Sade considered in their reciprocal relations." He also finds Wordsworth's "allusion" to Sade "a pleasing instance of W.'s consistent enmity to the first Bonaparte, persecutor of his venerable fellow-author" (*Letters,* 2:95). Swinburne immediately goes on to discuss, in all seriousness, his recently completed political poems for *Songs before Sunrise.*

These passages from Swinburne's letters, like the new poems he proceeds to explain to Rossetti, are clearly ideological, and they uniquely display the humorous effects of Wordsworthian intertexts operating seriously elsewhere in Swinburne's work. His play on the "reciprocal relations" between Wordsworth and Sade demonstrates Swinburne's characteristic preoccupation with matters of intertextuality (as does, for instance, his insistence in a letter discussing Wordsworth and Shelley upon "the quite incalculable obligations of the younger poet to the elder" [*Letters,* 5:63]). But more than this, the first passage demonstrates how Swinburne (by 1876) sees the Intimations Ode in exclusively ideological terms: the poem has, in his view, become a literary mainstay of middle-class values. More specifically, its mythology has been wholly appropriated by religious orthodoxy, and stands therefore in fundamental opposition to de Sade's ostensibly antibourgeois, antiphilistine ideology. As a defense of a doctrine of immortality compatible with that of

Christianity, the Ode is "unwholesome" to Swinburne. For him, clearly, questions of mortality and immortality are decidedly *political*. It follows that the outrageous comic ironies of the second passage record even more visibly Swinburne's skepticism about Wordsworth's later political values, especially in light of the laureate's cooptation, exemplified in *The Excursion,* by religious orthodoxy and, more generally, a "Philistine" system of values.

In Swinburne's letters written between 1856 and 1898 we begin to see how his relationship with the work of Wordsworth was, like his relationship with nature, long and fruitful. It helped him generate both poetry and ideology. Although his treatment of Wordsworth insistently suggests that he was *not* one of Swinburne's masters—as Blake, Shelley, and Hugo were—Wordsworth nonetheless served him, at least until 1880, as a negative model, a poet whose practice was sanctioned by philistia through its ultimate token of recognition, the laureateship. It was the power of Wordsworth's "evil influence" that first inspired Swinburne to confront the laureate's work and its "perverse" theories. If we follow the development of Swinburne's attitudes toward Wordsworth as they emerge in his essays and poems, however, it becomes clear that, as Swinburne aged, he was increasingly able to admire Wordsworth's work and accommodate its ideology. In "Byron," published the same year as his revisionist poetic treatments of the Immortality Ode's mythology in "The Triumph of Time" and the Proserpine poems (1866), he began his concerted anti-Wordsworthian campaign. He continued the offensive in "Matthew Arnold's New Poems," *Songs before Sunrise,* and works that appeared in *Poems and Ballads, Second Series* (1878). (These include "Thalassius," "Ave Atque Vale," and "The Forsaken Garden.") His epistolary satires of the same period must be seen as minor skirmishes in the fray. By the 1880s, however, as Swinburne's own productions became more politically conservative, indeed often xenophobic and jingoistic, his appropriations of Wordsworth become visibly less subversive. "Wordsworth and Byron" (1884) appears to acknowledge Swinburne's inevitable seduction by the Romantic giant whose ideological power he had ardently resisted in the 1860s and 1870s: "the direct or indirect influence . . . will end," he admits, "only when there is not a man left in the world who understands a word of the dead English language" (*Works*, 14:157). Thus, while the earlier essays and poems attempt to establish an ideological beachhead against Wordsworth's "incalculable power . . . on certain minds for a certain time" (*Works*, 15:83), his last substantial discussion of Wordsworth in prose, along with a number of late poems, but preeminently "Neap-Tide," exposes his all but complete surrender to that power.

In "Matthew Arnold's New Poems" (1867) Swinburne attributes Wordsworth's phenomenal "power" over his readers to "the might of will, the solid individual weight of mind . . . [as well as] the strong assumption and high self-reliance which grew in him so close to self-confidence and presumption . . . [and] the sublimity and supremacy of his genius in its own climate and proper atmosphere" (*Works*, 15:83). Indeed, even in this most highly iconoclastic period of Swinburne's career, his admiration for Wordsworth at his best as a poet (rather than an ideologue) must not be underestimated. In the same essay, he freely acknowledges that "the incommunicable, the immitigable might of Wordsworth when the god [of poetry] has . . . fallen upon him cannot but be felt by all. . . . what he has of greatest is his only. His concentration, his majesty, his pathos have no parallel" (*Works*, 15:87). But for Swinburne in 1867, as in the previous year, Wordsworth's theism serves virtually to undercut the greatness he otherwise acknowledges in his work. In "Byron" Swinburne had been harsh and explicit on this point when discussing Wordsworth's particular "method of contemplating and interpreting the splendours and terrors of nature." He denounces Wordsworth for using nature "as a vegetable fit to shred into his pot and pare down like the outer leaves of a lettuce for didactic . . . purposes." Swinburne cannot resist the urge to extend this metaphor and strengthen the attack in a footnote: "after the somewhat early subsidence of that 'simple, sensuous, and passionate' delight in nature . . . the place of this rapturous instinct of submission and absorption . . . in sight of natural glory and beauty, was taken by a meditative and moralising spirit too apt to express itself in the tone of a preacher to whom all the divine life of things outside man is but as raw material for philosophic or theological cookery" (*Works,* 15:126).

Several pages of Swinburne's essay on Arnold serve to refine upon this statement of his ideological objections to Wordsworth.[12] Inspired by Arnold's denunciation in *Culture and Anarchy* of the Victorian middle classes as philistines, Swinburne throughout the essay employs the biblical story of Samson as an elaborate conceit to discuss the largely antitheist and antibourgeois work of Arnold in both poetry and prose, while he nonetheless laments the residuary and paradoxical philistine influence on Wordsworth (as well as the headmaster of Rugby) upon Arnold: "It will be a curious problem for the critics of another age to work . . . out, this influence of men more or less imbued with the savour and spirit of Philistia upon the moral Samson who has played for our behoof the part of Agonistes or protagonist in the new Gaza where we live. From the son of his father and the pupil of his teacher none would have looked for such efficient assault and battery of the Philistine outworks." But this is due, in Swinburne's view, to the spirit of reaction in Arnold, who nonetheless is incapable of wholesale rebellion against his philistine fathers "of Rugby or of Rydal" (*Works,* 15:84). This conflicted discussion of the influence of Wordsworth upon Arnold is symptomatic of the profound difficulties Swinburne confronts when trying, in his essays, to do justice to the Romantic giant and when attempting revisionist maneuvers in his poems: Wordsworth is an unquestionably great poet who is, with equal certainty, a philistine. In one breath Swinburne exalts the "sublimity and supremacy of his genius"; in the next he decries his "indomitable dullness and thickness of sense," as well as his "violent and wearisome perversities." The one quality "which no other great poet ever shared or can share with" Wordsworth is his "inveterate and invincible Philistinism, his full community of spirit and faith, in certain things of import, with the vulgarest English mind." And this trait is politically dangerous: "what makes his poetry such unwholesome and immoral reading for Philistines" is that "they can turn round upon their rebukers," including Swinburne, "and say, 'Here is one of us who by your own admission is also one of the great poets.'" And, he concedes, "no man can give them the lie"

(*Works,* 15:83–84). Fortunately, nonetheless, Arnold's poetry demonstrates that he has "inherited the soothing force of speech and simple stroke of hand with which Wordsworth assuaged and healed the weariness and the wounds of his time," while largely resisting "Wordsworth's spirit of compromise with the nature of things, [along with] his moral fallacies" (*Works,* 15:86–87).

Seventeen years later, in nearly fifty pages of commentary on Wordsworth, Swinburne's attitude toward Arnold's (and his own unacknowledged) precursor is significantly changed. In fact, Arnold's literary stock is dramatically down, while Wordsworth's is up: "it is a fact which for some time past has been growing only too perceptible to some of Mr. Arnold's most cordial and earliest admirers—that to him, in spite of all of Wordsworth's guidance, years have brought the unphilosophic mind" (*Works,* 14:200). Swinburne attacks Arnold's recent work for "eccentricity, whimsicality, [and] caprice," while he exalts Wordsworth's "peculiar power" discovered "oftenest . . . in such poems as partake almost equally of the lyric and elegiac tone." These works, such as "Resolution and Independence," embody the "true, the sublime and profound genius which redeems all his unaccountable shortcomings and effaces all recollection of his besetting and obtrusive infirmities" (*Works,* 14:231–32). The crucial term here is *unaccountable.* Swinburne would like to be able to revere Wordsworth unequivocally, and he makes repeated gestures to do so. But Wordsworth's philosophizing, his theism, and, more equivocally, his politics remain sticking points. The increased extent of Swinburne's seduction by Wordsworth in 1884 is, nonetheless, measured by notable ambivalences and even apparent self-contradictions in his essay.

Effusive as his general evaluation of Wordsworth's poetry is, here Swinburne is at pains to expose what we might appropriately term "the Wordsworthian ideology," that is, the image of his work Wordsworth self-consciously propagated and that had been uncritically accepted by readers and disciples alike. His Victorian admirers, Swinburne explains with some care, have been "misled . . . by their more or less practical consent to accept Wordsworth's own point of view as the one and only proper or adequate outlook from which to contemplate the genius and the work, the aim and the accomplishment of Wordsworth" (*Works,* 14:213). Swinburne's project with his essay is, in part, to correct this fallacious "outlook." Specifically he argues that Wordsworth "was wrong in thinking himself a poet because he was a teacher, whereas in fact he was a teacher because he was a poet" (*Works,* 14:213).

However, his true teaching as a lyric and elegiac genius remains distinct from his theism, his philosophical doctrines, and to a significantly lesser extent, his political values. Swinburne's condemnation of Wordsworth's religious poetry (and religion in his poetry) is unrelenting: he is "one of the feeblest and flattest of religious poetasters." In such work the wings of his muse are "imped with plumes of religious doctrine—or . . . shall we say, clogged by the spiritual birdlime of a stupefying cant?" (*Works,* 14:232–33). As a corollary to this view, Swinburne wholly embraces Arnold's earlier pronouncement that, in the case of Wordsworth, "poetry is the reality, philosophy the illusion." He agrees fully that *"we cannot do [Wordsworth] justice until we dismiss his formal philosophy"* (quoted in *Works,* 14:212; emphasis in the original). Swinburne therefore directs his energies to descriptions of "the highest distinctive qualities of Wordsworth's genius" (*Works,* 14:217). In this attempt, however, his equivocations obtrude as he repeatedly confronts the problem of politics in Wordsworth's poetry and his life.

Twice in his essay Swinburne asserts that Wordsworth in his mature years altogether lacked vision in matters of European politics. By contrast with Shelley, who "looked steadfastly forward to the peaceful and irreversible advance of republican principle . . . throughout Europe," Wordsworth "showed himself the befogged, befooled, self-deluded, unpractical dreamer among the clouds and sunsets of his chosen solitude and his chosen faith" (*Works,* 14:195–96). In his reactionary conservatism, he could "see nothing between existing Georgian or Bourbonian society and a recrudescence of revolutionary chaos but the maintenance of such divine institutions as rotten boroughs and capital punishment" (*Works,* 14:195). Additionally, Wordsworth lacked "the good sense, the high principle, the far-sighted and impartial reason, which made the Holy Alliance appear to men like Landor more despicable than

Bonaparte and no less hateful than Napoleon" (*Works*, 14:211). There is nothing unexpected in these arch-republican Swinburnian diatribes. The political fine distinctions Swinburne tries to draw later in his essay, however, *are* surprising.

These distinctions emerge in discussions of Wordsworth's patriotism, an issue of vital concern to Swinburne by the eighties. In an extraordinary feat of logic Swinburne reconstructs Wordsworth as a humanitarian whose powerful empathies provided the foundations of his patriotism and, in the abstract, an unimpaired republicanism:

> *As the poet of high-minded loyalty to his native land, Wordsworth stands alone. . . . royalist and conservative as he appeared, he never really ceased . . . to be in the deepest and most literal sense a republican; a citizen to whom the commonweal—the 'common good of all' . . . was the one thing worthy of any man's and all men's entire devotion. The depth and intensity, the fixity and the fervour of his interest in personal suffering and individual emotion did but help to build up, to fortify and consolidate, this profound and lofty patriotism.*

(*Works*, 14:219)

Swinburne understands Wordsworth's "haughty and high-minded confidence in England" as "but the natural outgrowth of his early sympathy with France, while France was as yet undebased into an empire" (*Works*, 14:235). The conservative self-image that the late Wordsworth projected, in fact, becomes a belated component of the Wordsworthian ideology that Swinburne is bent on debunking. As he had facetiously envisioned a reincarnation of the Marquis de Sade in his letter to William Michael Rossetti of 1876, here, in all seriousness, he attempts to regenerate William Wordsworth (and immortalize him) as a lifelong republican.

Swinburne strains to resuscitate the young poet of 1790 and insists that at political heart Wordsworth never changed. As evidence, Swinburne cites his sonnet to Italy, "From the Alban Hills," which "unconsciously anticipated the message of Mazzini." This is the case, Swinburne argues in an extraordinary passage of revisionist biography, despite the fact that Wordsworth "was considered and believed himself to be" a "conservative and reactionary." For

Swinburne the moral is clear: "a high-minded man can no more be consistent in an evil creed, or constant to the submissive doctrine whose keynote is degradation and despair, than a base man can be constant to the faith of heroes, or consistent in his advocacy of political or spiritual freedom" (*Works,* 14:236). On such grounds, rather than on the transcendent and universal grounds elaborated by Wordsworth himself in his great Ode, Swinburne initiates Wordsworth into his pantheon of immortal poets: "the spirit and the body of [his republican] poems must be alike imperishable" (*Works,* 14:236). In Swinburne's final analysis, it is ironically on "account [of his patriotism and republicanism] above all . . . [that] his immortal words of sympathy [will] find immortal application to himself: there is not a breathing of the common wind which blows over England that ever shall forget him" (*Works,* 14:237). This (in every sense) radical rhetorical maneuver is at the heart of Swinburne's essay. Its political (and psychological) cunning resides in the new power over Wordsworth's image, reputation, memory, and influence that it yields to Swinburne, even beyond that of Wordsworth's previously acknowledged successor, Arnold (whom Swinburne has taken care wholly to subvert from the outset of his discussion in this essay). The great Romantic visionary is no longer quite what he himself or his admirers and disciples thought he was. Swinburne has also taken care, along the way, to disempower "that famous, ambitious, and occasionally magnificent poem," the Intimations Ode, that "reveals the partiality and inequality of Wordsworth's inspiration as unmistakably as its purity and its power" (*Works,* 14:223). For that work articulating a mythos unquestioned by Swinburne's contemporaries has in his mind been appropriated and superseded in a series of his own antiphonal poems (beginning in 1866) that—as his sensitivity to Wordsworth's insistent "influence" and "power" must surely have made him realize—was still unfinished in 1884.

Wordsworth in Swinburne

The keynote of Swinburne's finest poetry is elegiac. In this work resignation to time's triumph is the inevitable conclusion to all man's immortal aspirations and all passionate impulses that inspire them. Great poetry, the record of those frustrated aspirations and impulses, is for Swinburne the unique source of an immortality that is decidedly *not* Wordsworthian transcendence, belief in which would sanction the misguided pursuit of "something evermore about to be." Jerome McGann has treated the issue with clarity and precision. For Swinburne, "only in the poetic ability to perceive reality in terms of aesthetic transformations can the mind hope to overcome the tyrannies of time, death, and all the pains of loss and absence." Insofar as life's mutable joy and pain is transformed into great art, McGann explains, "Swinburne . . . has found his own way of showing . . . that, in the continuous process of death which is the human world, an endless fullness of life is for ever born; but that . . . fullness never for a moment cancels the reality and pain of that same world's unending entropic processes."[13] Swinburne's poetry through the 1870s inscribes this belief and, as I have insisted, sets out to challenge and subvert the ubiquitous power and influence of Wordsworth's great Ode in Victorian England.

To the extent that Swinburne's work operates upon the philosophical premise McGann articulates, it is not only poetry of loss, but it is also often poetry of suicidal despair, as is clear in poems such as "The Triumph of Time," "The Garden of Proserpine," and "The Forsaken Garden." These poems are optimistic only insofar as they argue that the frustrations and agonies of life can be resolved, sanctioned, and made meaningful only in death. For,

("Genesis," *Poems,* 2:118)

. . . if death were not, then should growth not be,
    Change, nor the life of good nor evil things,
Nor were there night at all nor light to see,
    Nor water of sweet nor water of bitter springs.

The very continuation of natural cycles demands the absolute death of the individual. In "A Nympholept" (1894) Swinburne recalls the "godhead innate in the fair world's life" that he had fully defined twenty-three years earlier in "Hertha," but now it is "dark" and "dumb"; he acknowledges that "No service of bended knee or humbled head / May soothe or subdue [this] God who has change to wife." We are inevitably its victims: "Life with death is as morning with evening wed" (*Poems,* 6:136). And in "By the North

Sea" (1880)—a clearer response to the Intimations Ode—we are gloomily assured that "the land has two lords that are deathless; / Death's self, and the sea."[14] Metaphorically, these interact as husband and wife but generate only a sort of metamortality that intertextually consumes all Wordsworthian promises of immortality:

> Death, and change, and darkness everlasting
>
> . . . . .
>
> These, above the washing tides and wasting,
>
> Reign, and rule this land of utter death.

(*Poems,* 5:104)

In such fashion Swinburne's anti-Wordsworthian poems deliberately set out to valorize the certainty, finality, and necessity of death.

The philosophical premises behind Swinburne's repeated challenges to Wordsworth's mythos of immortality are most fully articulated in the political poems of *Songs before Sunrise.* This fact is not surprising, given the extent to which issues of mortality, especially in their relations with Wordsworth's influence on Victorian literary culture, are, as we have seen, issues of "power" for Swinburne. Nor is it unexpected that such issues emerge with special urgency in Swinburne's poetry written at a time when the political ideals Wordsworth had in his youth attached to the French Revolution appeared to be reviving not only in Italy (under the guidance of Mazzini and Garibaldi) but also once again in France. From at least 1868 Swinburne had been at work on the poems of *Songs before Sunrise,* not published until January of 1871, and during most of that period France was for him a cause hopelessly lost to the tyranny of Napoleon III. On August 6, 1870, Swinburne lamented that "it is horrible to be unable to disengage France and Bonaparte—that she should play the succubus to so infernal an incubus!" (*Letters,* 2:118). But hope revived with the outbreak of the Franco-Prussian war and the capture of Napoleon III. We recall Swinburne's euphoric response to the declaration of the Third Republic on September 4: "I feel inclined to go out and kiss everybody I meet—to roll on the ground and 'come naked in contact with the earth' as Whitman says somewhere. . . . An Ode literally burst out of me. . . . I do think the rejoicings and salutations, tears and embraces, of the people at such a time, in the jaws of ruin *and* in sight of the Republic, the most glorious thing in democratic history" (*Letters*, 2:125). Swinburne ends his letter on a note that could not but recall Wordsworth's celebrations of the Revolution seventy years before: "But think what this is to me, who have never known but by tradition of a pre-imperial France—who cannot remember it other than fallen. . . . now to see France for the first time!" (*Letters*, 2:126). Swinburne's excitement is reminiscent of Wordsworth's in book 11 of *The Prelude*: "Bliss was it in that dawn to be alive / And to be young was very Heaven!" (*Wordsworth*, p. 570), a passage whose metaphors are borrowed repeatedly in the poems of *Songs before Sunrise*. Swinburne learned from Wordsworth the proper language for commemorating responses to events perceived as millennial. The same note of ecstacy is struck, as one might expect, in Swinburne's "Ode on the Proclamation of the French Republic":

> O loved so much so long,
> O smitten with such wrong,
> O purged at last and perfect without spot or stain,
> Light of the light of man,
> Reborn republican,
> At last, O first Republic, hailed in heaven again!
> Out of the obscene eclipse
> Rerisen.

(*Poems*, 2:282)

As is clear from such poems in *Songs before Sunrise*, the rebirth of France is of profound importance to the world, in part because it points to philosophical issues that emerge precisely where republican political values converge with the poetics of mortality. This is, for Swinburne, a narrow literary space in which individual immortality can be achieved in art that records and celebrates mankind as a historically developing organism, genuinely free and immortal despite most men's blindness to this form of freedom and immortality. It is a space that allows for the celebration of "The earth-god Freedom,"

("To Walt
Whitman in
America,"
Poems, 2:124)
> The soul that is substance of nations,
> Reincarnate with fresh generations;
> The great god Man, which is God.

This "God" Swinburne also identifies as Hertha, the primordial and universal life-force of which man is the most highly evolved, and the only self-conscious, embodiment. Hertha has "need of [men] free" and recognizes that time eventually yields mankind the ideal social formation, "Even . . . the beloved Republic, that feeds upon freedom and lives" (*Poems*, 2:79). In prophesying the rebirth of the Republic and grounding his celebrations of human freedom in abstract and idealized philosophical language rather than particularized historical terms, as Wordsworth had done in *The Prelude*, Swinburne is able to accomplish a Shelleyan transvaluation of Wordsworth that nonetheless transumes the political work of Shelley and subsumes that of Wordsworth. Unable to extricate his ideals from the failure of the French Revolution, that is, from the inescapable historical events to which he anchored his ideals, Wordsworth had been compelled finally to deplore and repudiate these events and seek refuge in an "abyss of idealism" paradoxically enabled by experiences in another order of the material world, experiences in nature that revealed his immortality precisely by insisting upon his ostensible mortality.

If, simply understood, Swinburne emphatically denied all myths of immortality in the poems of his 1866 volume (as he again does in *Poems and Ballads, Second Series* [1878]), then many works in *Songs before Sunrise* mediate the Wordsworthian influence upon him in more specifically political terms. The prospect of immortality and liberation from material constraints, including historical contingency, is allowed for the individual only as a mutable component of the species. Although any number of the poems of this volume thereby abstractly revise Wordsworthian philosophical commonplaces, "On the Downs" is one poem that more visibly replicates the structural patterns and images, and more audibly echoes the language of the Intimations Ode than other works in the volume.

Structurally, "On the Downs" conflates the Ode with "Tintern Abbey." The speaker, "sitting chambered," recalls a past hour of despondency at the seaside: "So is it now as it was then." He envisions "spread on either hand / Sky, sea, and land," where all "life hopeless lies," but his attention is focused particularly on the sea:

> Scarce wind enough was on the sea,
> Scarce hope enough there moved in me,
>   To sow with live blown flowers of white
> The green plain's sad serenity.

(*Poems,* 2:192)

Unsuccessfully he "send[s his] eyes out as for news . . . [for] Tidings of light or living air." Contemplating mankind's past, as Wordsworth contemplates his own in the Ode, the speaker's mind is "sterile," "unsatisfied," "hopeless." The sea becomes, among other things, a visual symbol of human history, triggering a quasi-allegorical vision:

> Out of time's blind old eyes were shed
> Tears that were mortal, and left dead
>   The heart and spirit of the years,
> And on man's fallen and helmless head
>   Time's disanointing tears
>   Fell cold as fears.

(*Poems,* 2:193)

As in the first four stanzas of Wordsworth's Ode, "hope flowering" is undercut by what in human experience the images from nature now represent: loss, mortality, and endless suffering. But these are described in clearly political, rather than personal, Wordsworthian terms: "my soul hears the songs and groans / That are about and under thrones."

Epiphany occurs, however, midway through the poem, as the "news" and "tidings" wished for at its beginning come, not to the speaker's eyes surveying the sea, but to his ears, as "the wise word of the secret earth." Though this speaker's interrogations of the world have been less explicit than Wordsworth's questions—"Whither is fled the visionary gleam? / Where is it now, the glory and the dream?" (*Wordsworth,* p. 460)—the answer allows him to commune with nature, at least "in thought" as Wordsworth had done, and it has the same rejuvenating effect upon him, expressed in direct echoes of Wordsworth:

> So my soul sick with watching heard
> That day the wonder of that word,
> And as one springs out of a dream
> Sprang, and the stagnant wells were stirred
> Whence flows through gloom and gleam
> Thought's soundless stream.

(*Poems,* 2:194)

Having arrived at the "unconquerable hour" of liberation from despair through understanding the larger operations of the world, the speaker now perceives the beneficent aspect of "One forceful nature uncreate / That feeds itself with death and fate" (*Poems,* 2:195). More somberly, perhaps, than Wordsworth in his Ode, but through the same compensatory intellectual process, Swinburne's speaker comes to realize that "freedom fills time's veins with power, / As, brooding on that sea, / My thought filled me" (*Poems,* 2:195). For Wordsworth thoughtful "questionings / Of sense and outward things" generated intimations of individual immortality. For Swinburne's speaker who also "hath kept watch o'er man's mortality," thought self-reflexively generates awareness that, in the larger scheme of mankind's history, accepting mortality is necessary to a liberated existence. As McGann has observed, "those who freely give themselves to mortality are Swinburne's 'enduring dead,' whose lives are known through . . . correspondences. Giving themselves to life, they are caught up in it and transformed through it. On the other hand, those who aim to escape mortality . . . find that even what they have been given will be taken away."[15] This poem moves toward its conclusion borrowing from the final stanza of Wordsworth's Ode the image of "clouds that gather round the setting sun." But in a subversive revisionist move that cancels Wordsworth's solipsism, Swinburne hails "Time's deep dawn" as "the sun smote the clouds and slew" (*Poems,* 2:195). A radiant awakening, he suggests, is available to every man who liberates himself from mortality by accepting it, and who commits himself to the inevitable processes of growth and evolution in human history.

Such reinscriptions of the Intimations Ode as we discover in "On the Downs" are forecast from the outset of *Songs before Sunrise*. The volume's "Prelude" proleptically celebrates "one whose will sees clear," a hero as poet whose

> . . . heart is equal with the sea's
> And with the sea-wind's, and his ear
>   Is level to the speech of these,
> And his soul communes and takes cheer
>   With the actual earth's equalities,
> Air, light, and night, hills, winds, and streams,
> And seeks not strength from strengthless dreams.

(*Poems*, 2:4)

Unlike the Wordsworthian hero who has unquestionably repudiated the historical world and embraces the natural world only temporarily for the purposes of "theological cookery," Swinburne as poet-hero sees the natural, historical, and spiritual worlds as contiguous and contingent, and these worlds now converge in his sea symbol so as to accentuate the deficiencies and limitations of the same trope in Wordsworth's Ode. Swinburne's true seer is one of those "who think long,"

> Till they discern as from a hill
>   At the sun's hour of morning song,
> Known of souls only, and those souls free,
> The sacred spaces of the sea,

(*Poems*, 2:9)

sacred precisely because they are at once spaces of liberation and mortality.

Like "On the Downs," "Neap-Tide"—written nearly a decade later—appears to be a conceptual and imagistic, antiphonal bricolage of fragments from the Intimations Ode. In this brief lyric, as in the earlier poem, the emotional movement is from desolation to optimism of a tentative, but more recognizably Wordsworthian, variety. In the last years of the 1870s Swinburne's ambivalent attitudes toward Wordsworth moved in the direction of greater sympathy, as we have witnessed in the evidence of the essays. Clearly borrowing from the Ode, in "Neap-Tide" Swinburne presents the irrecoverable past as a dream symbolized by the

land "All glorious with flowerlike weeds," which is at a distance
from the poem's speaker, who stands quite literally "stranded" at
the lowest tide of the month between land and sea. The things that
he has once seen, he now can see no more: "shadows of shapeless
dreams abide / Where life may abide no more." Indeed,

. . . the spell were broken that seems
To reign in a world of dreams
Where vainly the dreamer's feet make forward
And vainly the low sky gleams.

(*Poems,*
3:239)

From his perspective, only "the sea remains, / A shadow of dream-
like dread." Here, as in "On the Downs," the speaker's present and
past experience is depersonalized and universalized in abstract symbols, most of them borrowed from Wordsworth's Ode. He recalls
days when "ripples that kissed" the shore generated the "sweetest
of songs that the world may sing," songs tacitly appropriated from
the Ode's third and tenth stanzas (*Poems,* 3:239). If not wholly
"apparelled in celestial light," this speaker's past dependably saw
"the light from the sundawn [spring]" (*Poems,* 3:239). But "Now
no light is in heaven." Wordsworth's "fountain-light of all our
day," the "master-light of all our seeing," has gone out. Nonetheless, without undertaking elaborate Wordsworthian processes of
thought and recollection, in an abrupt maneuver of self-reversal
and closure, Swinburne finally goes far in recapturing the light and
thus appropriating the mythos of Wordsworth's Ode.[16] A mood of
optimism concludes the poem. It is achieved by a structural reversal of the Ode's central syntactic and rhetorical device: the penultimate stanza of "Neap-Tide" articulates a single question, whose
subsequent justification serves to affirm a Wordsworthian belief in
immortality and to generate a strain of joy akin (albeit pallidly) to
that celebrated in Wordsworth's poem:

Outside the range of time . . .
Who knows if haply the shadow of death
May be not the light of life?

(*Poems,*
3:240)

For the storm and the rain and the darkness borrow
But an hour from the suns to be,

> But a strange swift passage, that we
> May rejoice, who have mourned not to-day, to-morrow,
>   In the sun and the wind and the sea.

A conditional joy is the final note struck here, as "the sunset dies for dread" surrounded by gathering clouds viewed by the speaker's clearly "sober" eye. Still twenty years from the sunset of his own life, with "Neap-Tide" Swinburne thus appears largely to have succumbed, albeit tentatively and perhaps unwittingly, to Wordsworth's "direct or indirect influence" and the cultural "power" of the ideology propagated in the mythos of his great Ode.

Mortality, Aesthetics, Ideology

> *Prophets of Nature, we to them will speak*
> *A lasting inspiration, sanctified*
> *By reason, blest by faith: what we have loved,*
> *Others will love, and we will teach them how;*
> *Instruct them how the mind of man becomes*
> *A thousand times more beautiful than the earth*
> *On which he dwells, above this frame of things*
> *(Which, 'mid all revolutions in the hopes*
> *And fears of men, doth still remain unchanged)*
> *In beauty exalted, as it is itself*
> *Of quality and fabric more divine.*
>   *The Prelude*, bk. 14, ll. 444–54

> *Art for art's sake first, and then all things shall be*
> *added to her. . . . The worth of a poem has nothing*
> *to do with its moral meaning or design . . . but on*
> *the other hand we refuse to admit that art of the*
> *highest kind may not ally itself with moral or re-*
> *ligious passion. . . . The doctrine of art for art is*
> *true in the positive sense, false in the negative;*
> *sound as an affirmation, unsound as a prohibition.*
>   *Essays and Studies*, pp. 40–41

While insisting, in "Wordsworth and Byron," that Wordsworth was "a teacher because he was a poet," Swinburne nonetheless acknowledges that the author of the Intimations Ode was "a teacher no less beneficent than great" (*Works*, 14:213). As in the

conclusion to *The Prelude,* in his prefaces and in the notes to many
of his poems Wordsworth himself insists upon his role as ped-
agogue and ideologue. As we have seen, much of Swinburne's
work, too, is overtly ideological, often iconoclastic. Although,
early in his career, the "theological cookery" of his great precursor
is often the object of Swinburne's scornful iconoclasm, it is not
unexpected that he should eventually have come more or less
completely under Wordsworth's power and influence. This is so
because Swinburne (despite his frequent assertions to the contrary),
like Wordsworth, ultimately saw art as the only means of escape, in
the social and political sphere, from historical contingency. For
him, poetry constituted a discursive space in which the ideal of
freedom could be apprehended and a form of immortality attained.

In one of the most perceptive general criticisms of Swinburne
written during his lifetime, William Morris attacked his work for
its unyielding literariness. The commentary (in a letter to Georgiana Burne-Jones in 1882) is worth quoting in full, because it
speaks directly to the relations between aesthetics and ideology as
they in fact operate in the work of both Swinburne and Wordsworth:

> [Y]ou know I never could really sympathize with Swinburne's
> work; it always seemed to me to be founded on literature, not on
> nature. . . . Now I believe that Swinburne's sympathy with liter-
> ature is most genuine and complete. . . . he is most steadily enthu-
> siastic about it. Now time was when the poetry resulting merely
> from this intense study and love of literature might have been . . .
> very worthy and enduring: but . . . under the mass of material
> riches which civilization has made and is making more and more
> hastily every day; riches which the world has made indeed, but
> cannot use to any good purpose: in these days the issue between art,
> that is, the godlike part of man, and mere bestiality, is so momen-
> tous, and the surroundings of life are so stern and unplayful, that
> nothing can take serious hold of people, or should do so, but that
> which is rooted deepest in reality and is quite at first hand.[17]

Morris wrote this letter when he was just beginning to read Karl
Marx. What Morris might in 1882 have perceived but apparently

did not is that Swinburne's aestheticism was, in a sense, the necessary corollary of his libertarian political values, just as Wordsworth's fundamental idealism was, given his profound disillusionment with the French Revolution, his inevitable alternate mode of teaching and changing the world. Neither poet could aspire to alter his social and political world except through his art, but historically poetry has seldom been a successful impetus for such change. More often, it is discovered to be an abstracted and idealized discursive alternative to the social and political action "rooted deep[ly] in reality" that Morris calls for.[18]

In recent years a convincing argument has been made that in his major poetry Wordsworth deliberately elided topical, political issues and idioms—or at least successfully disguised or displaced them[19]—generating an ostensibly universalized and dehistoricized poetic discourse. McGann has used poems by Wordsworth as exemplary texts to argue the general case that "Romantic poems . . . tend to develop different sorts of artistic means with which to occlude and disguise their own involvement in a certain nexus of historical relations." And "this act of evasion . . . operates most powerfully whenever the poem is most deeply immersed in its . . . ideological materials and commitments." The Intimations Ode is a case in point, a poem which "annihilates its history, biographical and socio-historical alike, and replaces these particulars with a record of pure consciousness." As a result, "an ideology is born out of things which (literally) *cannot* be spoken of," but "if Wordsworth's poetry elides history, we observe in this 'escapist' or 'reactionary' move its own self-revelation. It is a rare, original, and comprehensive record of the birth and character of a particular ideology," one that denies its own sociohistorical determinations.[20]

Ironically, as Swinburne succumbed to the influence of Wordsworth, his poems became increasingly particularized, both politically and historically. His volumes of the 1880s and 1890s are filled with poems on political topics and figures, including the constitution of Parliament, the expansion and maintenance of the Empire, Irish Home Rule, the Franco-Russian alliance, Mazzini, Gladstone, Gordon, and Louis Blanc. Although commentators most often ignore these works or dismiss them as nationalistic (if not xenophobic), jingoistic, and artistically weak, they tell us a good deal about the developing relations between aesthetics and ideology in Swinburne's work. These poems reveal the extent to which his belief that poetry could at once engage and, as a body of purist formal structures, transcend sociopolitical values was as illusory as his insistent antagonism in the 1860s and 1870s to Wordsworth's philistinism. The conservatism of both poets in their "mature" and later years was, it seems paradoxically, determined by their early faith in the radical reformist and libertarian function of poetry, a faith inevitably undermined by both historical events and the social roles of poets (who are compelled just as inevitably to succumb to the cultural power of the texts and ideologies of their dominant precursors). The trajectory of Swinburne's career is ideologically parallel to that of Wordsworth. While Wordsworth after 1794 attempted with some success to disguise his youthful radicalism (or at least overthrow it) with a poetry of displacement, Swinburne appears to have been virtually blinded, by his own dexterous rhetorical ellipses, to the conflict between the philistine conservatism of his later poetry and the political radicalism of his work during the first two decades of his career. He thus stands out in telling relief as the Victorian poet who, with acknowledgment or without, most fully absorbed Wordsworth's ideological influence and transmitted it, reconstituted, to the next generation of influential poets.[21]

Indicative of the developing relations between aesthetics and ideology over the course of Swinburne's poetry is the altered function of sea imagery in Swinburne's late poems. Instead of remaining an anti-Wordsworthian symbol of release, oblivion, utter dissolution, and thus liberation into an originary generative matrix, it becomes a formulaic trope in the service of specifically political ideology. Repeatedly, the sea is associated with ideals such as truth, brotherhood, and liberty, but also with a uniquely English, indeed imperialist and thus philistine brand of patriotism. The sea now renders the immortality of Swinburne's nation rather than the insuperable mortality of all men and women.

On June 30, 1886, for example, Swinburne wrote "The Commonweal," a poem that denounces the collaboration between Gladstone and Parnell in advancing the cause of Home Rule for Ireland. This poem's title recalls Swinburne's comment two years earlier that Wordsworth was "a citizen to whom the common-weal—the 'common good of all' . . . was the one thing worthy of any man's and all men's entire devotion" (*Works,* 14:219). In Swinburne's view Home Rule would mean "Perfect ruin, shame eternal, [and] everlasting degradation" for the commonwealth, exposing "Freedom bought and sold, truth bound and treason free" (*Poems,* 6:358). But to this prospect, he concludes, "Yet an hour is here for answer; now, if here be yet a nation, / Answer England, man by man from sea to sea!" Fifteen years later, in his sonnet "Stratford-on-Avon" memorializing Shakespeare, Swinburne envisions the great bard as a symbol of England through history, and he figures freedom, empire, and Shakespeare's comprehensive soul in a subtle transposition of Wordsworth's "immortal sea":

> . . . None that hate
> The commonweal whose empire sets men free
> Find comfort there, where once by grace of fate
> A soul was born as boundless as the sea.

(*Poems,* 6:349)

In "Apostacy," another denunciation of Gladstone, Swinburne identifies the freedom of England's people—indeed, the principle of freedom itself—with the country's encircling sea. England is "The sole sweet land found fit to wed the sea," and all "loyal-souled / And true-born sons that love her" are "Free as winds and waters." How, he asks, should a nation whose "ancient fame / Burn[s] from the heavenward heights" of history "Cower, and resign her trust of empire?" (*Poems,* 6:364–65). Similar examples proliferate in his last three volumes.

Swinburne's early acceptance of Blake's, Hugo's, and Gautier's creed of art for art's sake (as he interprets these precursors) thus very often gives way in his late work to art exclusively for the sake of ideology. The provincial and narrowly nationalistic elements of philistine values that he attacked so relentlessly in the 1860s and 1870s came to dominate his work of the 1880s and 1890s.

The historical irony of his apotheosis of freedom in the early decades is that—as the ideological shifts in his own poetry demonstrate—none truly existed for him in his chosen medium of expression, in part because of the growing influence upon him of the single precursor whose power he attempted most vigorously but unsuccessfully to resist, William Wordsworth.

Notes

Index

Notes

Introduction

1. David G. Riede, "Recent Studies in the Nineteenth Century," *Studies in English Literature* 28 (1988): 713.
2. See, for instance, Dominick LaCapra, *History and Criticism* (Ithaca, N.Y.: Cornell Univ. Press, 1985), and A. Leigh DeNeef, "Of Dialogues and Historicisms," *The South Atlantic Quarterly* 86 (1987): 497–517.
3. David Simpson, "Literary Criticism and the Return to History," *Critical Inquiry* 14 (1988): 747.
4. Ibid., p. 743.
5. Louis Althusser, *Lenin and Philosophy* (New York: Monthly Review Press, 1971), p. 171.
6. David McLellan, *Ideology* (Minneapolis: Univ. of Minnesota Press, 1986); Lennard J. Davis, *Ideology and Fiction: Resisting Novels* (New York: Methuen, 1987), pp. 24–51. See also Frederick Jameson, *The Ideologies of Theory: Essays, 1971–86,* vols. 1–2, (Minneapolis: Univ. of Minnesota Press, 1988).
7. Claus Uhlig, "Literature as Palingenesis: On Some Principles of Literary History," *New Literary History* 16 (1985): 503.
8. See the following discussions: Thaïs E. Morgan, "Is There an Intertext in This Text? Literary and Interdisciplinary Approaches to Intertextuality," *American Journal of Semiotics* 3 (1985): 1–40; Owen Miller, "Intertextual Identity," in *Identity of the Literary Text,* ed. Mario J. Valdes and Owen Miller (Toronto: Univ. of Toronto Press, 1985), pp. 19–40; and Linda Hutcheon, *A Theory of Parody: The Teachings of Twentieth-Century Art Forms* (New York: Methuen, 1985).
9. Morgan, "Intertext" pp. 1–2.
10. The work of Barthes, Kristeva, and Bakhtin clearly support this assertion, sometimes in ways that subvert the premises of their own intertextual projects.
11. Robert Weimann, *Structure and Society in Literary History* (Baltimore: Johns Hopkins Univ. Press, 1984), p. 8.
12. Hans Robert Jauss, *Toward an Aesthetic of Reception,* trans. Timothy Bahti (Minneapolis: Univ. of Minnesota Press, 1982), p. 45. (Hereafter cited as *Reception.*)
13. Jauss and Wolfgang Iser are currently perceived as the foremost theorists of the "Constance School" and the early formulators of reception theory and reader-response criticism. Robert Holub in 1984 explained the historical importance of Jauss's "Provocation" essay: "Using the criterion of its own reception [in Europe] as a chief indicator of significance, . . . one would have to consider

[it] the most significant document of literary theory in the last few decades"
(Robert Holub, *Reception Theory: A Critical Introduction* [London: Methuen,
1984], p. 19).

14. "The received form of literary history scarcely scratches out a living for itself
in the intellectual life of our times," Jauss insists (*Reception,* p. 3). His explanation of this phenomenon in most European critical circles applies equally to
the fate of traditional historical criticism in American and English.

15. Jauss, *Reception,* p. 5.

16. "Included within the influence of a work is that which is accomplished in the
consumption of the work as well as in the work itself. . . . The work is a work
and lives as a work for the reason that it demands an interpretation and '*works*'
[influences, *wirkt*] in many meanings." *Geschicthe der poetiscen Nationalliteratur
der Deutschen,* p. 123 (Karl Kosik quoted in Jauss, *Reception,* pp. 15–16).

17. Jauss, *Reception,* pp. 15–16.

18. Ibid., p. 20.

19. "Raising newly articulated experiences to the level of consciousness," aesthetic
distance can be "objectified historically along the spectrum of the audience's
reactions and criticism's judgment" of it. These might include immediate
success or rejection, "scattered approval, gradual or belated understanding"
(Jauss, *Reception,* pp. 22–25).

20. Jauss, *Reception,* pp. 23, 25, 28, 32, 34.

21. Jauss, *Reception,* pp. 36–39. "The social function of literature," Jauss insists,
appears fully "only where the literary experience of the reader enters into the
horizon of expectations of his lived praxis, performs his understanding of the
world," and thereby also affects his social behavior (p. 39).

22. The Marxist origins of the new historicism are clear from the work of Jauss;
from the commentaries of Holub and Simpson, cited above; and from the
work of Butler, McGann, and Lindenberger, cited below. Despite problems
presented by Jauss's last two theses, Marilyn Butler has observed that his
theory "promises great things." But for her it is seriously flawed. His last two
theses present particular problems because "he is here clearly bent on retaining
[the] belief that literature has its own distinct history ['special history'], which
evolves in an autonomous series within the study or the academy, rather than
in society at large." Further, he has "formalized and institutionalized" the
initially "democratic tactic [of] giving the text to the reader to remake, so that
it is all too clearly the critic or professor whose authoritative readings we are to
study." Jauss's approach to the project would not be *truly* historicist and
contextual, therefore, but rather, restricted and delimited. It would "surely in
practice turn out to be an unskeptical, conservative reconstituting of literary
history." Marilyn Butler, "Against Tradition: The Case for a Particularized
Historical Method," in *Historical Studies and Literary Criticism,* ed. Jerome J
McGann (Madison: Univ. of Wisconsin Press, 1985), p. 36.

23. Butler, "Against Tradition," p. 44.

24. These principles in no way conflict with Herbert Lindenberger's description
of "A New History in Literary Study" that appeared in 1984 or with Jerome
McGann's more highly theorized program. Lindenberger's primary goal is to
distinguish "old" historicist criticism from the work of the "new" historicists

The conceptions of their respective projects are deeply opposed. "Traditional literary historians viewed themselves in a relatively subservient role" as "essentially guardians of a tradition . . . whose task was to preserve and transmit what had long since passed as sanctified." They adopted a characteristic stance of self-effacement, most often refusing to recognize the "cultural biases and the interpretive conventions" built into their method. Rooted in nineteenth-century German philological traditions, the "older history . . . sought to emulate the objectivity that the natural sciences of that time conceived for themselves," hoping to construct a "temple of knowledge that would last into perpetuity," and they did so most often with a decidedly nationalist bias, whether German, English, or American (Herbert Lindenberger, *Profession '84* [New York: MLA, 1984], pp. 16–23). For McGann's work, see "Introduction: A Point of Reference," in McGann, ed., *Historical Studies,* pp. 3–21; the essays in *The Beauty of Inflections: Literary Investigations in Historical Method and Theory* (Oxford: Clarendon Press, 1985), pp. 343–44; *The Romantic Ideology* (Chicago: Univ. of Chicago Press, 1983); and most recently, *Social Values and Poetic Acts: The Historical Judgment of Literary Work* (Cambridge, Mass.: Harvard Univ. Press, 1988).
25. McGann, "Introduction," pp. 11, 15.
26. Ibid., pp. 13–14.
27. See Simpson, "Literary Criticism," pp. 744–45.

I. Arnold, Keats, and the Ideologies of Empedocles on Etna

1. See especially George Ford, *Keats and the Victorians* (New Haven: Yale Univ. Press, 1944), pp. 51–89; William A. Jamison, *Arnold and the Romantics* (Copenhagen: Rosenkilde and Bagger, 1958), pp. 84–104; Leon Gottfried, *Matthew Arnold and the Romantics* (Lincoln: Univ. of Nebraska Press, 1963); Barbara Fass Levy, "Iseult of Brittany: A New Interpretation of Matthew Arnold's *Tristram and Iseult,*" *Victorian Poetry* 18 (1980): 1–22; Andrew Hickman, "A New Direction for 'The Strayed Reveller,'" *Victorian Poetry* 21 (1983), 133–44; and William Ulmer's series of articles, "'Thyrsis' and the Consolation of Natural Magic," *The Arnoldian* 12 (1984): 22–43; "Romantic Modernity in Arnold's *Tristram and Iseult,*" *Texas Studies in Literature and Language* 27 (1985): 62–65; and "The Human Seasons: Arnold, Keats, and 'The Scholar-Gipsy,'" *Victorian Poetry* 22 (1984): 247–61.
2. Ford, *Keats and the Victorians,* p. 88.
3. Ibid., p. 89.
4. *The Letters of John Keats,* ed. Hyder E. Rollins, 2 vols. (Cambridge, Mass.: Harvard Univ. Press, 1958), 1:266–67.
5. *Byron's Letters and Journals,* ed. Leslie A. Marchand, 12 vols. (Cambridge: Harvard Univ. Press, 1973–82), 7:200.
6. *The Letters of Matthew Arnold to Arthur Hugh Clough,* ed. H. F. Lowry (London: Oxford Univ. Press, 1932), 96–97. Hereafter cited as *Letters to Clough.*
7. Geoffrey Hartman, "Poem and Ideology: A Study of Keats's 'To Autumn,'" in his *The Fate of Reading* (Chicago: Univ. of Chicago Press, 1975), 124–46.

8. All references to Arnold's prose works are from *The Complete Prose Works of Matthew Arnold,* ed. R. H. Super, 11 vols. (Ann Arbor: Univ. of Michigan Press, 1960–77). The present quotation is from 1:8. Future citations to this edition in this chapter will appear parenthetically in text to *Prose,* with volume and page numbers.

9. Though it remains impossible to date the composition of some of Arnold's poems with precision, it is clear that only a few of his major works were composed after 1853. These include "Thyrsis," *Merope,* "Heine's Grave," "Rugby Chapel," and "Obermann Once More."

10. A friend of Arnold's father-in-law, Judge Wightman, Croker had even dragged himself from a sickbed to attend Arnold's wedding. Park Honan, *Matthew Arnold: A Life* (New York: McGraw-Hill, 1981), pp. 186, 230.

11. For the best survey of the political contexts of Keats's work, see *Studies in Romanticism* 25 (1986), a special issue devoted to "Keats, Politics, and Then Some."

12. J. G. Lockhart, "The Cockney School of Poetry, no. IV," *Blackwood's Edinburgh Magazine* 3 (Aug. 1818): 522.

13. William Keach, "Cockney Couplets: Keats and the Politics of Style," *Studies in Romanticism* 25 (1986): 183–85.

14. J. G. Lockhart quoted in G. M. Mathews, ed., *Keats: The Critical Heritage* (New York: Barnes and Noble, 1971), p. 109.

15. As David Bromwich has observed. See "Keats's Radicalism," *Studies in Romanticism* 25 (1986): 201.

16. *The Poems of John Keats,* ed. Jack Stillinger (Cambridge, Mass.: Harvard Univ. Press, 1978), pp. 163–64.

17. *Letters of Keats,* 2:176.

18. Patrick J. McCarthy, *Matthew Arnold and the Three Classes* (New York: Columbia Univ. Press, 1964), p. 55.

19. Bromwich, "Keats's Radicalism," p. 201.

20. G. B. Shaw quoted ibid., p. 198.

21. Gramsci quoted by John Storey in "Matthew Arnold: The Politics of an Organic Intellectual," *Literature and History* 11 (1985): 217.

22. Karl Marx, *The German Ideology* (London, 1963), pp. 40–41.

23. Honan, *Matthew Arnold,* p. 301.

24. P. J. Keating argues against any radical shift in Arnold's political values in "Arnold's Social and Political Thought," in *Writers and Their Background: Matthew Arnold,* ed. Kenneth Allott (Athens: Ohio Univ. Press, 1976), pp. 207–35.

25. McCarthy, *Matthew Arnold,* pp. 52–53.

26. Honan, *Matthew Arnold,* p. 341.

27. McCarthy, *Matthew Arnold,* p. 51.

28. Honan, *Matthew Arnold,* p. 306.

29. For the best brief, general discussion of the rise and fall of Spasmodicism, see Jerome Hamilton Buckley, *The Victorian Temper* (Cambridge: Harvard Univ. Press, 1951), pp. 41–65.

30. Sidney Coulling usefully discusses the interactions among Arnold, the re-

viewers, and the reputation of the Spasmodics in *Matthew Arnold and His Critics* (Athens: Ohio Univ. Press, 1974), pp. 23–40.

31. W. M. Rossetti quoted Ibid., p. 27.
32. See ibid., pp. 22–40.
33. See ibid., p. 27.
34. Clough's review-essay "Recent English Poetry," was first published in the *North American Review* 77 (July 1853), and was reprinted in *Poems and Prose Remains of Arthur Hugh Clough* (London, 1869), 1:360.
35. See Robert A. and Elizabeth S. Watson, *George Gilfillan: Letters and Journals with a Memoir* (London: Hodder and Stoughton, 1892), p. 194.
36. *Letters to Clough,* p. 136.
37. G. H. Lewes quoted in Coulling, *Matthew Arnold,* p. 47.
38. Noted ibid., p. 311.
39. See ibid., pp. 28–34.
40. Kenneth Allott and Miriam Allott, "Arnold the Poet," in *Writers and Their Background: Matthew Arnold,* p. 102. Although Byron's *Manfred* might, at first glance, appear to be the dominant pre-text for *Empedocles,* the resemblances remain superficial. Arnold's appropriation of Manfred's despair, utter alienation, and suicidal impulses in his own hero—like Empedocles' allusions to a Wordsworthian system of values no longer tenable—serve finally as deliberate intertextual strategies to foreground Arnold's more detailed and extensive allusions to and critique of Keats (and, implicitly, the Spasmodic poets). Just as the associations with *Manfred* (in act 2) can be seen to subvert perceptions of Empedocles's high-mindedness (in act 1), so his inaccessibility to the restorative power of nature condemns him as an irredeemable and unsympathetic solipsist.
41. Paul Zietlow, "Heard but Unheeded: The Songs of Callicles in Matthew Arnold's *Empedocles on Etna,*" *Victorian Poetry* 21 (1983): 241–56.
42. Lionel Trilling, *Matthew Arnold* (1939; reprint, New York: Meridian, 1955), p. 135.
43. Zietlow, "Heard but Unheeded," p. 254.
44. Rollins, ed., *Letters of Keats,* 1:193–94.
45. For a complementary commentary on the dialogical operations of *Empedocles,* see David Riede, *Matthew Arnold and the Betrayal of Language* (Charlottesville: Univ. Press of Virginia 1988), pp. 78–93.
46. *Matthew Arnold,* ed. Miriam Allott and R. H. Super (Oxford: Oxford Univ. Press, 1986), p. 79 (1.1.113). Future citations to this edition of Arnold's poetry will appear parenthetically in text by act, scene, and line numbers for *Empedocles on Etna* and by line numbers for other poems.
47. Zietlow, "Heard but Unheeded," pp. 242–43.
48. See Kenneth Allott, "Matthew Arnold's Reading-Lists in Three Early Diaries," *Victorian Studies* 2 (1959): 254–66.
49. Keats to George and Georgiana Keats, Oct. 14–31, 1818; in Richard Monckton Milnes, ed., *Life, Letters, and Literary Remains of John Keats,* 2 vols. (London, 1848), 1:235–36. Rollins, *Letters of Keats,* 1:404.
50. *Letters to Clough,* pp. 66, 99.

51. Keats to Richard Woodhouse, Oct. 27, 1818, in Rollins, *Letters of Keats,* 1:387.
52. For the best discussions of Arnold and Wordsworth see U. C. Knoepflmacher, "Dover Revisited: The Wordsworthian Matrix in the Poetry of Matthew Arnold," *Victorian Poetry* 1 (1963): 17–26, and Thaïs Morgan, "Rereading Nature: Wordsworth between Swinburne and Arnold," *Victorian Poetry* 24 (1986): 427–39.
53. Book 1 of *Hyperion* concludes with the "bright Titan, frenzied with new woes, / Unused to bend" bending "his spirit to the sorrow of the time" (ll. 299–301). He "arose, and on the stars / Lifted his curved lids, and kept them wide . . . / And still they were the same bright, patient stars" (ll. 350–53).
54. Rollins, *Letters of Keats,* 1:184.
55. Manfred Dietrich suggests rather different reasons for the inevitable fate of *Empedocles* in Arnold's mind. See "Arnold's *Empedocles on Etna* and the 1853 Preface," *Victorian Poetry* 14 (1976), especially pp. 320–24.
56. In his selections from Keats in Ward's *English Poets,* Arnold chose to include the following lines from *Hyperion:* book 1, ll. 1–51, book 2, ll. 167–243, and book 2, ll. 346–78 (*Prose* 9:323). He could not have known *The Fall of Hyperion,* since it was not published until 1856 (by Milnes).
57. Zietlow, "Heard but Unheeded," p. 249.
58. Bromwich, "Keats's Radicalism," p. 205.
59. *Letters to Clough,* p. 99.

II: *"Cleon" and Its Contexts*

1. For the most helpful recent theoretical commentary on how the dramatic monologue operates, see Ralph Rader, "Notes on Some Structural Varieties and Variations in Dramatic 'I' Poems and Their Theoretical Implications," *Victorian Poetry* 22 (1984): 103–20.
2. Dramatic monologues have been the subject of much theoretical discussion in recent years. Among the best commentaries are: Dorothy Mermin, *The Audience in the Poem: Five Victorian Poets* (New Brunswick, N.J.: Rutgers Univ. Press, 1983); Linda K. Hughes, *The Manyfaced Glass: Tennyson's Dramatic Monologues* (Athens: Univ. of Ohio Press, 1987); and the essays in *Victorian Poetry* 22, no. 2 (1984) on *The Dramatic "I" Poem* (ed. Linda M. Shires), including Rader's cited in note 1, above.
3. Roland Barthes, *S/Z* (Paris: Editions du Seuil, 1970), pp. 16–17.
4. Owen Miller, "Intertextual Identity," in *Identity of the Literary Text,* ed. Mario J. Valdes and Owen Miller (Toronto: Univ. of Toronto Press, 1985), p. 21.
5. Harold Bloom, Introduction to *Robert Browning,* ed. Bloom (New York: Chelsea House, 1985), pp. 1–3.
6. Pettigrew says that "Cleon" was probably composed in 1854 (*Robert Browning: The Poems,* ed. John Pettigrew, supplemented and completed by Thomas J. Collins, 2 vols. [New Haven: Yale Univ. Press, 1981], 1:1140). William DeVane is more specific in positing that the poem "was written in the summer of 1854, after Browning had written *Karshish* and had meditated upon Arnold's *Empedocles* of 1852, and its omission from [the] volume of 1853" (*A Browning Handbook* [New York: Appleton-Century-Crofts, 1955], p. 265).

7. All citations to Browning's poetry and his essay on Shelley are from volume 1 of *Robert Browning: The Poems,* ed. John Pettigrew. "Cleon" appears on pages 712–20. The words I quote in text conclude the poem. Future citations of line numbers from this edition of "Cleon" will appear parenthetically in text as *Poems.* Other poems by Browning and his "Introductory Essay" (on Shelley) will be cited parenthetically in text to *Poems,* with page numbers.

8. For a generalized discussion of these influences on the composition of "Cleon," see Adrienne Munich, "Emblems of Temporality in Browning's 'Cleon.'" *Browning Institute Studies* 6 (1978): 117–36.

9. A. W. Crawford, "Browning's 'Cleon,'" *Journal of English and Germanic Philology* 26 (1927): 485–90. See also John Coates, "Two Versions of the Problem of the Modern Intellectual: 'Empedocles on Etna' and 'Cleon,'" *Modern Language Review* 79 (1984): 770–82; Park Honan, "Robert Browning and Matthew Arnold," *Studies in Browning and His Circle* 3 (1975): 123; and Munich, "Emblems of Temporality," pp. 124–26.

10. *Dearest Isa: Robert Browning's Letters to Isabella Blagden,* ed. Edward C. McAleer (Austin: Univ. of Texas Press, 1951), p. 278.

11. For discussions of Arnold's Preface as an oblique attack on the Spasmodics, especially Alexander Smith, see H. W. Garrod, "Matthew Arnold's 1853 Preface," *Review of English Studies* 17 (1941): 310–21, and Mark Weinstein, *William Edmondstoune Aytoun and the Spasmodic Controversy* (New Haven: Yale Univ. Press, 1968), pp. 99–108.

12. *The Complete Prose Works of Matthew Arnold,* vol. 1, ed. R. H. Super (Ann Arbor: Univ. of Michigan Press, 1960), pp. 8, 9, 15. Future citations to this edition in this chapter will appear parenthetically in text to *Prose,* with volume and page numbers.

13. See Munich, "Emblems of Temporality," pp. 119, 126–28.

14. With "Dejection: An Ode," now generally accepted as Coleridge's response to the first four stanzas of the Intimations Ode, Coleridge also clearly participated in this dialogue, but his contribution is not as demonstrably fundamental to the operations of "Cleon" as the poems of Wordsworth and Keats.

15. *Matthew Arnold,* ed. Miriam Allott and R. H. Super (Oxford: Oxford Univ. Press, 1986), p. 102. Future citations to *Empedocles* in this chapter will appear parenthetically in text with act, scene, and line numbers. Citations to other poems will appear by line numbers.

16. Jerome J. McGann makes this point in "Matthew Arnold and the Critical Spirit: The Three Texts of *Empedocles on Etna,*" in *Victorian Connections,* ed. McGann (Charlottesville: Univ. Press of Virginia, 1989), pp. 146–71.

17. Keats to Benjamin Bailey Nov. 22, 1817, in *The Letters of John Keats,* ed. Hyder E. Rollins, 2 vols. (Cambridge: Harvard Univ. Press, 1958), 1:185.

18. Walter Pater, *The Renaissance,* ed. Donald L. Hill (Berkeley: Univ. of California Press, 1980), pp. 188–90.

19. On composition dates, see Pettigrew, ed., *Robert Browning: The Poems,* 1:1103. The only critic I know who has argued that Browning envied the success of the Spasmodics is Jerome Thrale in "Browning's 'Popularity' and the Spasmodic Poets," *Journal of English and Germanic Philology* 54 (1955): 353–54.

20. *A Life-Drama* appeared late in 1852 but was dated 1853. See Weinstein, *William*

Edmondstoune Aytoun, p. 76. For the reception of *A Life-Drama,* see Thrale, "Browning's 'Popularity,'" pp. 348–52.

21. See Thrale, "Browning's 'Popularity,'" p. 351; *Life and Letters of Herbert Spencer,* ed. David Duncan (New York, 1908), 1:87; and Jerome Hamilton Buckley, *The Victorian Temper* (New York: Vintage Books, 1951), p. 52.
22. *New Monthly Magazine* 100 (March 1854): 292, quoted by Thrale in "Browning's 'Popularity,'" p. 351.
23. Thrale, "Browning's 'Popularity,'" p. 353.
24. "Introduction," *Browning: The Critical Heritage,* ed. Boyd Litzinger and Donald Smalley (London: Routledge and Kegan Paul, 1970), pp. 2–3.
25. Ibid., pp. 3–15.
26. Ibid., p. 6.
27. Browning to Joseph Milsand, quoted in DeVane, *A Browning Handbook,* p. 207.
28. Weinstein, *William Edmondstoune Aytoun,* pp. 184–86.
29. *New Letters of Robert Browning,* ed. William C. DeVane and Kenneth L. Knickerbocker (New Haven: Yale Univ. Press, 1950), pp. 92–93.
30. For a full discussion of the Spasmodic and Keatsian contexts of "Popularity," see Thrale, "Browning's 'Popularity,'" passim.
31. Donald Hair, *Browning's Experiments with Genre* (Toronto: Univ. of Toronto Press, 1972), pp. 4–19.
32. Weinstein, *William Edmondstoune Aytoun,* p. 183. Theodore Watts later inverted that relationship and insisted upon Bailey's *Festus* as a work derivative from Browning's *Paracelsus.* But Weinstein quotes a letter from Bailey claiming ignorance of *Paracelsus* when he composed *Festus.*
33. Weinstein, *William Edmondstoune Aytoun,* pp. 184–85.
34. Anonymous review of *Men and Women, Saturday Review* 1 (1855): 69–70.
35. *Blackwood's* 79 (1856): 136–37.
36. Browning to Edward Chapman, Jan. 5, 1857, in *New Letters,* p. 99.
37. This group of poems includes "Fra Lippo Lippi," "A Toccata at Galuppi's," "How It Strikes a Contemporary," "Master Hughes of Saxe-Gotha," "Memorabilia," "Andrea del Sarto," "Old Pictures in Florence," "Cleon," "Popularity," "'Transcendentalism: A Poem in Twelve Books,'" and "One Word More."
38. See Thrale, "Browning's 'Popularity,'" p. 348–50.
39. Dorothy Donnelly, "Philistine Taste in Victorian Poetry," *Victorian Poetry* 16 (1978): 104.
40. Alexander Smith, *Poems* (Boston, 1852), p. 24.
41. For commentary on the formlessness and other weaknesses of poetry by these Spasmodics, see Buckley, *Victorian Temper,* pp. 40–65.
42. All citations to Wordsworth's poetry will appear by stanza and/or line number and are taken from *Wordsworth: Poetical Works,* ed. Thomas Hutchinson, rev. Ernest de Selincourt (London: Oxford Univ. Press, 1969).
43. Marjorie Levinson, "Wordsworth's Intimations Ode: A Timely Utterance," in *Historical Studies and Literary Criticism,* ed. Jerome J. McGann (Madison: Univ. of Wisconsin Press, 1985), pp. 48–75.
44. Eleanor Cook notes *Sordello*'s debt to the Intimations Ode and echoes of *The*

Prelude in *One Word More* (*Browning's Lyrics: An Exploration* [Toronto: Univ. of Toronto Press, 1974], pp. 27, 236). Cook also cites Browning's unpublished letter to Charles Eliot Norton (Florence, May 9, 1850): "Yet let us hope that your gift of the 'Prelude' is an excellent omen" (Houghton Library, Harvard University), a sentence that also suggests Browning's aspirations to the laureateship soon after Wordsworth's death in April. The post remained opened until November, when Tennyson was selected to fill it.

45. Quoted by Pettigrew, ed., *Robert Browning: The Poems,* p. 1091.
46. John Maynard, *Browning's Youth* (Cambridge: Harvard Univ. Press, 1977), p. 169.
47. Anya Taylor, "Religious Readings of the Immortality Ode," *Studies in English Literature* 26 (1986): 645–47. W. D. Shaw, "Browning's Intimations Ode: The Prologue to Asolando," *Browning Society Notes* 8 (1978): 9–10. Stanza two of the "Prologue" further reveals, through its metaphors, the inextricable interrelationships among Wordsworth, Keats, and the Spasmodics that Browning apparently found inescapable when considering issues of poetic accomplishment and poetic supremacy. Writing verses that echo Wordsworth to figure the inherent spirituality of natural objects, Browning uses the same image of dyes that he employs in "Popularity" to figure the essence of the poet's (specifically Keats's) genius—"that dye of dyes / Whereof one drop worked miracles"—which popular imitators (the Spasmodics) intrinsically lack (Pettigrew, *Robert Browning: The Poems,* p. 723). In stanza two of the "Prologue" to *Asolando* Browning's titular hero laments:

> "And now a flower is just a flower:
>   Man, bird, beast are but beast, bird, man—
> Simply themselves, uncinct by dower
>   Of dyes which, when life's day began,
> Round each in glory ran." (*Poems,* 2:875)

48. *Byron,* ed. Jerome J. McGann (Oxford: Oxford Univ. Press, 1986), p. 375. Byron's denunciations of Wordsworth began, of course, with *English Bards and Scotch Reviewers*. As Maynard observes, "Byron's influence on Browning was probably as great as that of any modern poet except Shelley" (*Browning's Youth,* p. 175).
49. See Maynard, *Browning's Youth,* p. 195.
50. Coincidentally, Wordsworth had just completed his thirty-third year when he finished writing the Immortality Ode.

III: Irony and Ideology in Tennyson's "Little Hamlet"

1. See Jerome J. McGann, "Tennyson and the Histories of Criticism," in his *The Beauty of Inflections: Literary Investigations in Historical Method and Theory* (Oxford: Clarendon Press, 1985), pp. 188–90.
2. Hallam Tennyson, *Alfred Lord Tennyson: A Memoir by His Son,* 2 vols. (New York, 1898), 1:396.
3. All references to *Maud* (and other poems by Tennyson) will be taken from *The Poems of Tennyson,* ed. Christopher Ricks (London: Longman, 1969). Future citations of *Maud* in this chapter will appear parenthetically in the text as

Poems, with part and line number. The present quotations are from 3.19 and 51.

4. Henry Van Dyke, *Studies in Tennyson* (New York: Scribners, 1920), p. 97.

5. The best recent studies of *Maud* include the following: Chris Vanden Bossche, "Realism versus Romance: The War of Cultural Codes in Tennyson's *Maud*," *Victorian Poetry* 24 (1986): 69–82; Henry Kozicki, *Tennyson and Clio: History in the Major Poems* (Baltimore: Johns Hopkins Univ. Press, 1979), pp. 98–111; David F. Gosslee, " 'Fairer than aught in the world beside': The Speaker's Invocation of Maud," *Victorian Poetry* 23 (1985): 391–402; Robert E. Lougy, "The Sounds and Silence of Madness: Language as Theme in Tennyson's *Maud*," *Victorian Poetry* 22 (1984): 407–26; Marilyn Kurata, " 'A Juggle Born of the Brain': A New Reading of *Maud*," *Victorian Poetry* 21 (1983): 369–78; James R. Bennett, "*Maud*, Part III: Maud's Battle-Song," *Victorian Poetry* 18 (1980): 35–49; James R. Bennett, "The Historical Abuse of Literature: Tennyson's *Maud: A Monodrama* and the Crimean War," *English Studies* 62 (1981): 34–45; and Linda K. Hughes, *The Manyfaced Glass: Tennyson's Dramatic Monologues* (Athens: Ohio Univ. Press, 1987), pp. 158–74. Each earlier major critic of *Maud* has tried to perceive integrity and meaning in the poem by emphasizing just one or two aspects of it, although a number of these earlier treatments of *Maud* are discursive and do not argue a narrow thesis. Philip Drew's "Tennyson and the Dramatic Monologue: A Study of *Maud*" is typical of these (in *Tennyson,* ed. D. J. Palmer [Athens: Ohio Univ. Press, 1973], pp. 115–46). Unlike Drew, F. E. L. Priestly (*Language and Structure in Tennyson's Poetry* [London: Andre Deutsch, 1973], pp. 106–19), Christopher Ricks (*Tennyson* [New York: Macmillan, 1972], pp. 246–63), A. S. Byatt ("The Lyric Structure of Tennyson's *Maud*," in *The Major Victorian Poets: Reconsiderations,* ed. Isobel Armstrong [Lincoln: Univ. of Nebraska Press, 1969], pp. 69–92), and A. Dwight Culler (*The Poetry of Tennyson* [New Haven: Yale Univ. Press, 1977]) have dwelt at length on the complex structure of the poem, usually beginning with Tennyson's own description of his speaker's passage through numerous phases of passion. Priestly and Culler, along with John Killham ("Tennyson's *Maud*—The Function of the Imagery," in *Critical Essays on the Poetry of Tennyson,* ed. D. J. Palmer [New York: Barnes & Noble, 1960], pp. 219–38) also attempt to define, or at least to describe, the "monodramatic" form of the poem and its historical origins. Kilham's discussion of *Maud,* however, deals primarily with the patterns of meaning that are rendered through Tennyson's imagery and symbolism, an approach to the poem which derived from Jerome Buckley (*Tennyson: The Growth of a Poet* [Cambridge, Mass.: Harvard Univ. Press, 1960], pp. 140–49) and E. D. H. Johnson ("The Lily and the Rose: Symbolic Meaning in Tennyson's *Maud*," *PMLA* 64 [1949]: 1222–27), and which is taken to its extreme in the Burkean analysis of *Maud*'s language undertaken by W. D. Shaw (*Tennyson's Style* [Ithaca, N.Y.: Cornell Univ. Press, 1976], pp. 168–90). The work of four different critics has fairly exhausted two other approaches to *Maud.* The first half of Rick's chapter on *Maud* recapitulates the biographical origins of the poem which Ralph Rader has fully discussed in *Tennyson's Maud: The Biographical Genesis* (Berkeley:

Univ. of California Press, 1963), while Roy Basler in 1948 initiated incisive psychoanalytical studies of the poem (*Sex, Symbolism, and Psychology in Literature* [New Brunswick, N.J.: Rutgers Univ. Press, 1948], pp. 73–93), and Jonas Spatz ("Love and Death in Tennyson's *Maud*," *Texas Studies in Literature and Language* 16 [1974], 504–10) has concluded the work Basler began. Another helpful psychological approach to *Maud* appears in Jonathan Wordsworth's "'What is it that has been done?': The Central Problem of *Maud*" (*Essays in Criticism* 24 [1974]; 356–62). Despite the special thesis of each of the above essays, almost all of them at some point or other discuss *Maud*'s dominant pattern of despair and regeneration that becomes the central concern of a number of important commentaries. James Kincaid (*Tennyson's Major Poems: The Comic and Ironic Patterns* [New Haven: Yale Univ. Press, 1975]) and Dorothy Mermin ("Tennyson's *Maud*: A Thematic Analysis," *Texas Studies in Literature and Language* 15 [1973]: 267–77) present perhaps the most forceful case for *Maud* as a "comic" poem, but Ward Hellstrom (*On the Poems of Tennyson* [Gainesville: Univ. of Florida Press, 1972], pp. 68–88) takes this case too far in arguing that Maud is the speaker's Virgil and Beatrice combined, guiding him to redemption.

6. Vanden Bossche, "Realism versus Romance," p. 82.

7. *Maud*'s Spasmodicism is most fully discussed by Joseph J. Collins in "Tennyson and the Spasmodics," *Victorian Newsletter* 43 (Spring 1973): 24–28; Jerome H. Buckley, *The Victorian Temper* (New York: Vintage, 1951), pp. 41–65; Culler, *Poetry of Tennyson*, pp. 191–92; and Edgar F. Shannon, "The Critical Reception of Tennyson's *Maud*," *PMLA* 68 (1953), 397–417. The most useful recent commentaries on the Spasmodic phenomenon are Mark A. Weinstein's *William Edmondstoune Aytoun and the Spasmodic Controversy* (New Haven: Yale Univ. Press, 1968) and Dorothy F. Donnelly's "Philistine Taste in Victorian Poetry," *Victorian Poetry* 16 (1978): 100–111.

8. Collins, "Tennyson and the Spasmodics," p. 26.

9. See Shannon, "The Critical Reception." As Collins has demonstrated and as critics earlier in this century acknowledged, the Spasmodics were more likely imitating early Tennyson than vice versa. See especially Paul F. Baum, *Tennyson Sixty Years After* (Chapel Hill: Univ. of North Carolina Press, 1948), p. 310.

10. Hallam Tennyson, *A Memoir*, 1:468.

11. See Collins, "Tennyson and the Spasmodics," and Donnelly, "Philistine Taste." W. A. Rossetti, ed., *The Collected Works of Dante Gabriel Rossetti*, 2 vols. (London: Ellis and Elvey, 1890), 1:407.

12. Margaret Oliphant, *Blackwood's Edinburgh Magazine* 92 (Nov. 1892): 758.

13. Priestly, *Language and Structure*, pp. 108–9.

14. For the standard discussion of how the dramatic monologue form operates, see Robert Langbaum, *The Poetry of Experience* (New York: Norton, 1963), pp. 73–108. But more recent and complex analyses of the monologue form include Hughes, *Manyfaced Glass* and essays in *Victorian Poetry* (22, no. 2, 1984), on "The Dramatic 'I' Poem," ed. Linda M. Shires.

15. Shaw, *Tennyson's Style*, p. 170.

16. Northrop Frye, quoted ibid., p. 170.
17. Thomas Harrison, "Tennyson's *Maud* and Shakespeare," *Shakespeare Association Bulletin* 17 (1942): 80.
18. *The Tragedy of Hamlet Prince of Denmark* in *The Riverside Shakespeare* ed. G. Blakemore Evans, (Boston: Houghton Mifflin, 1974), pp. 1135–97. All future references to *Hamlet* will cite act, scene, and line numbers from this edition parenthetically after a quotation in the text. For a useful commentary on the "rottenness" of Denmark, see David Bevington's Introduction to *Twentieth Century Interpretations of Hamlet*, ed. David Bevington (Englewood Cliffs, N.J.: Prentice Hall, 1968), p. 2.
19. Philip Henderson, *Tennyson: Poet and Prophet* (London: Routledge and Kegan Paul, 1978), pp. 47, 58.
20. For remarks on Tennyson's general use of irony, see Kincaid, *Tennyson's Major Poems*, pp. 1–14 and passim; and Jerome H. Buckley, "Tennyson's Irony," *Victorian Newsletter* 31 (1967): 7–10.
21. Harry Levin, *The Question of Hamlet* (New York: Oxford Univ. Press, 1959), p. 82. Levin quotes John Weiss.
22. Bevington, Introduction, pp. 9, 4–5.
23. Mermin, "Tennyson's *Maud*," p. 267.
24. This comment by one reviewer is recounted by Jerome H. Buckley (among others) in *Tennyson: The Growth of a Poet*, p. 140.
25. Kozicki, *Tennyson and Clio*, pp. 103–4.
26. Jerome Hamilton Buckley, *The Victorian Temper* (New York: Vintage, 1951), p. 42.
27. Sydney Dobell, *Balder*, in *Poetical Works* (London, 1875), 2:17.
28. Thomas Carlyle, *Past and Present*, ed. Richard D. Altick (Boston: Houghton Mifflin, 1965), p. 155.
29. See McGann, "Tennyson," pp. 177–78.

IV: Dante Rossetti: Parody and Ideology

1. Claus Uhlig, "Literature as Textual Palingenesis: On Some Principles of Literary History," *New Literary History* 16 (1985): 503.
2. On this topic see, for instance, the recent work of Jerome J. McGann and Hayden White, as well as that of Marilyn Butler, Terry Eagleton, Frederick Jameson, and Jane Tompkins.
3. Elliot Gilbert, "The Female King: Tennyson's Arthurian Apocalypse," *PMLA* 48 (1983): 866. Also see A. Dwight Culler, *The Victorian Mirror of History* (New Haven: Yale Univ. Press, 1985), and Peter Allen Dale, *The Victorian Critic and the Idea of History: Carlyle, Arnold, Pater* (Cambridge, Mass.: Harvard Univ. Press, 1977).
4. Gilbert, "The Female King," p. 866.
5. See Herbert Sussman, "The Pre-Raphaelite Brotherhood and Their Circle: The Formation of the Victorian Avant-Garde," *The Victorian Newsletter* 57 (1980): 7–9, and, by the same author, *Fact into Figure: Typology in Carlyle, Ruskin, and the Pre-Raphaelite Brotherhood* (Columbus: Ohio State University Press, 1979), pp. 44–45, 55.
6. In *Michael*, for instance, Wordsworth dedicates his work expressly to "youth-

ful Poets, who . . . / Will be my second self when I am gone." *Wordsworth: Poetical Works,* ed. Thomas Hutchinson, rev. Ernest de Selincourt (Oxford: Oxford Univ. Press, 1969), p. 104.

7. Terry Eagleton, *Literary Theory: An Introduction* (Minneapolis: Univ. of Minnesota Press, 1983), p. 15.

8. Dante G. Rossetti, *The Early Italian Poets,* ed. Sally Purcell (Berkeley: Univ. of California Press, 1981), p. 1.

9. David Riede, *Dante Gabriel Rossetti and the Limits of Victorian Vision* (Ithaca, N.Y.: Cornell Univ. Press, 1983), pp. 34–35.

10. *The Complete Poetical Works of Dante Gabriel Rossetti,* ed. William Michael Rossetti (Boston: Roberts Brothers, 1887), pp. 132–33. Hereafter all poems by Rossetti will be cited parenthetically in the text to page numbers from this edition.

11. Jerome J. McGann, "Rossetti's Significant Details," *Victorian Poetry* 7 (1969): 41–54; reprinted in *Pre-Raphaelitism: A Collection of Critical Essays,* ed. David Sambrook (Chicago: Univ. of Chicago Press, 1974).

12. An essay which also concerns itself with matters of fantasy and one which takes a view of "The Blessed Damozel" opposed to my own is D. M. R. Bentley's " 'The Blessed Damozel': A Young Man's Fantasy," *Victorian Poetry* 20 (1982): 31–43.

13. Keats to Benjamin Bailey, Nov. 17, 1817, in *The Letters of John Keats,* ed. Hyder E. Rollins, 2 vols. (Cambridge: Harvard Univ. Press, 1958), 1:185.

14. Linda Hutcheon, *A Theory of Parody* (London: Methuen, 1985).

15. Ibid., p. 54.

16. Ibid., p. 57.

17. Ibid., p. 75.

18. See McGann, "Rossetti's Significant Details."

19. *The Poems of John Keats,* ed. Jack Stillinger (Cambridge: Harvard Univ. Press, 1978), p. 365.

20. See Riede, *Dante Gabriel Rossetti,* p. 273.

V: In the Shadow of E. B. B.: Christina Rossetti and Ideological Estrangement

1. Quoted by Mackenzie Bell in *Christina Rossetti: A Biographical and Critical Study* (London: Thomas Burleigh, 1898), pp. 329–30.

2. See ibid., pp. 321–30; among recent discussions that attempt to demonstrate Rossetti's superiority over Browning, see Joan Rees, *The Poetry of Dante Gabriel Rossetti: Modes of Self-Expression* (Cambridge: Cambridge Univ. Press, 1981), pp. 146–60; and Antony H. Harrison, *Christina Rossetti in Context* (Chapel Hill: Univ. of North Carolina Press, 1988), pp. 156–57.

3. William Michael Rossetti, ed., *Dante Gabriel Rossetti: His Family Letters, with a Memoir,* 2 vols. (London: Ellis, 1895), 2:323.

4. Bell, *Christina Rossetti,* p. 324.

5. Quoted ibid., p. 93.

6. William Michael Rossetti, ed., *The Family Letters of Christina Georgina Rossetti* (New York: Scribners, 1908), p. 31. W.M.R. dates the letter as April 1870, but

it was doubtless written before 1865. In it Christina refers to her "one first, last, and only book."

7. *The Complete Poems of Christina Rossetti,* ed. R. W. Crump, 2 vols. (Baton Rouge: Louisiana State Univ. Press, 1979–86), 2:93. Future citations to this standard edition of Rossetti's poetry in this chapter will appear parenthetically in text as *Poems,* with volume and page numbers.

8. See Harrison, *Christina Rossetti in Context,* pp. 152–57.

9. Bell, *Christina Rossetti,* pp. 90–91.

10. *The Complete Works of Elizabeth Barrett Browning,* ed. Charlotte Porter and Helen A. Clarke, 6 vols. (New York: Thomas Y. Crowell & Co., 1900; reprint, New York: AMS Press, 1973), 4:53. Future citations to this standard edition of Browning's works in this chapter will appear parenthetically in text as *Works,* with volume and page numbers.

11. Quoted by Mary Sandars in *The Life of Christina Rossetti* (London: Hutchinson, 1930), p. 85.

12. *The Letters of Elizabeth Barrett Browning,* ed. Frederick G. Kenyon, 2 vols (London: John Murray, 1898), 1:232.

13. For the most extensive argument that Browning's work is deeply feminist in its impulses, see Angela Leighton, *Elizabeth Barrett Browning* (Bloomington: Indiana Univ. Press, 1986); in *Intellectual Women and Victorian Patriarchy: Harriet Martineau, Elizabeth Barrett Browning, George Eliot* (Ithaca, N.Y.: Cornell Univ. Press, 1987), Deirdre David asserts Browning's "firm identification with male modes of political thought and aesthetic practice, whatever feminist sympathies she may be said to possess" (p. 98); Helen Cooper adopts the moderate position in *Elizabeth Barrett Browning, Woman and Artist* (Chapel Hill: Univ. North Carolina Press, 1988).

14. See, for instance, Harrison, *Christina Rossetti in Context;* Dolores Rosenblum, *Christina Rossetti: The Poetry of Endurance* (Carbondale: Southern Illinois Univ. Press, 1986); and Jerome J. McGann, "Christina Rossetti's Poems: A New Edition and a Revaluation," *Victorian Studies* 23 (1980): 237–54, for discussions of Rossetti's "feminist" subversiveness. But compare Margaret Homans, "'Syllables of Velvet': Dickinson, Rossetti, and the Rhetorics of Sexuality," *Feminist Studies* 11 (1985): 569–93; and Sandra Gilbert and Susan Gubar, *The Madwoman in the Attic* (New Haven: Yale Univ. Press, 1979), pp. 549–54, 564–75, who lament her acquiescence in conventional Victorian roles for women.

15. Henry Mayhew, "Home Is Home, Be It Never so Homely," in Viscount Ingistre, ed., *Melioria; or, Better Times to Come: Being the Contributions of Many Men Touching the Present State and Prospects of Society* (London, 1852), p. 263.

16. John Ruskin, *Sesame and Lillies* (London, 1865), p. 147. For a helpful introduction to the Victorian ideal of motherhood, see Lynda Nead, *Myths of Sexuality: Representations of Women in Victorian Britain* (Oxford: Basil Blackwell, 1988), p. 28. For an extended discussion of the relations between Victorian ideals of motherhood and the profession of writing for women in Victorian England see Margaret Homans, *Bearing the Word: Language and Female Experience in Nineteenth-Century Women's Writing* (Chicago: The Univ. of Chicago Press, 1986), especially chapter 7, "The Author as Mother: Bearing the Word as Nineteenth-Century Ideology," pp. 153–88.

17. Nead, *Myths of Sexuality,* pp. 26–27.
18. Sarah Stickney Ellis, *The Daughters of England* (London, 1845), p. 7, quoted in Nead, *Myths of Sexuality,* p. 28.
19. Mrs. Roe, *A Woman's Thoughts on the Education of Girls* (London: 1866), p. 39.
20. For a brilliant analysis of the genuine power accorded to women in the domestic sphere throughout the nineteenth century, see Nancy Armstrong, *Desire and Domestic Fiction: A Political History of the Novel* (Oxford: Oxford Univ. Press, 1987).
21. David, *Intellectual Women,* pp. 98, 143.
22. For a full discussion of Browning's debt to Wordsworth, see Kathleen Blake, "Elizabeth Barrett Browning and Wordsworth: The Romantic Poet as a Woman," *Victorian Poetry* 24 (1986): 387–98.
23. *The Poetical Works of William Wordsworth,* ed. Thomas Hutchinson, revised by Ernest de Selincourt (London: Oxford Univ. Press, 1969), p. 590.
24. For an alternate reading of "The Lowest Room," see Rosenblum, *Christina Rossetti,* pp. 162–66.
25. Jerome J. McGann, Introduction to *The Achievement of Christina Rossetti,* ed. David A. Kent (Ithaca, N.Y.: Cornell Univ. Press, 1988), p. 7. Surprisingly, McGann does not discuss "The World."
26. Ibid., p. 11.
27. For the most extensive discussion to date of Eve figures in Rossetti's work see Diane D'Amico, "Eve, Mary, And Mary Magdalene: Christina Rossetti's Feminine Triptych," in Kent, ed., *The Achievement of Christina Rossetti,* pp. 175–91.
28. For commentary on this topic see "The Poetics of Conciseness," chapter 2 in Harrison, *Christina Rossetti,* (pp. 23–63).
29. See D'Amico, "Eve, Mary, and Mary Magdalene," p. 177.
30. Christina Rossetti, *Letter and Spirit: Notes on the Commandments* (London: SPCK, 1883), pp. 17–18.
31. Christina Rossetti, *The Face of the Deep* (London: SPCK, 1892), pp. 310–11.
32. Ibid., p. 410.
33. Rossetti to Augusta Webster, quoted in MacKenzie Bell, *Christina Rossetti,* p. 112; my italics.
34. Rossetti, *Face of the Deep,* p. 310.
35. Rossetti quoted by Lona Mosk Packer in *Christina Rossetti* (Berkeley: Univ. of California Press, 1963), p. 330.
36. Among numerous examples, see "An Apple-Gathering," "Cousin Kate," "Twice," "Maude Clare," "Wife to Husband," "May," "A Pause of Thought," "Mirage," "Dead before Death," "Rest," "The Convent Threshold," "A Portrait," "Light Love," "Beauty Is Vain," "Autumn," and "Memory."
37. Bell, *Christina Rossetti,* p. 112.
38. For discussions of Browning's poems relating to motherhood, see Sandra Donaldson, "'Motherhood's Advent in Power': Elizabeth Barrett Browning's Poems about Motherhood," *Victorian Poetry* 18 (1980): 51–60; and Virginia V. Steinmetz, "Images of 'Mother-Want' in Elizabeth Barrett Browning's *Aurora Leigh,*" *Victorian Poetry* 21 (1983): 351–67.
39. For a complementary reading of Rossetti's headnote, see William Whitla,

"Questioning the Convention: Christina Rossetti's Sonnet Sequence "*Monna Innominata*," in Kent, ed., *The Achievement of Christina Rossetti*, pp. 87–93. The most thorough commentaries on the *Monna Innominata* to date are those by Whitla (pp. 82–131) and Harrison (*Christina Rossetti in Context*, pp. 142–86).

40. W. M. Rossetti, ed., *Family Letters*, p. 98.
41. My reading of the *Sonnets* opposes Leighton's feminist argument that in it Browning asserts "the woman's right to speak" (*Elizabeth Barrett Browning*, p. 110).
42. *The Letters of Robert Browning and Elizabeth Barrett Barrett, 1845–46*, ed. Elvan Kintner, 2 vols. (Cambridge, Mass.: Harvard Univ. Press, 1969), 2:116.
43. David, *Intellectual Women*, p. 157.

VI: Art Is Enough: Morris, Keats, and Pre-Raphaelite Amatory Ideologies

1. E. P. Thompson, *William Morris: Romantic to Revolutionary* (New York: Pantheon, 1977), p. 153.
2. J. W. Mackail, *The Life of William Morris*, 2 vols. (London: Longmans, Green, and Co., 1901), 1:281, 287.
3. Ibid., pp. i, 242, 272. Morris had studied the Icelandic language and Icelandic culture since 1868 under the tutelage of Eirikr Magnusson.
4. The first volume alone went through five editions in two years. See Introduction to *William Morris: The Critical Heritage*, ed. Peter Faulkner (London: Routledge and Kegan Paul, 1973), p. 4. For the reception of *The Earthly Paradise*, see Introduction, pp. 9–13, and 79–151.
5. Morris collected many of these lyrics in *A Book of Verse*, which he produced by hand and illuminated for Georgiana Burne-Jones's birthday in 1870. Concerned that *Love Is Enough* also be as beautiful an artifact as possible, Morris had originally intended that Burne-Jones prepare elaborate illustrations for it.
6. *The Letters of Dante Gabriel Rossetti*, ed. Oswald Doughty and John Robert Wahl, 4 vols. (Oxford: The Clarendon Press, 1965), p. 1014.
7. *The Collected Letters of William Morris*, ed. Norman Kelvin, 2 vols. + (Princeton: Princeton Univ. Press, 1984–), 1:153.
8. Morris's comment, after reading "The Willow and the Red Cliff" to an assembled company in 1855, is well known. "Well, if this is poetry, it is very easy to write," he is reported (by Canon Dixon) to have responded to accolades from his auditors (Mackail, *Life of William Morris*, 1:52).
9. Kelvin, ed., *Collected Letters*, 1:155.
10. Faulkner, ed., Introduction, *William Morris*, pp. 13–14.
11. Ibid., pp. 204–10.
12. Frederick Kirchhoff, "*Love Is Enough:* A Crisis in William Morris's Poetic Development," *Victorian Poetry* 15 (1977): 306.
13. Philip Henderson, *William Morris: His Life, Work, and Friends* (New York: McGraw-Hill, 1967), pp. 128–29.
14. Thompson, *William Morris*, pp. 151–52.
15. Kelvin, ed., *Collected Letters*, 1:100.
16. *The Letters of William Morris to His Family and Friends*, ed. Philip Henderson (London: Longmans, Green, 1950), p. 186.

17. Mackail, *Life of William Morris,* 1:285; my italics.
18. Morris confessed to Georgiana Burne-Jones on August 9, 1882, that after "two or three attempts" to read *Tristram of Lyonesse,* he had "failed." In remarks significant to my later comments on the intertextual relations between the two poets' work, he further explains: "you know I never could really sympathize with Swinburne's work; it always seemed to me to be founded on literature, not on nature. In saying this I really cannot accuse myself of any jealousy on the subject. . . . in these days . . . nothing can take serious hold of people, or should do so, but that which is rooted deepest in reality and is quite at first hand: there is no room for anything which is not forced out of a man of deep feeling, because of its innate strength and vision" (Kelvin, ed., *Collected Letters,* 2a:119).
19. *The Collected Works of William Morris,* ed. May Morris, 24 vols. (London: Longmans, Green, 1910–15; reprint, New York: Russell and Russell, 1966), 9:3. Future citations to this edition in this chapter will appear parenthetically in text to *Works,* with volume and page numbers.
20. Carole Silver, *The Romance of William Morris* (Athens: Ohio Univ. Press, 1982), p. 99.
21. The Keatsian backgrounds to the work of the Pre-Raphaelite poets have been extensively, which is not to say exhaustively, explored. See, for example, on Morris: Thompson, *William Morris,* 10–21; David G. Riede, "Morris, Modernism, and Romance," *ELH* 51 (1984): 85–106; and Elizabeth Strode, "The Crisis of *The Earthly Paradise:* Morris and Keats," *Victorian Poetry* 13 (1975): 71–81. On Swinburne, see: Georges Lafourcade, *Swinburne's "Hyperion" and Other Poems: With an Essay on Swinburne and Keats* (London: Faber and Gwyer, 1927) and Cecil Y. Lang, "Swinburne and Keats: A Fragment of an Essay," *Modern Language Notes* 64 (1949): 168–71. See also George Ford's discussions of both writers, along with his definitive commentary on Keats and Dante Rossetti, in *Keats and the Victorians* (New Haven: Yale Univ. Press, 1944).
22. Mackail, *Life of William Morris,* 1:200.
23. Kelvin, ed., *Collected Letters,* 1:65.
24. Walter Pater, "Poems by William Morris," in Faulkner, ed., *William Morris,* p. 89.
25. *Rossetti's Poems,* ed. Oswald Doughty (London: Dent, 1961), xiii.
26. *The Collected Works of Dante Gabriel Rossetti,* ed. William Michael Rossetti, 2 vols. (London: Ellis and Elvey, 1890), 1:339.
27. This theme is clearly derived as much from Keats's life as from his poetry.
28. Doughty, ed., *Poems,* p. 128. Future citations to this edition in this chapter will appear parenthetically in text to Doughty, with page numbers. I use this edition rather than the standard one (cited above, n. 26) because it usefully presents Rossetti's poems in chronological order of their publication.
29. David G. Riede, *Dante Gabriel Rossetti and the Limits of Victorian Vision* (Ithaca, N.Y.: Cornell Univ. Press, 1983), p. 122.
30. Morris's review appeared in the *Academy,* May 14, 1870.
31. Kelvin, ed., *Collected Letters,* 1:116.
32. Morris quoted in May Morris, *William Morris, Artist, Writer, Socialist,* 2 vols. (1936; reprint, New York: Russell and Russell, 1966), 1:101–3.

33. Ibid., p. 103.
34. Algernon Charles Swinburne, "Matthew Arnold's *New Poems,*" in *Swinburne as Critic,* ed. Clyde K. Hyder (London: Routledge and Kegan Paul, 1972), p. 87. For extended commentary on Swinburne and Keats see Ford, *Keats and the Victorians,* and Lafourcade, *Swinburne's "Hyperion."*
35. Terry Meyers, "Shelley and Swinburne's Aesthetic of Melody," *Papers on Language and Literature* 14 (1978): 290.
36. *The Complete Works of Algernon Charles Swinburne,* Bonchurch edition, ed. Sir Edmund Gosse and Thomas J. Wise, 20 vols. (London: Chatto and Windus, 1925–27), 18:295–96.
37. *The Poems of Algernon Charles Swinburne,* 6 vols. (London: Chatto and Windus, 1904), 1:34.
38. Silver, *Romance of William Morris,* pp. 75–76.
39. *The Poems of John Keats,* ed. Jack Stillinger (Cambridge, Mass.: Harvard Univ. Press, 1978), pp. 126–27. Future citations to this edition of Keats's poetry in this chapter will appear parenthetically in text to *Keats,* with page numbers.
40. See, for instance, Kelvin, ed., *Collected Letters,* 2a:110.
41. *The Poems of Algernon Charles Swinburne,* 6 vols. (London: Chatto and Windus, 1904), 4:7. Future citations to this standard edition of Swinburne's poetry in this chapter will appear parenthetically in the text as *Poems,* with volume and page numbers.
42. Walter Pater, "Poems by William Morris," in *Pre-Raphaelitism: A Collection of Critical Essays,* ed. James Sambrook (Chicago: Univ. of Chicago Press, 1974), p. 113.
43. Mackail, *Life of William Morris,* 1:338.
44. Kelvin, ed., *Collected Letters,* 1:28.
45. Ibid., 1:xlv.
46. Thompson, *William Morris,* p. 196.
47. Doughty and Wahl, eds., *Letters,* p. 976.
48. *The Swinburne Letters,* ed. Cecil Y. Lang, 6 vols. (New Haven: Yale Univ. Press, 1959–62), 2:125.
49. Ibid., 2:146.
50. Thompson, *William Morris,* p. 197, 196.
51. Doughty and Wahl, eds., *Letters,* p. 1015.
52. Lang, ed., *Swinburne Letters,* 2:186.
53. Kelvin, ed., *Collected Letters,* 1:xlvii.
54. Bromwich makes the points I cite in "Keats's Radicalism," pp. 197–201. For extended discussions of the politics of Keats's poetry, see *Keats and Politics: A Forum,* ed. Susan Wolfson, which is *Studies in Romanticism* 25 (1986).

VII: Swinburne, Wordsworth, and the Politics of Mortality

1. *Wordsworth: Poetical Works,* ed. Thomas Hutchinson, rev. Ernest de Selincourt (London: Oxford Univ. Press, 1969), p. 462. Future citations to Wordsworth's poems will be from this edition and will appear parenthetically in the text as *Wordsworth,* with page numbers.

2. In "The 'Intimations' Ode and Victorian Romanticism," Lawrence Kramer presents a helpful preliminary discussion of the widespread cultural power of the ode (*Victorian Poetry* 18 [1980]: 316). But see also Carl Dawson, *Victorian Noon: English Literature in 1850* (Baltimore: Johns Hopkins Univ. Press, 1979, p. 133), for a suggestive remark on Dickens's debt to the Intimations Ode in *David Copperfield;* and the essays in a special issue of *Victorian Poetry* (vol. 24 [1986], ed. Thaïs E. Morgan) entitled *Wordsworth among the Victorian Poets.*

3. *The Poetical Works of William Wordsworth,* ed. Ernest de Selincourt and Helen Darbishire, 5 vols. (Oxford: Clarendon Press, 1940–49), 4:463.

4. Marjorie Levinson has analyzed the historically specific political origins and ramifications of the ode in her important essay "Wordsworth's Intimations Ode: A Timely Utterance" in Jerome J. McGann, ed., *Historical Studies and Literary Criticism* (Madison: Univ. of Wisconsin Press, 1985), pp. 48–75. Her general point, that "the object of the poem is precisely to pose and answer political questions at the level of abstract idea," is directly relevant to my own argument in this chapter.

5. *The Swinburne Letters,* ed. Cecil Y. Lang, 6 vols. (New Haven: Yale Univ. Press, 1959–62), 1:xxi. Future citations to this edition of Swinburne's letters in this chapter will appear parenthetically in the text as *Letters,* with volume and page numbers. David G. Riede is the only critic who frequently, albeit fragmentarily, discusses Wordsworthian strains in Swinburne's poetry. See *Swinburne: A Study of Romantic Mythmaking* (Charlottesville: Univ. Press of Virginia, 1978). Throughout this chapter my understanding of the issue of mortality in Swinburne's poems is indebted to Riede's clear-minded treatment of it.

6. "Anactoria," *The Poems of Algernon Charles Swinburne,* 6 vols. (London: Chatto and Windus, 1904), 1:65–66. Future citations to this standard edition of Swinburne's poems in this chapter will appear parenthetically in the text as *Poems,* with volume and page numbers.

7. In "Matthew Arnold's New Poems," *The Complete Works of Algernon Charles Swinburne,* ed. Sir Edmund Gosse and Thomas J. Wise, 20 vols. (London: William Heineman: 1926), 15:83. Future citations of Swinburne's prose works in this chapter will be to this edition and will appear parenthetically in text as *Works,* with volume and page numbers.

8. See especially Michael Sprinker, *Imaginary Relations: Aesthetics and Ideology in the Theory of Historical Materialism* (London: Verso, 1987); Jerome J. McGann, "Poetic Ideology and Nonnormative Truth" in his *Social Values and Poetic Acts* (Cambridge, Mass.: Harvard Univ. Press, 1988), pp. 73–92; and David Simpson, "Literary Criticism and the Return to 'History,'" *Critical Inquiry* 14 (1988): 721–47.

9. Edmund Gosse, *The Life of Algernon Charles Swinburne* (London: Macmillan, 1917), p. 15.

10. See *Letters,* 4:281 and 6:130.

11. The deep influence of Swinburne on later generations of poets and novelists from the aesthetes to Hardy, Lawrence, Kate Chopin, Pound, Eliot, and Faulkner has hardly begun to be traced. But see Ross Murfin, *Swinburne, Hardy, Lawrence, and the Burden of Belief* (Chicago: Univ. of Chicago Press,

1978), and my own "Swinburne and the Critique of Ideology in Kate Chopin's *The Awakening,*" in *Gender, Voice, and Image in Victorian Poetry and Art,* ed. Antony H. Harrison and Beverly Taylor (forthcoming).

12. For a preliminary discussion of relations among Wordsworth, Swinburne, and Arnold, especially as they bear upon Arnold's "Resignation," see Thaïs E. Morgan, "Rereading Nature: Wordsworth between Swinburne and Arnold," *Victorian Poetry* 24 (1986): 427–39.

13. Jerome J. McGann, *Swinburne: An Experiment in Criticism* (Chicago: Univ. of Chicago Press, 1972), p. 235.

14. Riede explains that in "By the North Sea" "the eroding coast is an emblem of change and destruction, of the triumph of time, where death and the eternal sea are the deathless lords of the land. . . . The shore is an emblem of mortal life; its constant erosion represents the inevitability of death and change." Appropos of my concern here with Wordsworthian myths of immortality, Riede further notes that "the purpose of all myths of salvation is to slay death, but Swinburne demonstrates that natural law does this, that no myth is necessary. . . . Unlike the Christian cycle, however, the movement is not from life through death to a higher form of life, but from nonbeing through life and back to nonbeing." One consolation for mortality, nonetheless, "proceeds from a recognition of the eternality of death. The only immortality we achieve is the eternality of the elements to which we return. This is a strictly reductive immortality consisting of no more than the realization that after the first death there is no other" (*Swinburne,* pp. 163–64, 167).

15. McGann, *Swinburne,* p. 251.

16. My reading of "Neap-Tide" challenges that of Kerry McSweeney in *Tennyson and Swinburne as Romantic Naturalists* (Toronto: Univ. of Toronto Press, 1981), who concludes that "at the end of 'Neap-Tide' Swinburne turns away from the brink of transcendence" (p. 136).

17. *The Collected Letters of William Morris,* 2+ vols., ed. Norman Kelvin (Princeton, N.J.: Princeton Univ. Press, 1984–), 2a:119.

18. Ironically, what Morris could not yet have understood is that, in Michael Sprinker's words, "classical Marxism shares with bourgeois aesthetics the conviction that in art one attains freedom, and that this freedom consists, among other things, in the liberation from ideological determination and historical contingency." But this conviction is an illusion: "the ingenuity of the individual artist is the outcome of socio-economic determinations which have provided him with certain materials and have, as well, produced him. . . . the human subject is a text that is produced, not a natural entity with historically invariant features and capacities" (Sprinker, *Imaginary Relations,* pp. 13, 146). One force active in every poet's social determination is the body of literary pre-texts in which he has immersed himself, as Morris appears to have perceived in Swinburne's case. Swinburne himself, of course, conceived of the artist in a precisely opposite fashion, as one "with historically invariant features and capacities" who may advance mankind's awareness of the certain and evolving principle of freedom active in human history, while attaining his own freedom from mortality by producing great art. The progress of his intertextual relations with Wordsworth, however, demonstrates that Swin-

burne's conception is, despite his antiphilistinism, merely an idiosyncratic version of the general "bourgeois" illusion.

19. See especially Levinson, "Wordsworth's Intimations Ode"; Jerome J. Mc-Gann, *The Romantic Ideology* (Chicago: Univ. of Chicago Press, 1983), pp. 81–92; and David Simpson, *Wordsworth's Historical Imagination* (London: Methuen, 1987).

20. McGann, *Ideology,* pp. 82, 90, 91. Levinson ("Wordsworth's Intimations Ode") and Simpson (*Wordsworth's Historical Imagination*) both expand upon McGann's argument, though in Simpson's case with significant reservations.

21. Not surprisingly, at least two of them, Pound and Eliot, turned out to be extreme political conservatives, in the tradition of the later Swinburne, rather than the earlier, iconoclastic and republican, Swinburne.

INDEX

Habermas, Jurgen, 7
Hair, Donald, 58
Hallam, Arthur Henry, 86
Harrison, Thomas, 75
Hartmann, Geoffrey, 19
Hegel, Friedrich von, 7
Hemans, Felicia, 113
Henderson, Philip, 146
Homer, 16
Honan, Park, 30
Howard, Jean, 5
Hugo, Victor, 184
Hunt, Leigh, 25
Hutcheon, Linda, 97–98

Ideology, 6–7, 91, 100, 113–14
Ingelow, Jean, 111
Ingram, John, 112
Intertextuality, 1, 7–9, 44, 90, 91, 92
Irish Home Rule. *See* Swinburne, Algernon Charles

Jauss, Hans Robert, 10–13

Keach, William, 25
Keats, John, 3, 16, 17, 91, 92, 96, 101, 102; as poet of natural magic, 19–20; "sensory ideology," 19–20; aesthetic ideology of, 23, 33, 36, 153; radical politics, 25–28; and Spasmodic poetry, 30–32, 60, 62, 66–67; Pre-Raphaelite appropriations of, 144, 148, 159, 162, 171; equation of love and death, 155, 159, 161, 162; *see also,* Arnold, Matthew; Browning, Robert; Morris, William; Rossetti, Dante Gabriel
— WORKS: *Endymion,* 25, 48, 49, 66, 148, 150, 157, 162–65, 176; "Eve of St. Agnes," 157, 161; *The Fall of Hyperion,* 163; *Hyperion,* 35, 37, 40–43; *Isabella,* 19, 27, 48, 157; "La Belle Dame sans Merci," 150–51,

157, 158, 161, 165; *Lamia,* 158; *Letters to Fanny Brawne,* 22–23, 24, 38; "Ode on a Grecian Urn," 103, 161; "Ode on Melancholy," 49, 156, 157, 161; "Ode to a Nightingale," 155–56; "Ode to Psyche," 103; *Sleep and Poetry,* 37, 163; "To Autumn," 157, 165–66
Kelvin, Norman, 175
Kingsley, Charles, 59
Kosik, Karl, 10–11
Kristeva, Julia, 1
Kozicki, Henry, 87
Kramer, Lawrence, 177

Landon, Laetitia, 115
Lang, Andrew, 108
Lang, Cecil, 178
Levin, Harry, 79
Levinson, Marjorie, 63, 255 n. 4
Lewes, G. H., 31
Lockhart, J. G., 25, 27
Lotmann, Juri, 8
Louis Blanc, 201
Lucretius, 34
Ludlow, J. M., 48, 59

McClellan, David, 7
McGann, Jerome, 5, 69, 94, 127, 191, 201; and the new historicism, 13–14
Mackail, J. W., 147, 172
Macready, William Charles, 78
Magnusson, Eirikr, 145
Mannheim, Karl, 7
Marcus, Leah, 5
Marston, J. Westland, 30, 62
Martin, Patchett, 109
Martineau, Harriet, 121
Marx, Karl, 7, 200
Mason, Bertie, 182
Mayhew, Henry, 116
Maynard, John, 64
Mazzini, Giuseppi, 201
Meredith, George, 145, 170
Mermin, Dorothy, 79–80

Victorian Literature and Culture Series
is a series of monographs on literature
covering the years from 1830 to 1914.
Contributions may be editorial, critical
(historical or theoretical), biographical,
bibliographic, comparative, or
interdisciplinary.

DANIEL ALBRIGHT, *Tennyson: The Muses' Tug-of-War*

DAVID G. RIEDE, *Matthew Arnold and the Betrayal of Language*

JAMES RICHARDSON, *Vanishing Lives: Style and Self in Tennyson, D. G. Rossetti, Swinburne, and Yeats*

ANTHONY WINNER, *Culture and Irony: Studies in Joseph Conrad's Major Novels*

JEROME J. McGANN, ed., *Victorian Connections*

ANTONY H. HARRISON, *Victorian Poets and Romantic Poems: Intertextuality and Ideology*